Language and Gnosis

HARVARD DISSERTATIONS IN RELIGION

Number 18

Language and Gnosis

Michael LaFargue

LANGUAGE AND GNOSIS:
The Opening Scenes of the
Acts of Thomas

Michael LaFargue

Fortress Press   Philadelphia

Library of Congress Cataloging in Publication Data

LaFargue, Michael
    Language and gnosis.

    (Harvard dissertations in religion; no. 18)
    1. Acts of Thomas—Criticism, interpretation, etc.
2. Gnosticism I. Title. II. Series.
BS2880.T5L34 1985 229'.92 84–45191
ISBN 0–8006–7016–7

K900I84 Printed in the United States of America 1–7015

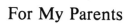

For My Parents

CONTENTS

PREFACE

This study is a somewhat revised version of my Harvard doctoral dissertation. It began as an exercise in hermeneutics, an attempt to find better ways to go about understanding ancient religious texts. Principally, I wanted to carry forward Rudolf Bultmann's "demythologizing" project in a way that does more justice to the terms and images used in the texts themselves.

Aside from a scholar's concern for accuracy, my aims arose partly out of my experience teaching in a secular and heterogeneous environment where terms have to be understandable to people from many different backgrounds, and where no philosophical or religious framework can be assumed as a framework for interpretation. More importantly, they arose out of an essentially political concern with the role of interpretative scholarship in the cultural situation now facing us. Thrust upon us today is the necessity of understanding other cultures' ways of experiencing reality fundamentally different from our own. And at the same time we have to recognize that much of what has gone on in this area in the past is a kind of cultural imperialism proceeding from an overconfidence in the universal validity of our own basic assumptions and standards.

Western scholarship has developed hermeneutical method to a very high degree of sophistication, largely due to the immense amount of work and reflection invested in biblical criticism in recent centuries, and also because of recent developments bearing on hermeneutics in philosophy, literary criticism, linguistics, and psychology. The tools are there for a sophisticated hermeneutics, sensitive and versatile in its application of intepretative frameworks and capable of guiding us to an accurate and in-depth appreciation of culturally foreign visions of life and ways of experiencing reality. But the tools have been too little used for serious and disciplined interpretation of works outside the mainstream of the western tradition.

In the project as I originally planned it, the *Acts of Thomas* was to be a demonstration text. I had suspected that Gnosticism was a rejected element in our tradition that was not appreciated, primarily because its imaginative and linguistic style (reflecting its particular way of construing experience) was too foreign to the literary and logical standards imposed on it by even the more self-conscious and sophisticated of modern interpreters. I wanted to probe that style and get at the relation between Gnostic literary style and the Gnostic vision, the relation between language and saving *Gnosis*.

As I began this project, I had only vague conjectures as to the nature of the connection between literary style and Gnostic thinking in the *Acts Thom.* It was only in the process of working out a controlled way of understanding the real intention of the text that I came to realize how immensely sophisticated this work is, both in the artfulness of its construction and in the thought which underlies it. Further, the "demonstration text" I chose for the purpose of illustrating and developing a better hermeneutic method turned out to be precisely about hermeneutics—a Gnostic hermeneutics for which I would not claim "universal validity," but which nonetheless has a great deal to offer as a method of interpreting major themes from the Judeo-Christian tradition.

The main body of the present work (Chapters 1–6) is a reproduction of my 1977 doctoral dissertation with only minor changes. The Introduction and Chapter 7 are substantially rewritten and partially represent subsequent reflections on the nature and importance of the methodology worked out here and of the message of the *Acts Thom.*

Thanks for help in this study must go first of all to my advisor, Dieter Georgi, who first introduced me to Gnosticism, to the *Acts of Thomas*, and to many of the methodological insights and attitudes that motivate and inform this work. He was and is a great inspiration to me as a scholar, and he was a very patient listener and counsellor during the time I was struggling with this project. I owe a good deal to Claudio Naranjo whose vision helped restore my faith in the usefulness of this kind of work and encouraged me at a crucial time, and also to Wendy Orange for her personal support. The methodology employed here I worked out to a great extent through conversations with my students at the Cambridge Center for Adult Education, and I received valuable help as well from my other professors at Harvard: John Strugnell, Helmut Koester, and George W. MacRae. I also wish to thank the editors of Harvard Dissertations in Religion for making the publication of this work possible. Finally, I want to thank Joe Snowden for his very thorough work in the preparation of the manuscript.

ABBREVIATIONS

Abbreviations used in this volume for sources and literature from antiquity are the same as those used in Gerhard Kittel, ed., *Theological Dictionary of the New Testament*, vol. 1 (Grand Rapids: Eerdmans, 1964) xvi–xl. Some abbreviations are adapted from that list and can be easily identified. In addition, the following abbreviations have been used:

BAG	Walter Bauer, *A Greek-English Lexicon of the New Testament and Other Early Christian Literature* (2d ed.; rev. Frederick W. Danker; trans. William F. Arndt and F. Wilbur Gingrich; Chicago/London: University of Chicago Press, 1979).
1 Clem.	*1 Clement*
Corp. Herm.	*Corpus Hermeticum*
Disc. 8–9	*Discourse on the Eighth and Ninth*
DS	Heinrich Denzinger and Adolfus Schönmetzer, *Enchiridion symbolorum* (Freiburg: Herder, 1967).
DThC	*Dictionnaire de theologie catholique*
EncJud	*Encyclopaedia judaica*
Enn.	*Ennead*
Epiph.	Epiphanius
Pan.	*Panarion*
Eus.	Eusebius
Hist. eccl.	*Historiae ecclesiasticae*
Exc. Theod.	*Excerpts of Theodotus*
Exeg. Soul	*Exegesis on the Soul*
Gos. Thom.	*Gospel of Thomas*
Ign.	Ignatius
Trall.	*Letter to the Trallians*
Iren.	Irenaeus
Adv. haer.	*Adversus haereses*
JR	*Journal of Religion*

JTS	*Journal of Theological Studies*
LSJ	Henry George Liddell and Robert Scott, *A Greek-English Lexicon*, rev. Henry Stuart Jones (Oxford: Clarendon, 1940).
NovT	*Novum Testamentum*
NPNF	*Nicene and Post-Nicene Fathers*
NTApo	Edgar Hennecke, ed., Wilhelm Schneemelcher, rev., R. McL. Wilson, trans. ed., *New Testament Apocrypha* (2 vols.; Philadelphia: Westminster, 1963–65).
Ps. Sol.	*Psalms of Solomon*
1QapGen	*Genesis Apocryphon* of Qumran Cave 1
SC	Sources chrétiennes
Seph. Yez.	*Sepher Yezirah*
TDNT	Gerhard Kittel, ed., *Theological Dictionary of the New Testament* (10 vols.; Grand Rapids: Eerdmans, 1964–76).
ThR	*Theologische Rundschau*
ZAW	*Zeitschrift für die alttestamentliche Wissenschaft*
ZNW	*Zeitschrift für die neutestamentliche Wissenschaft und die Kunde der älteren Kirche*
ZWTh	*Zeitschrift für wissenschaftliche Theologie*

SHORT TITLES

Information appears here for frequently used works which are cited by short title. A few short titles do not appear in this list, but in each instance full bibliography is given on the page(s) preceding such references.

Bonnet, *Acta*
> Maximilianus Bonnet, *Acta Apostolorum Apocrypha* (part 2; Darmstadt: Wissenschaftliche Buchgesellschaft, 1959).

Bornkamm, *Mythos*
> Günther Bornkamm, *Mythos und Legende in den apokryphen Thomas-Akten: Beiträge zur Geschichte der Gnosis und zur Vorgeschichte des Manichäismus* (FRLANT n.s. 31; Göttingen: Vandenhoeck & Ruprecht, 1933).

Bornkamm, "Acts of Thomas"
> Günther Bornkamm, "The Acts of Thomas," in *NTApo* 2. 425–531.

Bousset, "Manichäisches"
> W. Bousset, "Manichäisches in den Thomasakten," *ZNW* 18 (1917) 1–39.

Chadwick, *Origen*
> Henry Chadwick, *Origen: Contra Celsum* (Cambridge: Cambridge University Press, 1953).

Charlesworth, "Paronomasia"
> J. H. Charlesworth, "Paronomasia and Assonance in the Syriac Text of the Odes of Solomon," *Semitics* 1 (1970) 12–26.

Herrmann, "Gedanken"
> Wolfram Herrmann, "Gedanken zur Geschichte des altorientalischen Beschreibungsliedes," *ZAW* 75 (1963) 176–97.

Hoffmann, *Zwei Hymnen*
    G. Hoffmann, "Zwei Hymnen der Thomasakten," *ZNW* 4
    (1903) 273–309.
Jonas, *Gnostic Religion*
    Hans Jonas, *The Gnostic Religion* (2d ed.; Boston: Beacon,
    1963).
Klijn, *Acts of Thomas*
    A. F. J. Klijn, *The Acts of Thomas* (Leiden: Brill, 1962).
Lipsius, *Acta*
    Ricardus Adelbertus Lipsius, *Acta Apostolorum Apocrypha* (part
    1; Darmstadt: Wissenschaftliche Buchgesellschaft, 1959).
Lipsius, *Apostelgeschichten*
    Richard Adelbert Lipsius, *Die Apokryphen Apostelgeschichten und
    Apostellegenden: Ein Beitrag zur Altchristlichen Literaturgeschichte*
    (Braunschweig: Schwetschke, 1883).
Preuschen, *Hymnen*
    Erwin Preuschen, *Zwei gnostische Hymnen* (Giessen: Töpel-
    mann, 1904).
Reitzenstein, *Wundererzählungen*
    R. Reitzenstein, *Hellenistische Wundererzählungen* (Stuttgart:
    Teubner, 1963).
Reitzenstein, *Mystery-Religions*
    R. Reitzenstein, *The Hellenistic Mystery-Religions: Their Basic
    Ideas and Significance* (Pittsburgh: Pickwick, 1978).
Scholem, *Jewish Gnosticism*
    Gershom G. Scholem, *Jewish Gnosticism, Merkabah Mysticism,
    and Talmudic Tradition* (New York: The Jewish Theological
    Seminary of America, 1965).
Scholem, *Major Trends*
    Gershom G. Scholem, *Major Trends in Jewish Mysticism* (2d ed.;
    New York: Shocken, 1946).
Scholem, *Ursprung*
    Gershom G. Scholem, *Ursprung und Anfänge der Kabbala* (Ber-
    lin: DeGruyter, 1962).
Söder, *Apostelgeschichten*
    Rosa Söder, *Die apokryphen Apostelgeschichten und die
    romanhafte Literatur der Antike* (Würzburger Studien zur Alter-
    tumswissenschaft 3; Stuttgart: Kohlhammer, 1932).
Thilo, *Acta*
    Joannes Carolus Thilo, *Acta S. Thomae Apostoli* (Lipsiae: Vo-
    gelli, 1823).

Wetzstein, "Dreschtafel"
  J. G. Wetzstein, "Die syrische Dreschtafel," *Zeitschrift für Ethnologie* 5 (1873) 270–302.
Wilson, "Acts of Thomas"
  R. McL. Wilson, "The Acts of Thomas" in Werner Foerster, ed., *Gnosis: A Selection of Gnostic Texts* (2 vols.; Oxford: Clarendon, 1972) 1. 337–64.

INTRODUCTION

The Practical Problem

The *Acts of Thomas* (hereafter *Acts Thom.*) is one among several apocryphal books describing the deeds or "Acts" of various apostles. It is commonly supposed to have been composed in Syria sometime in the second century C.E. It is known today primarily because of many Gnostic ideas and motifs found in it, more especially in two of its many hymns, the Wedding Hymn found in chapters 6–7, and the so-called Hymn of the Pearl found in chapters 108–13.

The book is organized as a narrative, telling the story—or rather a series of very colorful but probably entirely legendary stories—of Thomas's adventures as a missionary in India. But the narrative is interrupted quite often by long monologues (i.e., sermons, prayers, and hymns) whose contents are at first sight only loosely connected with the narrative action. Adding to this sense of discontinuity, the narrative itself is full of odd and unexplained events or remarks that seem to have little to do with the plot of the story in which they occur.

Most previous scholars who have studied the book have assumed that the discontinuities in it, particularly in its narrative sections, are of no great significance for interpretation. What one could not make immediate sense of should be ignored as simply the result of the ineptness of the book's author—or perhaps, as R. Reitzenstein suggested, of successive inept interpolators.[1] I began this study with the same assumption. My initial hypothesis was similar to Rudolf Bultmann's regarding the discourses in the Gospel of John:[2] the sermons, prayers, and hymns, in the *Acts Thom.* were originally composed independently of the present narrative framework and reflected the worship of some

---

[1] Reitzenstein, *Hellenistische Wundererzählungen* (Stuttgart: Teubner, 1963) 149.

[2] Bultmann, *The Gospel of John: A Commentary* (Philadelphia: Westminster, 1971) 6–7.

semi-Gnostic community. I planned to ignore the narrative and to reconstruct the beliefs, practices, and structure of this community on the basis of the sermons and prayers.

In trying to establish the hypothesis that the long monologues were originally composed independently of the narrative, however, I discovered a great deal of evidence pointing in the opposite direction, evidence suggesting that there is indeed a great deal more connection between these spoken parts and the narrative than meets the eye. Some connections of this kind had already been suggested by Günther Bornkamm, who showed that in quite a few cases it can be demonstrated that the Gnostic motifs in the prayers and hymns give an allegorical interpretation to otherwise puzzling events and remarks in the narrative.[3] But Bornkamm's work was very selective in this regard. He simply chose cases in which this connection could be fairly clearly shown and ignored everything else. The basic impression of most readers that a great deal of the *Acts Thom.* was simply incoherent was left unchallenged. But the evidence I gathered went further than this and made me suspect that there is a great deal more coherence in the work than even Bornkamm suspected.

The specific details to which I am alluding here will be presented in the body of this study beginning in Chapter 2. However, the extraordinary character of the *Acts Thom.* suggested by this evidence requires that some fundamental issues in hermeneutical and exegetical theory be dealt with also, issues which will be discussed in the remainder of the Introduction.

The Theoretical Problem

The basic issue can be put in this way: if we read the *Acts Thom.* in the light of any of the ordinary literary conventions familiar to us from the ancient world, it appears only partially coherent at best. Bornkamm suggested that with a little stretching of some ancient conventions, one can make sense of several features which might originally appear incoherent. The material presented in Chapters 1 and 2 suggests a great deal more than this, raising some hope that if one is ingenious enough at interpretation, all the apparent incoherence in the *Acts Thom.* will disappear and one will thus be able to make sense of this work in all its details.

---

[3] Bornkamm, *Mythos und Legende in den apokryphen Thomas-Akten* (FRLANT n.s. 31; Göttingen: Vandenhoeck & Ruprecht, 1933) 17–18, 23, and 32–33.

But here of course caution is clearly in order. With enough ingenuity, one can make sense of almost anything, including works that are indeed genuinely incoherent, creating sense and coherence where there really is none. A means of controlling ingenuity is needed, insuring that the attempt to make sense of the *Acts Thom.* is not overly creative, going beyond the intention of its author or authors.

One is tempted to simply fall back on some sense of "moderation" accepting interpretations that are in accord with our sense of literary conventions of the Hellenistic period and respecting certain boundaries beyond which one should not venture to apply ingenuity in an effort to save the text. But moderation is a questionable strategy, particularly in the case of Gnostic writings. One always has to contend with the possibility that these are genuinely "esoteric" writings in which not merely the content but also the literary conventions are perhaps peculiar and relatively unique, familiar to a small community of initiates, employing conventions not understandable even to the contemporary educated public outside the group.

It is in this context that the project of interpreting the *Acts Thom.* raises many basic questions that have excercised hermeneutical and literary-critical theorists so greatly in recent times: (a) Do literary texts generally have determinate meaning, and if so how does one discover it? (b) What is the role of creativity in the work of interpretation, and what are its limitations? (c) What is the nature of the "author's intention" and how does it relate to the "meaning" of the text?

These points must be raised at a fundamental level in the interpretation of the *Acts Thom.* This study tries to make a virtue of this necessity and to make these theoretical and methodological problems part of its subject matter. What is proposed here is a somewhat novel model of how to go about interpreting a text, a model which has more general applications beyond the *Acts Thom.* The general thrust of the thesis in this respect is to develop a method by which, first, one can establish through fairly rigorous argumentation the fact that a given text does in fact require a close reading that gets at relatively hidden meanings not directly stated on the surface. (I do not assume that all texts require this kind of reading; this is a matter always to be established.) Secondly, the thesis develops a method by which one can discover, with some certainty and through controlled argument, the nature of these hidden meanings. Not just any interesting ideas suggested by a suggestive text represent a good interpretation of that text. Suggestive texts suggest something very definite, and good interpretation needs a controlled method of ascertaining what this definite but hidden meaning is.

Let me now outline the main features of the interpretative method developed to accomplish this task.

Outline of a Theoretical Solution

The basic problem facing interpretation in almost every literary or religious text is the indeterminacy in the meaning of the words on the page taken simply by themselves. Everyone is aware that the same words can be interpreted in many different ways by different readers. It is obvious that the words on the page are, so to speak, only one half—the external or "objective" half—of what goes into producing meaning. Equally important are the linguistic skills and habits and the assumptions and concerns that the readers bring to the reading. These factors are the "subjective" half of what it is that brings about meaning, determining the way in which the readers construe words and phrases and make connections within the text and between the text and their own experience.

Bultmann gives special attention to the "existential" dimension of these subjective factors that influence interpretation, the way in which our personal concern for meaning in life determines the meaning the text has for us. For Bultmann, the "demand that the interpreter must silence his subjectivity . . . in order to obtain an objective knowledge is . . . absurd . . . only those who are stirred by the question of their own experience can hear the claim which the text makes."[4]

Recently, hermeneutics and literary criticism of a "structuralist" orientation has drawn attention to the semiotic dimension of the subjective factors that determine meaning. Jonathan Culler offers some helpful insights in this regard.[5] His proposals regarding structuralist literary criticism are based partly on some analogies between structure in a literary work as a whole and the more easily studied grammatical structure of sentences. The grammatical structure of a sentence, he points out, is not something given completely objectively in the sentence itself. With no prior knowledge of English grammar, for example, one could not discover the structure of "The child hit the ball." There is nothing in the words themselves, nor in their arrangement, which would let one know that the child is the one hitting the ball, and not

---

[4] Rudolf Bultmann, *Essays, Philosophical and Theological* (London: SCM, 1955) 255–56.

[5] Culler, *Structuralist Poetics: Structuralism, Linguistics, and the Study of Literature* (Ithaca: Cornell University Press, 1975) 3–6, 20–24, and 113–30.

vice versa. One must know by some means prior to reading the sentence that nouns preceding verbs are generally the subject of English sentences and nouns following are objects. It is this linguistic competence, existing in the readers' minds, which allows them to construe and "structure" the words on the page properly.

We tend, says Culler, to think of structure and meaning as objectively given properties of literary texts, a fact which one can discover by careful examination of the texts themselves; however, this is not so. A subjective component is also necessary in that a "work has structure and meaning because it is read in a particular way, because potential properties, latent in the object itself, are actualized by the [implicit] theory of discourse applied in the act of reading."[6]

Bultmann's existentialist hermeneutics and Culler's brand of structuralist poetics point us, in different ways, to the crucial importance of particular subjective factors present in the mind of the reader which give the reader the ability to understand the intended meaning of a given text. What Culler and Bultmann do not offer is an adequate method of discovering those particular subjective presuppositions with which we must approach a text when that text comes from a culture (or an esoteric subculture) which may be foreign and unfamiliar, both in the character of its existential concerns and in its use of language and literary genres. Any appeal to "universally valid" presuppositions appropriate to the reading of all texts of all cultures and subcultures of all eras is of course very questionable.[7]

This dilemma has sometimes led to treating literary texts as though they had no determinative meaning. The literary critic Stanley Fish, for example, argues that the presuppositions which a particular group of readers brings to the reading of a given text merely reflects the presuppositions of the community constituted by this group.[8] These readers simply take notice of those features of the text which are highlighted by these presuppositions, and whatever meanings suggest themselves as a

---

[6] Culler, *Structuralist Poetics*, 113.

[7] Hans Jonas (*The Gnostic Religion* [Boston: Beacon, 1958] 320–21) makes this point with regard to the Heideggerian presuppositions which he used in his interpretation of Gnostic thought. Initially, Jonas says, he assumed that these presuppositions provided the key to an interpretation of Gnosticism because they were universally valid and offered the key to interpreting religious texts generally. He later came to realize the somewhat coincidental nature of the fit: Heideggerian existentialism and early Gnostic thought simply happen to be worldviews with strong similarities to each other.

[8] Fish, *Is There a Text in This Class?: The Authority of Interpretative Communities* (Cambridge: Harvard University Press, 1980) 1–17 and 356–71.

result of this kind of reading are legitimate. Since there are no universally held or universally valid presuppositions, Fish says, there is no way of saying that any interpretation is more objectively accurate than any other. The meaning of a given text varies according to the presuppositions of the community in which it is being read.

This is the dilemma which the present study tries to solve, both theoretically and by showing how the theoretical model it proposes can be carried out in practice. The theoretical solution proposed is in itself a fairly simple one. The proposal is, first of all, that for any given text there is a definite set of presuppositions in the light of which this text must be read. This set of presuppositions is not universal. It is the set which governed the minds of the author or authors as they were composing the text.[9] The primary task of the interpreter is to discover the character of the presuppositions proper to the accurate understanding of this text. A thoroughgoing and systematic investigation focused primarily on this task, rather than immediately and directly on the interpretation of individual passages, is what distinguishes the method of the present study from the more usual approaches.

Culler borrows the technical term "competence" from the linguist Noam Chomsky to refer to the key subjective presuppositions necessary to make a given reader competent to understand a given literary genre.[10] "Literary competence" is thus the term he uses to describe what it is that should be the chief focus of one's setting about to interpret a given work. In the model of interpretation offered here, I incorporate also Bultmann's emphasis on the importance of existential concerns (though not necessarily existentialist concerns). Therefore, I use the somewhat broader term "reading competence," personified sometimes in the "competent reader." So a primary goal of this study can be described as discovering the nature of the reading competence appropriate to an accurate reading and interpretation of the *Acts Thom.*

---

[9] This proposal preserves the traditional idea that the "intention of the author" in some sense is indeed what we are trying to discover in interpreting a text. At the same time it avoids the justly criticized idea that this "intention" is some other set of conscious *ideas* authors have in addition to the ideas they set down on paper; see W. K. Wimsatt, Jr., *The Verbal Icon: Studies in the Meaning of Poetry* (Lexington, KY: University of Kentucky Press, 1954) 3–18. "What the author intends" is the meaning the words appear to have as they are set down because of the presuppositions which govern one's mind at the time of writing—presuppositions which in the typical case remain unconscious, in the same way that grammatical structures governing sentence formation typically remain unconscious as a person speaks.

[10] Culler, *Structuralist Poetics*, 10 and 113–30.

Of course, if there is no universally valid set of presuppositions which make one competent to read all texts, one might well wonder how the nature of the particular reading competence appropriate to a given text is to be discovered. My proposal here is that it can usually be discovered from clues indirectly given in the text. By "indirectly given" I mean that, although authors almost never state explicitly and directly the presuppositions necessary to construe their work properly, given a long enough piece of text which can be systematically mined for clues of this kind, the major elements of reading competence proper to the text can be discovered. This is what the body of the present study does for the opening scenes of the *Acts Thom*. Let me briefly mention, by way of example, two of the most important kinds of "indirect clues" which are basic to my argumentation.

First of all, there are some passages whose substantive meaning is fairly clear—so that we know in general how it is to be construed—but whose structure is somewhat unusual. This structure can be kept in mind as a possible model for construing the meaning of unclear passages sharing similar formal features. To use the grammatical analogy mentioned earlier, if we saw a ball hit a child, and someone described this by saying, "The child hit the ball," we would have reason to suspect that for some reason their sense of word order was the reverse of the usual one. And if the person made several like comments, one would have reason to start construing their other sentences accordingly, even where there were no external guides as to their substantive meaning. The person does not have to tell us directly about their particular grammatical sense. Under fortunate circumstances we can infer it indirectly from the way they speak. It is of course a somewhat different matter with regard to ancient texts, since there is no way to directly observe the concrete situation on which they comment. But as I have shown below, there are some cases in the *Acts Thom*. in which the substantive meaning of a given passage is fairly clear, despite rather unusual verbal devices that might appear in it.

Secondly, there are verbal patterns whose substantive meanings are not clear, but they are clearly significant because they stand out and recur frequently. An obvious example of this phenomenon involves the pleonasms of the type "joy and gladness" or "gazing and looking." In almost every passage in which this kind of construction occurs, one member of the pleonastic phrase occurs within one or two sentences of the pleonasm. As an example, we may note: "They will be at that eternal joy . . . and they will be in joy and gladness" (110.10 and 14). Again this is an indirect clue that, once noticed, should shape further reading. Having discovered on the basis of the above observations that this pattern has some special significance in this work, one should be alert for further occurrences and attempt to discover what significance the pattern might have.

An Outline of Method

A caution is necessary in regard to the second example. That is, although this example does involve looking for verbal patterns in the text, it is an important aspect of the method proposed here that not just any set of features one might observe forming some pattern serves as valid and conclusive evidence for a project of discovering the nature of reading competence proper to a given text. This is what differentiates the method proposed here from interpretative methods which, for example, focus on finding such patterns as recurrent groups of three or four members or recurrent symmetrical arrangements of elements in the sequence of a text. Such a method is frequently defended on the grounds that in a given text such patterns are clearly "there" if one only pays proper attention to them. On the contrary, the key question is not whether a given pattern is "there" in the sense that it can be found if one looks for it. In order for an observable pattern to serve as good evidence on this score, it must be a pattern which calls attention to itself in some fairly obvious way, and the case for seeing it as something one ought to look for must generally be supported by evidence drawn from other features in the text. So, in the example given above, a pleonastic construction like "joy and gladness" is a phrase that draws attention to itself to some degree even by ordinary reading conventions. The frequent recurrence of such phrases with nearby catchwords constitutes some initial evidence that such phrases have some significance in this work, and one ought to pay special attention to them. More conclusive argumentation that such phrases are significant and the discovery of what this significance might be comes later in the thesis through a convergence of many other observations supporting and filling out the initial suspicion generated by observing that pleonasms with nearby catchwords do occur frequently.

The method proposed here requires a certain kind of special carefulness in looking at the text of the *Acts Thom.* In particular, it requires that attention be paid to seemingly odd features of the text and elements that appear deviant from the point of view of good Greek usage and grammar. Normally, when reading "popular" works such as this, one tends to gloss over such irregularites, chalking them up to the authors' idiomatic eccentricities or carelessness or to textual corruption. One pays attention to what the authors probably meant, overlooking the odd way they actually phrase their account. In this study, however, I am operating on the basis that any such oddity may well contain some indirect clues as to unusual verbal structures or devices which we have to be alert for in the work as a whole. They need to be carefully noted to see whether they recur and also whether they fit into larger schemata of meaning.

A note must be added here in reference to the thesis of F. C. Burkitt who proposed another way of accounting for many of the oddities in the *Acts Thom.*[11] He pointed to a number of passages in which oddities in the Greek text could plausibly be explained as a result of clumsy or mistaken translation from Syriac into Greek. On this basis he proposed that the *Acts Thom.* was originally written in Syriac and that our present Greek text of the *Acts Thom.* is a translation of this now lost Syriac original. The present study does not come into direct conflict with Burkitt's explanation of specific passages—none of the passages he considered comes into play here. However, all the oddities in the passages which I do treat can be explained as deliberate literary devices used by those who composed the surviving Greek text of the *Acts Thom.* This renders other attempts to explain these phenomena unnecessary. This study suggests at a minimum that the Greek *Acts Thom.* is a carefully composed work in its own right, whatever its relation to a hypothetical Syriac original. And by showing that numerous oddities can be explained as deliberate devices by Greek authors, it tends to remove the principal basis on which this hypothesis of a Syriac original was intially proposed.

The systematic mining of the text for indirect clues as to the nature of reading competence requires a great deal of detailed textual analysis. It is largely for this reason that I have chosen to focus primarily on a relatively small stretch of the *Acts Thom.*, chapters 1 – 10, in order to be able to conduct the investigation with the thoroughness and attention to detail it requires and still remain within manageable boundaries of time and space. On the other hand, the first step is to use evidence from other passages in the *Acts Thom.*, primarily concerning links between narrative and monologues generally in this book and concerning the internal structure and unifying devices found in the longer monologues themselves.

Reading competence is a constant when moving within any given writing. Therefore, the account of its character given here, though based primarily only on a small section of text, should be able to be

---

[11] Burkitt, "The Original Language of the Acts of Judas Thomas," *JTS* 1 (1899/1900) 280 – 90.

applied (perhaps with some additions or modifications) to the rest of the *Acts Thom.* The requirements of space also dictate another methodological narrowness in this study as well. An investigation of the presuppositions necessary on the part of the reader of the *Acts Thom.* could well be based on the evidence beyond indirect indications given in the work itself. Ancient works contemporary with the *Acts Thom.* could also be used, as well as modern scholarly accounts of literary genres and of general cultural and religious currents. This study relies in several places on such sources as supplemental evidence and means of argumentation. The insights of form-criticism prove to be of considerable importance, for example, and the work of Gershom G. Scholem on Jewish mysticism,[12] and of Philip Merlan on Middle Platonism[13] provide much supportive and clarifying evidence as well. But for the most part this study proceeds on the basis of *scriptura ipsius interpres,* the text provides its own clues for its interpretation.

The General Plan of This Study

Due to the nature of the material and the requirements of the method just outlined, this study proceeds in a somewhat unusual fashion. The chief peculiarity perhaps is that the text of the *Acts Thom.* has basically two functions here. On the one hand, it is the text to be interpreted, and on the other hand, it is also the source to be systematically mined for clues as to how this interpretation should proceed. The general plan of the study begins with this latter task, gathering clues as to the nature of the reading competence appropriate to this work. There is a gradual shift from discovering the nature of reading competence to applying what we learn about it to the actual interpretation of chapters 1–10.

Specifically, Chapters 1 and 2 are devoted entirely to gathering both evidence about literary devices and principles which can be shown to have guided the composition of the work. Chapter 1 focuses on five speeches from various places in the *Acts Thom.* and on the narrative surrounding them. It points to literary devices linking speech and narrative and to the standard internal structure common to these speeches. Chapter 2 begins focusing more narrowly on the primary section of the

---

[12] Scholem, *Major Trends in Jewish Mysticism* (2d ed.; New York: Shocken, 1946); and idem, *Ursprung und Anfänge der Kabbala* (Berlin: De Gruyter, 1962).

[13] Merlan, *Monopsychism Mysticism Metaconsciousness: Problems of the Soul in the Neoaristotelian and Neoplatonic Tradition* (The Hague: Nijhoff, 1963).

text to be interpreted in the thesis, chapters 1 – 10, collecting evidence from various passages throughout these chapters concerning several different kinds of literary devices being used.

Chapters 3 and 4 move from this preliminary gathering of evidence to a more direct focus on the actual interpretation of the main text under consideration in this study, starting with the opening passage of the *Acts Thom.* These Chapters have a dual focus. They apply what has been learned in Chapters 1 and 2 to substantive interpretation while continuing to gather more evidence about the special way this text needs to be interpreted.

Chapter 5 interrupts the sequential interpretation and analysis of the text in order to give for the first time an account of the overall literary strategy and the substantive thought of the redactors. Chapter 6 finishes the exegesis of chapters 7 – 10, applying the account of reading competence gained earlier to this section of the text while putting some finishing touches on that account of competence. Chapter 7 concludes with some remarks on the character of the "Gnostic hermeneutics" implied in the way the redactors of the *Acts Thom.* use language and traditional religious imagery. They guide the reader to a more meaningful state of being and interpretation (gnosis) of experience.

This study has a cumulative character. The initial Chapters take up a considerable amount of spade work. This initial preparatory work establishes in a controlled way what is, on the face of it, a very implausible thesis: an incredible amount of artful and complex design has gone into the composition of the *Acts Thom.* Therefore, a great deal of attention to detail is required in order to understand its intended meaning, a meaning which is suggested and hidden rather than directly stated on the surface.

1

SPECIAL COMPOSITIONAL DEVICES
RELATED TO
SPEECHES, PRAYERS, AND HYMNS

There are many long accounts of monologues in the *Acts Thom.*, and these most often have the appearance of being only tangentially related to their narrative contexts. Likewise they often appear to consist of strings of clichéd phrases strung together without much order. The purpose of this Chapter is to show that, in both cases, appearances are deceiving. The speeches and prayers show quite deliberate internal organization and also relate to themes and motifs from the narrative context in consistent and predictable, if somewhat unconventional, ways.

1.1 General Principles of The Relationship of Narrative and Speech Material

Günther Bornkamm has already established one kind of relation between the narrative and the speeches: narrative "legends" allegorically reflect the same "myths" that are expressed in the monologues.[1] The following analyses can be looked upon partly as enlargements of his thesis extending its scope and giving more precise definition to the devices employed to indicate the relationships involved.

As to the actual principles of composition involved, they can be divided into two kinds. The first is the one Bornkamm has noticed, that is, that the speeches or prayers give mythical expression to a theme presented as a more realistic story ("legend") in the narrative. Two cases of this kind of relationship in chapters 1–10 would be: (1) the theme of the eschatological wedding banquet in the wedding hymn (110.9–15) can be read as a mythical version of the banquet given by the king of Andrapolis, and (2) the theme of the redeemer's descent into hell in the Christ prayer (115.4–8) can be read as a mythical version of the saving activity of the apostle Thomas in the "foreign" and "worldly" Andrapolis.

The second kind of compositional device involves catchword and motif recurrences. There are numerous examples in chapters 1–10:

1) the wedding hymn (109.5) has the striking image of the king seated "on top of the woman's head (κορυφή)" which recalls the odd reference in the narrative (107.5–6) to Thomas's anointing "the top of his head" (also κορυφή, not mentioned in ritual anointings elsewhere in the *Acts Thom.*);[2]

2) the door of the bride's bedroom in the hymn is oddly "decorated with reeds" recalling Thomas's unexpected gesture at the end of the anointing scene, "He took in his hand a reed branch" (107.11–108.1);

3) the blossoms in Thomas's crown (107.10), and the blossoms to which the woman's clothes are compared in the hymn (109.3–4);

---

[1] Bornkamm, *Mythos*, 17–18, 23, and 32–33.

[2] The Greek supplied throughout this work follows the text of Maximilianus Bonnet and Ricardus Adelbertus Lipsius, *Acta Apostolorum Apocrypha* (Darmstadt: Wissenschaftliche Buchgesellschaft, 1959). The citations (e.g., 109.6) refer to the page and line numbers in Bonnet, *Acta*. References to "chapters" and "Acts" also follow Bonnet's conventions for dividing the text.

4) the fact that Thomas very oddly anoints his teeth (107.8), while the woman's thirty-two teeth "sing her praises" (109.8–9);
5) the metaphorical motif of the journey in the opening lines (114.5–6) recalls Thomas's journey to Andrapolis;
6) Thomas's statement, "You know the future and bring it about through us" (114.10–11), is a recollection of his own prophecy of the servant's punishment and its fulfillment;
7) one's "making manifest secret words" (114.12–13) brings to mind the flutist's explaining Thomas's Hebrew words to the Andrapolitan guests who did not understand them (113.3–6); and
8) the image of "power destroying the enemy" (115.1–2) reminds one of the lion who killed the hostile servant.

In regard to these latter catchword connections, one is clearly in the area where more proof is needed. The first way of relating speech to narrative as an interpretative element stays pretty close to normal contemporary conventions and proceeds also according to a common contemporary practice, that of allegorical interpretation of legend. The second way, on the contrary, goes beyond this: the nature of its significance is much harder to grasp, and it presupposes conventions quite different from those with which one may be familiar in contemporary literature.

In order to show that the above examples indeed involve deliberate compositional devices and that they are not simply the result of coincidence, we shall look at five other long monologues in the *Acts Thom.* In several cases the analysis will show that deliberate principles are clearly being followed, and a high degree of plausibility in many other cases will support this argument.

What follows is a very selective analysis of some aspects of five sample speeches. Not every aspect even of organization will be treated. And it will at times appear that, as to substantive interpretation, the analyses raise more questions than they answer. It will be a general feature of the thesis that it will begin by showing that interpretation of this work is much more complex than it at first appears. Only after the analysis of the wedding hymn in Chapter 4 will it be possible to begin saying what the work is about and so to begin suggesting lines of substantive interpretation.

1.2 The Bride's Speech

The speech in chapter 14 is a good example with which to start. It shows some of the same kinds of unusual connections between speech and narrative in a context where they appear fairly clearly intentional.

The narrative situation is that of the first night of a newlywed couple who have during the night been visited by Jesus and converted to sexual abstinence. The parents enter in the morning and find them "sitting opposite each other, the bride unveiled, the bridegroom very happy (ἱλαρός)." The parents are surprised at this state of affairs and ask about it.

It is worth noting that both questions of the parents are somewhat unclear. The mother asks (119.8–9), "Why are you sitting like this, child, and have you no modesty, but are as though you had lived a long time with your own husband" (διὰ τί οὕτως καθέζῃ τέκνον, καὶ οὐκ αἰδῇ, ἀλλ᾽ οὕτως εἶ ὡς πολὺν χρόνον συμβιώσασα τῷ ἰδίῳ ἀνδρί)? Is she complaining that the daughter is sitting apart from her husband (οὕτως καθέζῃ) and thus appears like one who is no longer in love? Or does "have you no modesty" (οὐκ αἰδῇ) refer to the fact that she is not veiled so that we should understand οὕτως to mean "unveiled" (ἀσκέπαστον, line 7) ?

The father asks (119.10–11), "Because of your great love for your husband don't you even veil yourself" (διὰ τὴν πολλὴν ἀγάπην τὴν πρὸς τὸν ἄνδρα σου οὐδὲ σκεπάζῃ)? Does he mean "Don't you even [besides not sitting next to your husband] veil yourself because of the great love [you are supposed to be feeling] for your husband?" Or is the sense "Don't you even veil yourself [if for no other reason] because of your great love for your husband?" Or perhaps it is even "Is it because of your great love for [passion for, familiarity with] your husband that you don't even veil yourself?" The fact that there is unclarity in the wording of both questions is some reason to suspect that we are dealing not with an exegetical difficulty but with something deliberate on the part of the writers.

Following these questions the bride's answer (119.12–120.12) centers on the theme of conversion as a sacred marriage with Jesus. Already here we see how the speech not only gives a mythical interpretation (sacred marriage) to a narrative event (the conversion) but it takes over another theme from the narrative (earthly marriage and sexual union) as a metaphor leading to the myth.

In addition to this, the speech is very clearly organized according to themes from the narrative. This initially takes the very conventional and obvious form of taking up specific points from the parents' questions, repeating them and answering them:

> I *am indeed in great love*, father . . . and I shall ask for the husband I have experienced today.

And so, yes, I *shall no longer be veiled* because the mirror of shame has been taken from me.

And I *am no longer ashamed or modest* (αἰσχύνομαι ἤ αἰδοῦμαι) because the work of shame and modesty stands far from me. (119.12–120.5)

But then the bride, imperceptibly to the inattentive reader, begins speaking of matters not specifically asked by the parents. And what is noteworthy here is that care is taken, by the introduction of "that" (ὅτι), to continue to give the impression she is answering questions:

And that I am not upset— because my upsetness (ἔκπληξις) did not remain;

And that I am in happiness (ἰλαρότητι) and joy—because the day of joy was not disturbed;

And that I have set at naught this husband and this marriage which pass away from before my eyes—because I am joined in another marriage;

And that I did not have intercourse with this temporary husband, whose end comes about with tears and bitterness of soul—because I am yoked with the True Husband. (120.5–12)

One feature that is immediately obvious is that happiness (ἰλαρότης) in the second line is derived from the earlier narrative passage where it is, however, spoken of the bridegroom (119.7): "They found the bride unveiled and the bridegroom very happy (ἰλαρός)."

The way in which this becomes obvious is worth analyzing more closely because it provides a paradigm for the kind of argumentation which is fundamental to this thesis. The speech uses a particular organizational device, that of referring to specific points from the narrative and answering them. The device is obvious because it is a fairly conventional one and also because its features are so clearly marked and consistent (repeated three times) in the first lines of the speech.

The speech then continues to use one aspect of the device, the form of the sentences, even adding an additional feature ("that") to make clear that this is the intention. But the passage has now gone beyond what "makes sense" according to normal conventions, because normal conventions would assume that there are actual questions in the narrative to which reference is being made.

The attentive reader knows, then, that something is happening in the text different from what one normally expects. On the other hand, the expectation still lingers that narrative questions are being replied to, and one naturally makes the connection to ἱλαρός which is something like the same phenomenon. In fact, if ἱλαρός were said of the bride and not the bridegroom in the narrative, it still would not be a departure from normal conventions. We would probably understand the bride as addressing what the readers have heard of her, rather than what the parents have asked.

But as the text stands, it in effect leads us from a normally structured set of meanings over to an interpretation that is clearly intended but which assumes an abnormal literary structure (a reference to something not said of the bride as though it were).

If this were an isolated phenomenon in the speech it might be regarded as insignificant, attributed perhaps to the carelessness of the author. But this instance has several analogues in this same speech.

For example, the woman abruptly brings up the fact, "I am not upset," as though there were some expectation in the air that she would be. And that this indeed was a matter of concern for her is confirmed when she says, "My upsetness did not remain" and "The day of joy was not disturbed." Given the content of the first marriage night and the reference in the preceding line to the "work of shame" which is now far from her, these lines clearly imply that the woman had been originally upset in anticipation of intercourse. The conversion to sexual abstinence removed this anxiety and the "day of joy was not disturbed."

What is very remarkable here is that there is no hint at all in the narrative that the woman was upset or that anyone expected her to be. In other words we find here an extension, in a more radical form, of the peculiarity noticed above: we have moved from a normal convention, to a slightly abnormal extension of it, to a very abnormal extension.

This example and the one involving ἱλαρός support each other. On the one hand, the latter is a very clear case and encourages us to construe the former as we have. On the other hand, the elaborateness with which the "upsetness" passage is carried out precludes the assumption that the formulations are merely coincidental, careless on the part of the author.

It is clear then, that the writers intend to use the speech partly as a means of reading elements into the narrative situation that are not present in the text of the narrative. In the case of ἱλαρός, the speech transfers something said of one character, the bridegroom, to a different one, the bride. In the case of "upsetness" the speech seems to invent a completely new theme.

Further exploration of this passage shows that this intention of the writer extends not only to particular formulations in the speech itself, but to narrative formulations as well: there appear to be several cryptic suggestions in the narrative of themes that become more explicit in the speech.

One example of this is the wording of the passage about the couple's conversion (118.11–12): "They believed in the Lord and gave their surrendered selves to him" (ἐπίστευσαν τῷ κυρίῳ καὶ ἑαυτοὺς ἐκδότους ἔδωκαν αὐτῷ). "Surrendered" (ἐκδότους) is tautologous here. On the other hand one of the meanings of ἐκδιδόναι is "to give in marriage," and this word has in fact been used in this sense several times in preceding sections of this same story.[3] Given the fact that the bride's speech interprets the conversion as a marriage to Jesus, it appears very likely that the tautology in the narrative is intended to be an early hint of the same theme.

This calls to our attention the unclear wording of the parents' questions which may also be cryptic references to themes taken up in the speech. What is noticeable here is that at the end of her speech the bride says, "I have set at naught (ἐξουθένισα) this husband," whereas the narrative says nothing of this and implies instead a mutual decision on the part of the couple not to sleep together. But we saw earlier that the wording of both the mother's and the father's questions involves unclarity precisely on this point as to whether they are complaining about the bride's lack of respect for her husband or whether they are remarking on her apparent lack of modesty in being unveiled. The fact that both these themes are taken up in the speech makes it likely that there is some intentionality to the unclear wording of the questions. It is part of a compositional principle whereby subtle suggestions in the narrative prepare for the explicit treatment of the same themes in the speech that follows.

One final organizational principle involves the relation of this speech to those immediately preceding and following it. The bridegroom's speech (chapter 15) that follows immediately upon this one has a seemingly anticlimactic section at the end (121.15–122.5). Close attention to it reveals that the bridegroom here is using much of the language from the bride's speech: "He whom I have experienced (ἠσθόμην, see 120.1 and 2) . . . whose love (ἀγάπη, see 119.13; 120.1) burns in me . . . he will not blame me, unashamed (ἀναιδευόμενον, see 120.4) to

---

[3] The king "is giving his daughter in marriage" (105.2–3; 113.9–10).

speak of him. . . ." This last word, of course, is used in an entirely different context than its earlier counterpart, but the coincidence of all three words makes it likely that some intention lies behind the correspondences.

Looking back at the preceding speech (116.9–118.10), it centers on the theme of the trouble and worry brought on by sexual intercourse and children. Given the particular compositional principles observed so far, it seems not unlikely that the sex occasioned "upsetness" (ἔκπληξις) in the bride's speech is meant to be connected to the trouble and worry of the earlier speech, even though there it is related to sex in a very different way. This suggestion is supported by the fact that that speech ends by speaking of an "incorruptible and true marriage" (118.7–8) matching the bride's statement concerning "another marriage . . . the True Husband" (contrasted with the "temporary man," 120.10–12).

At this point we can pause to reflect on the kind of argumentation being employed here and the way different kinds of evidence are being evaluated.

First of all, there is the argument from implication. In a case where the intent of a passage is fairly clear, we can examine the passage for what it might imply about unusual organizational principles. In the case of ἱλαρός, for example, it is clear that the authors intend to continue picking up motifs from the narrative, though this implies a transference of this motif from the bridegroom to the bride.

Secondly, there is the argument from analogy. The fact that both the case of ἱλαρός and the case of the bride's "upsetness" imply analogously peculiar principles of composition strengthens the case regarding these as principles actually being followed by the writers.

Thirdly, there is the argument from puzzling abnormalities in the text. Unclear wording in the parents' questions makes one ask whether there is not some deliberate intention at work and what that intention might be. It will become more clear as we proceed that other devices as well (such as tautologies and word repetitions) are also meant to call one's attention to particular elements.

Finally, there is the argument from coincidence. The fact that there are plausible catchword or motif recurrences between three successive speeches makes one suspect that this too is a deliberate organizing principle.

These arguments, of course, do not function separately. One must rely most often on a convergence of probable indications from several kinds of evidence. The last-mentioned argument (from coincidence) is an especially weak one by itself unless it rests on features that in some way draw attention to themselves. On the other hand, once one example of an organizational device is established with some probability, other merely possible examples do have some weight in that, according to their respective degrees of plausibility, they help make a case for repeated use of the device. For example, the anticlimactic character of the end of the bridegroom's speech and the fact that it contains three different key words from the bride's speech make it very likely that the writers are going out of their way to connect this speech with the preceding one. On the other hand, in the case of the connection between the themes of upsetness and the "true man" from the bride's speech with the themes of worry and "true marriage" in the preceding speech, nothing in the text draws special attention to the features in question. By itself it could hardly be cited as evidence, and yet it does have some weight: it shows that if one does look for such connections they can be found without straining the text at all. And in the case of the theme of "upsetness," it actually helps to explain what is otherwise the anomaly of an important idea being read back into the narrative with no preparation at all.

These various kinds of arguments, in different combinations, will be implicit in all of the analyses carried out from this point through Chapter 6. It should be noticed that they really consist of a formalization of, and an attempt to establish methodological control over, what is often the natural process by which we come to grasp the special conventions of an unfamiliar literary genre or other art form.

1.3 Thomas's Address to the Demons

The next sample speech (161.12–20) is also one where a number of examples of the kind of organization described above are fairly obvious even on the surface, and close attention reveals several other examples not so clearly indicated but clearly analogous to the others and often pointed to by them.

The narrative situation (159.9–161.9) in which it occurs is this: as Thomas enters a city, a woman, "very beautiful" (πάνυ ὡραία), cries out and asks the apostle to listen to her story. She says (160.2), "I have been tormented by the Opponent (βασανίζομαι ὑπὸ τοῦ ἐναντίου) for five years." She was coming out of the baths one day when a "troubled and disturbed" (τεθορυβημένος καὶ ἐντάραχος) man confronted her, wanting to sleep with her (7). She refused, and she later said to the maid accompanying her (15–16), "Did you see that young man and his shamelessness, how without shame he spoke to me brashly?" But the maid had seen an old man, not a young one.

The woman reports that as she was going to sleep that evening, "My soul suggested a suspicion to me, especially since he appeared to me under two forms." She goes on to state (161.1), "Coming to me that night he united with me with his filthy intercourse." The next morning the woman woke, and she saw the man and fled. But she reports that he came again "in the night which is kin to him and used (παρεκρᾶτο)" her.

She has at present been "disturbed" (ἐνοχλουμένη) for five years by him, and she requests of Thomas (8–9), "Drive out the demon that possesses me" (ἀπέλασον ἀπ' ἐμοῦ τὸν διενοχλοῦντά μοι δαίμονα).

The story consistently refers to the woman's assailant as though he were a single figure, yet he undergoes many (unannounced) changes of form as the story progresses. He is first a crazy man at the baths, then there is a suggestion that he is a dream incubus (insinuating himself into the woman's mind by the "suspicion" she has (160.19), then she actually sees him after she wakes, and finally she seems to speak of a demon possessing her.

Already in the case of the narrative preceding the bride's speech we saw the likelihood that the writers inserted subtle suggestions in the narrative that are taken up by a subsequent speech, and here we have in fact a speech which speaks of the "many-formed one" stating "he appears however he wants" (161.14–15).[4] We also find in the narrative here the explicit remark that the man at the baths appeared under two forms. In other words, although there are other possible ways of explaining the passage to avoid the difficulties about apparent changes in the assailant's form, the culmination of other indications suggests that they be read as part of a deliberate device on the part of the writers of the text.

It will be helpful to proceed to other examples of compositional principles visible in the speech itself (161.12–20). The speech in this case very clearly presents a mythical interpretation of the narrative events. Here the form it takes is that Thomas treats the whole incident as an example of the way in which the "Enemy" (a mythical figure who appears often in the first part of the *Acts Thom.*) attacks people. It is also very obvious how this interpretation is already suggested in the narrative itself, particularly by the woman's opening statement (160.2) that she has been tormented by the "Opponent" (ἐναντίος).

---

[4] See also the alternation in the speech between "Oh . . ." and "Oh (the one) from . . ." at the beginning of the lines (161.16 and 19), probably a case of deliberate confusion between the mythical enemy and his representative manifestations.

Finally, there are many examples of motif recurrences between speech and narrative, some almost certainly intended, others with varying degrees of probability concerning intended connections. A number of these motifs occur in the opening lines of the speech:

O unrestrained Evil,
O shamlessness of the Enemy,
O envious one never resting,
O ugly one subduing the beautiful ones. . . .

The most obvious case here is "shamelessness" (ἀναίδεια, related also to "unrestrained," ἀκατάσχετος). It occurs again toward the end of the speech (161.19). Whereas here it refers to the Enemy himself, in the narrative it refers to the conduct of one of his manifestations, the crazy man at the baths. In the narrative, attention is drawn to this theme by tautologous repetition (160.16): "Did you see (his) shamelessness . . . how without shame he brashly spoke to me" (ἀναίδειαν . . . μὴ αἰδεσθεὶς παρρησίᾳ, 160.16)? In this case we also have explicit confirmation that the author intends the transfer of the motif from one figure to another: "O bitter tree whose fruits are like it" (161.16–17) reflects directly on the fact that the same qualities are shared by the Enemy and his manifestations.

This example also draws attention, by analogy, to another tautology (160.7–8), the pleonasm "troubled and disturbed" (τεθορυβημένος καὶ ἐντάραχος) referring to the crazy man. The plausible connection to the speech here is double: (1) it implies that the man is very unpleasant, leading to "O ugly one subduing the beautiful ones" (earlier [159.13–14] the woman was spoken of as "very beautiful"); and (2) it is plausibly related to "O envious one never resting" (161.13), though here the "troubled" quality of the man is given a new twist by being related to envy.

There are two cases in the speech where the introduction of a theme which is itself absent from the narration is occasioned by a narrative theme related to it. The speech's description of the "many-formed one" noting "he appears however he wants but his nature cannot be changed" (161.14–16) is followed by "O the one from the deceitful and untrustworthy one." That is, the demon's many changes of form are interpreted as an attempt to deceive. (The narrative has no hint of this.) Likewise "envy" (βάσκανος, 161.13) is not a theme in the narrative, but it immediately precedes "O ugly one, subduing the beautiful ones."

These two speeches provide key examples of compositional principles by which speeches and narratives are connected in the *Acts Thom.* They serve this purpose particularly well because of the way in which the more obvious relationships lead, by implication or analogy, to the ones that are not clearly significant and might be overlooked if we had not the obvious ones to draw our attention to them.

1.4 Internal Speech Organization

Before going to a more cursory analysis of three further speeches, I want to point out several features related to the internal structure of these two speeches.

They do not have a common "structure" as that term is often used in literary studies: there is no common schema of sections of certain types occurring in particular sequence and in special relation to each other. On the other hand, they are composed according to some common principles.

The individual lines of the speeches show very little originality by themselves. Taken in isolation, they are easily passed over as clichés. The interest of the speeches lies almost entirely in the particular way the lines relate to each other and to the narrative. This "reading between the lines" is sometimes necessary, not only to grasp what is interesting in the writing but even the substance of the message—as, for example, it is only the conjunction of several speech and narrative features which leads us to understand that the bride's anxiety was about sex.

This implies that there is more unity to the speech than might at first appear. Part of the reading competence is the general expectation that the speeches are not the unrelated strings of clichés that they might appear to be but are intended as interrelated wholes. Several specific remarks can be made on the character and indications of this unity. All the patterns mentioned are implicit in the interpretations of the speeches given above, unless otherwise noted.

The speeches are made up for the most part of small, thematically focused sections. Unity within these sections is often indictated by parallelism of structure:

And I am not veiled, because. . . .
And I am not ashamed, because. . . . (120.2 and 4)

At other times it is only a common theme, sometimes accompanied by repetition of catchwords, that indicates the unity:

O many-formed one—he appears however he wants but his nature cannot be changed. O one from the Deceitful One. ... (161.14–16)

I am in great love ... and I will ask that the love I have experienced may remain. (119.12–120.1)

The themes forming the focus of different sections are also linked to each other in several ways. One way is by the repetition of catchwords or synonyms. For example, both "shamelessness" and "evil" appear at the beginning of the demon speech and again at the end, both in connection there with another early theme, deceit:

O unrestrained Evil (πονηρία). . . .
O shamelessness (ἀναίδεια) of the Enemy. . . .
O one from the Deceitful One (δόλιος). . . .
O one from the Lie that practices shamelessness (ἀπὸ τῆς
   πλάνης τῆς χρωμένης τῇ ἀναιδείᾳ),
O one from Evil (πονηρία). . . . (161.12–19).

These catchword recurrences might, of course, be looked upon as merely coincidental. But the fact that catchword and/or motif recurrences can be observed in several other speeches as well makes it likely that we should see this as a deliberate compositional principle followed in the writing of this work.[5]

These recurrences within the speech are especially to be observed as links between the beginnings and ends of speeches. In the wedding hymn (chapters 6–7), for example, we shall observe the recurrence of the words φῶς, ἀμβροσία, and ἀλήθεια, as well as the repetition of the themes of the "king-father-master" and of the divine banquet—all links between the opening and the closing sections of the hymn. In the Christ prayer we shall observe the recurrence of the cognates ὁδηγός and ἄνοδος with the accompanying theme of a guide on a journey. Additionally, the recurrence of the motif of freeing captives will be noted—all again linking the opening section to the last one.

---

[5] We have already observed the role of catchword and motif recurrences as links between speech and narrative. Chap. 2 will show that this is a frequent device also in the narrative.

In the light of this common phenomenon, recurrences that might otherwise appear coincidental deserve attention as deliberate and hence significant. That is, reading this work alertly involves looking for such recurrences and integrating the connections they suggest into our interpretation in some way. For example, in the bride's speech the occurrence of ἀνήρ both at the beginning and at the end of the speech would not ordinarily seem to be of any special significance. But the fact that a competent reading requires one to notice such connections makes it likely that one should give some significance to this recurrence in interpreting the hymn.

Another way in which the sections of speeches are linked is by blurring of the boundaries between the sections. This is apparent in the middle section of the bride's speech:

> I am no longer veiled because the mirror of shame was taken
>   from me;
> And I am no longer ashamed because the work of shame stands
>   far from me;
> And . . . I am not upset because my upsetness did not remain;
> And . . . I am in happiness and joy because the day of joy is not
>   disturbed. (120.2–8)

What is noteworthy here is the way some features would lead one to read this as two separate two-line sections, while others tend to suggest the four lines are a unity.

The first two lines share "no longer," the catchword "shame," and the direct reference to shameful sex being removed from the woman. The second two lines both show the awkward "that," share the motif "upset-disturbed," and refer obliquely to the absence of sex. On the other hand, the four lines are constructed in parallel (though the retention of the simple "because" in the second pair makes for some awkwardness) and contain an underlying parallelism of thought. And the similarity, "ashamed-upset," occurring in the middle two lines helps give the impression of a smooth flow from one pair to the other.

A similar phenomenon occurs in the latter half of the demon speech of chapter 44:

> He appears however he wishes, but his nature cannot be
>   changed;
> O one from the deceitful and untrustworthy one;
> O bitter tree whose fruits are like it;
> O one from the devil who fights for the Aliens;

O one from the Lie who practices shamefulness;
O one from the Evil who creeps like a snake, from the one who
is kin to him. (161.15–20)

The first two lines quoted here seem to be united by the common idea of deceit. One could say, then, on the one hand, that there is a break between the second and third lines in that the idea of deceit does not appear in the next two lines. On the other hand, the fact that one of the main themes of the speech is the relation between the mythical Enemy and his manifestations makes it likely the tree-and-fruits metaphor is also related to this theme. Hence one can say that the third line takes up an idea related to the first line: "He appears [in his fruits] however he wants, but his nature [the tree] cannot be changed." Pursuing this same theme, one could read the following lines as carrying this demon-and-his-representatives theme to yet a third level. The plural "Aliens" (ἀλλότριοι) is meant to suggest a whole group of sinister beings that lie even behind the "devil" (διάβολος) who manifests ᾱmself in the woman's many-formed assailant. Whatever the case, it is evident that in the fifth line, the speech again explicitly takes up the theme of deceit (i.e., by the connection δόλιος/πλάνη).

Following this general style of organization, it becomes likely that "creeping like a snake" is also related to the theme of deceit. And perhaps part of the awkwardness of the last phrase (τούτου συγγενοῦς αὐτοῦ ὑπάρχοντος) is due to an attempt to make an association between the motif of "kin" (συγγενές) and that of "likeness" (ἔοικεν) mentioned in the third line.[6]

What the above examples suggest is that the appearance of disorder in many of the speeches is misleading. They are in fact composed of relatively small units focused on a single theme. What obscures this particular principle of organization is the fact that there is also a counterprinciple at work. There is an attempt to link these units to each other by blurring the boundaries between them or by interweaving one theme through more than one unit (or interspersing lines related to one theme between units related to another). The well-prepared reader, then, will construe the text in the light of these two counterbalancing tendencies—when this is done, the initial appearance of randomness in the composition largely disappears.

[6] Finally, as mentioned above, it is likely that the alteration of "Oh . . ." and "Oh (the one) from . . ." as line openings also carries the theme of the relation of the Evil One and his manifestations through all these lines.

The above analyses constitute the thrust of the argument in favor of seeing certain paradigms at work in the composition of the speeches and prayers of the *Acts Thom.* Given the probable case that they establish, we can now proceed to read the three remaining sample speeches (chapters 15, 25, and 27) in the light of the organizational paradigms observed in chapters 14 and 44. That is, for reasons of economy, analyses of the three remaining speeches will not be accompanied by detailed argumentation. The force of these examinations will be merely corroborative, limited to showing (a) that in many cases features that even in themselves are quite noticeable call attention to the same kind of speech organization, (b) that reading these speeches in the light of the organizational paradigms outlined above often suggests plausible solutions to otherwise puzzling details in the speeches, and (c) that construing the text in the light of these paradigms yields in every case a reading that in no way strains the text but instead is able to account for much of its form as we have it.

1.5 The Bridegroom's Speech

The first of the remaining samples (120.14–122.5) is the bridegroom's speech in chapter 15, immediately following that of the bride. We can begin this additional analysis by noticing three separate themes interwoven in the first part of the speech.

The first of these is conversion. It is given in four parallel lines:

> The one placing me far from corruption and sowing in me life
> . . .
> The one delivering me from that sickness and putting me in continent health (ὑγείαν σώφρονα) . . .
> The one redeeming me from the Fall and leading me to the better . . .
> The one changing me over from what is temporary and making me worthy of what is eternal and lasting forever. (121.1–9)

"Putting me in continent health" is a reference to the conversion to sexual abstinence implying, then, that the young man previously was somehow subject to the "sickness" of sexual indulgence. This thought is completely absent from the narrative as such. However, like the woman's anxiety, a takeoff point can be found in Jesus' earlier speech (116.9–118.10) in which he makes reference to physical sickness and immorality ("fornication" and "adultery" repeating the reference to sex) which in that context are said to plague children.[7]

The other motifs in the parallel lines expand on the contrasting characteristics of sexual indulgence and celibacy. The reference to the "Fall" in this connection follows the familiar pattern of placing a narrative theme (conversion) in the context of a myth.

The second theme has to do with instructing the man about his fallen condition. It is most visible in two lines obviously associated although they are separated in the speech by other lines:

> You, the one . . . revealing to me everything about myself, (the condition) in which I exist. (121.5–6)

> You warned me to seek myself and to know who I was and who and how I now am, so that I might become again what I was. (121.12–13)

The previous theme has already related sexual indulgence to the Fall. The latter motif is again clearly implied in the second line quoted here. Given this association, the reference to instruction in these lines is quite plausibly related to Jesus' earlier speech in which he spoke of the condition of those who indulge in the "filthy union." We should then include part of the first line in the list of references to this theme— "preached by the foreign man."

"Foreign man" most naturally refers to Thomas. On the one hand nothing is reported of Thomas in the narrative that could properly be called "preaching," but on the other there has already been a confusion in the narrative between Jesus and Thomas who are look-alike brothers there.

The third theme is that of the epiphany of Christ. It is again presented in lines somewhat separate from each other but clearly related in thought:

> The one showing me yourself. . . . (121.5)

> The one lowering yourself to me and my smallness, that you might . . . unite me to yourself. (121.9–11)

> The one not withholding your own mercy from me who was perishing. . . . (121.11–12)

---

[7] Note the attention called here (121.3) to the sickness theme by the pleonasm "hard to cure and hard to heal" (δυσίατος καὶ δυσθεράπευτος).

The fairly obvious narrative correlate to this theme is the epiphany of Jesus to the couple. Hence we should add to it the second half of the first line:

Lord . . . found in us.[8]

Having separately examined the material related to the three themes, we can now look at the speech as it exists as a whole (120.16–122.5) with the themes interwoven. They will be designated as follows: (i) = instruction, (e) = epiphany, (c) = conversion.

1   I thank you, Lord,

2 (i) Who was preached through the foreign man
    (e) and found in us,

3 (c) Who placed corruptions far from me
    and sowed in me life,

4   Who changed me over from that sickness hard to heal
    and hard to cure and lasting forever,
    and put into me healthy continence,

5 (e) Who showed himself to me
    (i) and revealed to me everything about myself,
    (the condition) in which I exist,

6 (c) Who redeemed me from the Fall
    and led me to the better,

7   Who changed me over from the temporary
    and made me worthy of what is immortal
    and lasting forever,

8 (e) Who lowered himself to me and my smallness,
    that setting me beside greatness
    (c) he might unite me with himself,

9 (e) Who did not withhold his own mercy
    from me the lost one,
    (i) but you showed me to seek myself
    and know who I was and who and how I now am,
    that I might become again what I was,

10 (i-e-c) Whom I did not know but you yourself sought me,

11   Whom I did not understand but you yourself received me,

12   Whom I have experienced . . .

13   Whose love burns in me. . . .

---

[8] Note the narrative question to Jesus (116.5), "How is it you are found here?"

We have already noticed an interweaving of themes in chapter 44. It is clear that we have the same phenomenon here. It takes two forms. One has to do with the way the lines relating to the themes are interspersed: the themes of epiphany and instruction appear combined in lines 2, 5 and 8–9, while that of conversion appears in lines 3–4 and 6–7.

Secondly, there are several cases where themes overlap. The most obvious is that the motif of the Fall occurs both in line 6, as an interpretation and generalization of indulgence in sex, and also in line 9, explicitly in the "lost one" to whom Jesus comes down and implicitly in the description of the content of the instruction. Another case involves the peculiar phrase (121.10): "Who lowered himself to me and my smallness, that setting me beside greatness ($\dot{\epsilon}\mu\dot{\epsilon}$ $\tau\hat{\eta}$ $\mu\epsilon\gamma\alpha\lambda\omega\sigma\dot{\upsilon}\nu\eta$ $\pi\alpha\rho\alpha\sigma\tau\dot{\eta}\sigma\alpha\varsigma$) he might unite me to himself." The peculiarity points to the possibility that this is an example of a device particular to this work, and another familiar thought suggests itself: encounter with the divine greatness shows up one's own "fallen" condition. That is, the peculiarity exists to call attention to the interweaving of the theme of instruction about humanity's unfortunate condition with that of the epiphany. This is already very slightly suggested in the combination of themes in line 5: "Who showed himself to me and (by doing so) revealed to me everything about myself."

On the other hand, the implication that this learning about oneself is related directly to salvation ("uniting me with himself") is supported by the following line in which knowing one's present fallen condition leads to "knowing who I was," another image for salvation. Thus complex indications of analogous thoughts also can help us see patterns. Lines 10–11 seem to combine all three themes.

Finally, it is also evident here how the theme of the divine visitation gradually merges into that of loving union, a theme, as we saw earlier, relating this speech to the previous one.

The pattern of mythical interpretation of narrative themes shows up in this speech in the fact that the three themes of the speech come gradually to be set in mythical contexts. Instruction about one's unfortunate condition gradually becomes knowledge about the Fall, and conversion to sexual abstinence becomes redemption from the Fall, while the epiphany motif merges with that of the divine descent of the savior and divine union (with overtones of a sacred marriage).

Finally, note that here, as in the previous speeches, most of the uniqueness and interest of the speech lies "between the lines"—what appears in each line taken by itself is commonplace ideas expressed in a rather commonplace manner.

1.6 Thomas's Prayer

The next speech to be treated is the prayer of Thomas for King Gundaphorous and Gad. The narrative preceding the prayer (124.5–139.14)
is about Thomas's distributing the king's money to the poor instead of
building a palace. The king imprisons Thomas, and the king's brother
is so upset at his brother's misfortune that he dies. He goes to heaven
and there finds that Thomas's alms have actually built the king a fine
palace in heaven. He returns to earth and tells his brother, whereupon
they both convert and ask to become servants of Thomas's God.

Thomas's speech which follows (140.1–141.9) opens with the theme
of how God reveals the truth to those who are "surrounded by error."
In the light of the patterns seen above, this can be seen as generalized
expansion on the narrative themes that the brothers are originally in
error about Thomas's supposed trickery, and that Gad learns the
"Truth" in heaven.

After this, Thomas speaks in his prayer (140.16–141.2) about how
the royal brothers are "pleased to be persecuted by (Christ's) enemies,
and . . . hated, and insulted, and put to death." Günther Bornkamm
points to this line as an example of the incongruities between the narrative and the speeches.[9] Who would be persecuting a king and his
brother?

However, with the organizational paradigms established earlier in
mind, we can see that this line is connected with a narrative theme,
though in a very unconventional way. Early on in the narrative
(133.4), Thomas is presented as persecuted by the king, condemned to
death and going "gladly" (χαίρων) into jail.

Several catchword recurrences linking speech and narrative are also
visible: διάκονος (139.3, 4, and 140.15); διακονία (139.12 and 141.8);
ὑπηρέτης (139.9 and 140.15); παροράω (139.5 and 140.7); ἱκετεύω
(139.11 and 140.8, 15). Note that in the case of διάκονος and
παροράω, the word in question is repeated in one or both of the passages where it occurs.[10] In one case we also are dealing with a particular
pleonastic construction (διακονία καὶ ὑπηρεσία, 139.12; cf. 140.15).
We have met both these phenomena as devices calling attention to a

---

[9] Bornkamm, Mythos, 4.
[10] The appearance of διακονίας can be noted in 139.3 and 4, and παροράω occurs twice
in 140.7.

particular motif, and many more cases will appear as we proceed. At this point, it would be helpful to include the entire speech:

1   I acknowledge you, Lord Jesus,
That you have revealed your truth to (or: in) these men.
For you are alone God of Truth, and there is no other.
And you are the one who knows everything, things unknown to the many.
5   You are, Lord, the one showing mercy and kindness to me.
For men because of the error in them forsook you, but you did not forsake them.
And now, as I pray and ask you, take the king and his brother and mix them into your flock, purifying them in your bath and cleansing them with your oil from the error which surrounds them.
Guard them also from the wolves, taking them into your pastures.
Give them to drink from your ambrosial spring which does not go bad or dry up.
10   For they entreat and ask you and want to become your servants and ministers,
And because of this they are pleased to be persecuted by your enemies, and hated and insulted and put to death, just as you suffered everything for us that you might get possession of us being Lord and truly a good shepherd.
Grant them that they may have confidence in you alone and might have help from you and the hope of their salvation which they expect from you alone,
And that they might be established in your mysteries, and will receive the perfect goods of your graces and gifts,
And that they will blossom in your service and bring forth fruit to maturity in your Father.

The opening section (lines 1–4) deals with God as revealer of secret truth. Line 5 begins a new theme, God's mercy and kindness, but leads back to the theme of revealing truth, indirectly stated in 7 as "cleansing them . . . from the error which surrounds them." ("Error" here is connected at least associatively with what is perhaps a different kind of "error" in line 6. πλάνη is used in both cases.) Line 7 begins the introduction of the "good shepherd" theme ("mix them into your flock"), which is probably connected with the theme of kindness (5). The good shepherd theme is the basis for metaphors in 8 and 9, and recurs again at the end of 11. Line 10 introduces, meanwhile, the new theme that the brothers want to become servants of Christ. However 11 is probably to be seen as relating this theme to one of the "good shepherd" metaphors in 8: the "enemies" of 11 are comparable to the "wolves" of 8.

Motifs linking the beginning of the prayer to the end are not obvious in this case, but one can see a plausible case in the connection between "mysteries" in line 13 and the revelation of hidden truth in lines 2–4.[11]

As to the previously cited compositional principle according to which the speech gives mythical interpretation to a narrative theme, this example suggests a modification. Neither the theme of freeing from error and revealing truth nor the theme of the good shepherd's care for his sheep would normally be called "mythical." Rather than speak of "myth," then, we should probably speak of general theological themes portraying direct dealings between divine (or demonic) figures and people. These themes may be expressed in mythical (the sacred marriage) or metaphorical (the shepherd and flock) terms, or they may deal with more general conventional themes (e.g., revelation and epiphany).

1.7 An Epiklesis

The final sample is the epiklesis following soon after Thomas's prayer for the brothers (142.13–143.4). This passage is of particular interest because the epikleses in the *Acts Thom.* provide the most difficult passages for interpretation, and they are certainly the most difficult passages in which to find unity. The epiklesis reads:

1 Come, name of Christ, above every name.
  Come, power of the most high and perfect compassion.
  Come, most high gift.
  Come, compassionate Mother.
5 Come, fellowship of the male.
  Come, one [fem.] who reveals hidden mysteries.
  Come, Mother of the seven houses that your rest might be in the eighth house.
  Come, eldest of the five members—understanding, thought, prudence, consideration, reasoning—have fellowship with these young men (or: give these young men a share in the five members).

---

[11] For the idea of hidden truths connected with μυστήρια and μύστης, see 114.12 and 156.13 respectively.

Come, Holy Spirit, and cleanse their loins and their heart and
seal them in the name of the Father and the Son and the
Holy Spirit.

First, the recurrence of themes within this passage is quite noticeable. "Most high" and "compassion" in line 2 are repeated in 3 and 4
respectively.[12] "Mother" from line 4 is repeated in 7. "Name" from
line 1 (repeated twice there) and "fellowship" from 5 both recur again
in 8. Thus this passage shows the special pattern of catchword
recurrences at the beginning and the end.

Connections with narrative motifs are also noticeable even without
detailed analysis. The narrative emphasizes how much the two brothers
loved one another. This is explicitly stated, "Gad loved him greatly"
(135.2–3), and it is strikingly dramatized when Gad becomes mortally
ill and dies because Thomas has apparently tricked his brother
(134.2–135.2). This partially explains the occurrence of "fellowship of
the male," for which it is difficult to find parallels in contemporary
literature, in the epiklesis.

The epiklesis reads, "Have fellowship with these young men
($\nu\epsilon\omega\tau\epsilon\rho\sigma\iota$)"—a strange way of referring to the king and his brother.
But immediately after the prayer a "young man" ($\nu\epsilon\alpha\nu\iota\alpha\varsigma$) appears in
a collective vision. "Hidden mysteries" has its correlate in the "mys-
teries" of the previous speech (141.7). One may also observe that two
references to "fellowship" in the epiklesis are preceded by "have fel-
lowship ($\kappa\sigma\iota\nu\omega\nu\eta\sigma\alpha\iota$) in the eucharist" in the narrative (141.20).
Additionally, "rest" ($\alpha\nu\alpha\pi\alpha\upsilon\sigma\iota\varsigma$) in the epiklesis (line 7) is preceded
by two narrative passages using this same motif. The first occurs in the
description of one "supplying those who were in need . . . giving rest
($\alpha\nu\alpha\pi\alpha\upsilon\sigma\nu\tau\epsilon\varsigma$) to all," and the second (141.15–16) is the statement,
"Our souls are at leisure ($\sigma\chi\sigma\lambda\alpha\zeta\sigma\upsilon\sigma\alpha\iota$) . . . give us the seal."

By looking further back in the narrative, one may discover "Mother
of the seven houses ($\sigma\iota\kappa\sigma\iota$)" is related to the "house" Thomas built
for Gundaphorous in heaven (135.10–136.3).

The central intent of this epiklesis is too unclear to say anything very
certainly about how it interprets the narrative in a new context.[13]

---

[12] Note also $\upsilon\pi\epsilon\rho$ in line 1 and $\upsilon\psi\iota\sigma\tau\sigma\varsigma$ in line 2.

[13] Given this text's concern with gnosis that is shown later in this study, it is probable
that lines 6 and 8 intend to interpret the sacramental proceedings in the narrative as
imparting special knowledge and understanding. See the line of the previous speech,
linking anointing to the freeing from $\pi\lambda\alpha\nu\eta$: $\alpha\lambda\epsilon\iota\psi\alpha\varsigma$ $\alpha\upsilon\tau\sigma\upsilon\varsigma$ $\tau\omega$ $\sigma\omega$ $\epsilon\lambda\alpha\iota\omega$ $\alpha\pi\sigma$ $\tau\eta\varsigma$
$\pi\epsilon\rho\iota\epsilon\chi\sigma\upsilon\sigma\eta\varsigma$ $\alpha\upsilon\tau\sigma\upsilon\varsigma$ $\pi\lambda\alpha\nu\eta\varsigma$ (140.10–11).

1.8 Summary

At this point it would be helpful to summarize the results of this Chapter:

1) So far as reading competence goes, the reader should approach the speeches and prayers in the *Acts Thom.* looking for motif and catchword recurrences that link speech to narrative.

2) Guided by similarities between elements of the speech and those of the narrative, one ought to look for ways in which the themes of the speech can be seen as taking up themes from the narrative—though these may be transposed or quite drastically reinterpreted—or as reading ideas or events into the narrative that fit the general situation but are not actually present in the text of the narrative (e.g., the idea that the bride was upset on her wedding night).

3) The reader should look for ways in which the foregoing device also might involve the reinterpretation of a narrative motif in terms of some theme related to the direct interaction of people and God or supernatural beings.

4) The reader should look at the internal composition of the speeches in the light of three organizational principles: (a) the grouping of several lines into a unit around a single theme; (b) the partial breakdown of the boundaries of these thematic units by several devices interspersing one theme through two or more units; and (c) the recurrence of catchwords and motifs, particularly at the beginning and end of the speech.

5) Finally, in reading the narrative itself one should be attentive to peculiarities, tautologous expressions, and word repetitions in close successions that might in subtle ways call attention to motifs or themes that are taken up more explicitly in the ensuing speech or prayer.

It seems best to view the above remarks as descriptions of paradigmatic structures, paradigmatic arrangements of textual elements, for which the alert reader looks when approaching the text. (They would be comparable, e.g., to the adjective-followed-by-noun and verb-followed-by-object paradigms in English sentence grammar.) These are paradigms that operate by structuring one's reading, determining how the relation between textual elements is construed.[14]

---

[14] Note that while we now know of several such paradigms appropriate to a reading of this text, we have only the beginnings of an understanding of how to convert the respective organizational patterns into substantive meaning. This will only gradually unfold in Chaps. 3–5.

The analyses in the foregoing Chapter are fundamental to this study in that they deal with some of the most important literary constructions. Additionally, they outline the major mode of argumentation used throughout the study. They show the way in which the prayers and speeches of the *Acts Thom.* are tightly constructed according to consistent principles both internally and in relation to the narrative. The focus of the following Chapter is on the ways in which the narrative itself is pervaded by devices similar to those pointed out in the earlier analyses.

2

COMPOSITIONAL DEVICES COMMON TO
NARRATIVE AND SPEECHES

This Chapter catalogues and categorizes several stylistic peculiarities found in the *Acts Thom.*, concentrating now on chapters 1–10, the section of text to be interpreted in this study. The aim is to show that there are certain literary devices to which the "competent readers" of the *Acts Thom.* must be especially sensitive, and for which they must be on the lookout. It will be seen that such devices are clearly deliberate and significant; however, their substantive significance is left to be treated further on.

2.1 Recurrence of Similar Elements

To begin with, we can simply note that many cases of recurrent words, phrases, or motifs appear even on the surface, though because they remain within normal conventions they may appear of trivial significance. Of such a nature, for example, are three pairs of similar phrases:

> As he was thinking over and saying these things. . . . (100.8)
> As he was saying and reflecting on these things. . . . (101.3)
>
> As they were eating and drinking. . . . (106.5)
> After they were eating and drinking. . . . (107.2)
>
> When he had sung and completed this song. . . . (111.1)
> When she had completed everything and fluted. . . . (111.9–10)

A somewhat less-noticeable example is the repetition of "foreigner" in two successive scenes:

> Let us set off (for the wedding) . . . especially since we are foreigners. (105.9–11)
>
> They looked at him as at a foreigner and one coming from a different land. (106.2–3)

Even less conspicuous but noteworthy, given the unconventional connections spoken of earlier, is the presence (105.12) of ξενοδοχεῖον (inn; literally "receiver of foreigners") between these two occurrences.

Many other examples could be given where the same or similar words, phrases, or motifs recur in the text. Some are of apparently conventional and fairly trivial significance. Others are seemingly mere coincidences. For example, is the repeated use of ἀποβλέπειν (to look at) in 111.2–7 related in any significant way to its use in the opening scene of the banquet much earlier (106.2)?

The questions raised by these observations lead us to look for less-obvious word and motif recurrences in other passages as well. It turns out that there are indeed particular devices that call attention to other such recurrences in an unmistakable way.

Parallel Descriptions

One such device is that in which two figures are described in very similar terms. The clearest example is one that stays within normal conventions acquiring a meaning, therefore, which is fairly clear.

Thomas implicitly claims to be a "king's herald" by parodying the earlier description of the Andrapolitan king's heralds:

The king has sent heralds to announce (κήρυκας ... κηρύξαι) ...
That everyone should come to the wedding ... whoever refuses
... will be answerable to the king (ὑπεύθυνος ἔσται τῷ βασιλεῖ).
(105.4–9)

The heralds announce (κήρυκες ... κηρύσσουσιν) the king's matters, and whoever does not listen to the heralds will be subject to the king's condemnation (ὑπόδικος ἔσται τῇ τοῦ βασιλέως κρίσει). (106.10–107.1)

But much more puzzling passages also occur. When Jesus sells Thomas the "craftsman" he goes out of his way to describe himself as "son of Joseph the craftsman."[1] In adjacent sentences, we find the statements: "(Thomas) took in his hand a reed branch and held (κατεῖχεν) it. And the flutist, holding (κατέχουσα) in her hand the flutes ..." (107.11–108.2). The similarity is more striking if we keep in mind that flutes were made of "reeds" (κάλαμοι) in the ancient world.

These examples draw attention, by analogy, to the parallel descriptions of Thomas and Abban, both of whom are "sent" (100.3 and 101.5).

Images Connected With Their Context in Unusual Ways.

A similar phenomenon is one in which an image has a striking yet puzzling appropriateness to a given context. Two passages involve allusions to traditions outside the *Acts Thom.* It can hardly be ignored that "Judas Thomas" is called simply "Judas" only once in these chapters (102.3), and that occurs in the scene where Jesus is selling him—as Judas Iscariot once sold Jesus.[2] At the banquet, where Thomas plays the part of a heaven-sent messenger vulnerable to hostile attacks from worldly Andrapolitans, he ends his anointing by crowning himself with blossoms and taking a reed in his hand (107.11–108.1). The latter gesture is particularly incongruous at a banquet, and several commentators have tried to devise an explanation for it. In light of the above example of Judas, I suggest that it is an allusion to the scene of the mocked

---

[1] Walter Bauer ("The Picture of the Apostle in Early Christian Tradition, I: Accounts," in *NTApo*, 2. 60) notices this and relates it, correctly I believe, to the "twin" motif common elsewhere in the *Acts Thom.*

[2] A. F. J. Klijn (*The Acts of Thomas* [Leiden: Brill, 1962] 151) also remarks on this similarity.

king Jesus in the passion account (Matt 27:27–31). This motif fits the
scene here where Thomas, like Jesus, is under attack from ungodly
enemies.

Finally, it is striking that as Thomas sits *in the boat* talking to Abban
about his trade, he speaks of three wooden articles (plows, yokes and
scales) and then of boats—he makes "boats and boat-oars, and masts
and pulleys" (103.10–11). In the last example, as in some of the earlier ones, it is far from clear what the purpose of the device might be.
On the other hand, it has already been sufficiently established on other
grounds that there is much more going on in this work than is immediately apparent. These analyses draw on, as well as support and extend,
that supposition.

In the above cases, evidence of significant connections of elements
consists in a complex convergence of indicators. The most important
of these indications overall is that several possible cases of such connections have the same literary structure. Two paradigms are involved.
One is the description of two figures in the same or similar terms. The
other is the introduction into a particular context of a theme connected
to that context but in a way not in accord with the surface logic of the
passage in question.

Pleonasms with Recurrent Catchwords

One finds evidence of another paradigm consisting of a certain type
of pleonastic construction made up of two synonyms joined typically by
"and" (e.g., "joy and gladness"), and a recurrence of one of the
members, most often in the nearby context.

Several examples here are fairly obvious:

> . . . having their gaze and vision (σκοπὸν καὶ θέαμα) toward
> the bridegroom, that by the vision (θεάματος) of him they
> might be enlightened. (110.8–9)

> We are foreigners. (105.11)

> . . . as at a foreigner and one coming from a different country.
> (106.2–3)

> They were looking (ἀπέβλεπον) at him. . . . (111.2)

> They were looking (ἀπέβλεπον) at his changed appearance.
> (111.3)

> She was gazing and looking (ἀφεώρα καὶ ἀπέβλεπεν) at him.
> (111.7)

. . . gazing and staring (ἀφορῶσα καὶ ἀτενίζουσα) at him. . . .
(111.11)

But he . . . gazed at no one nor fixed his attention on anyone
(εἰς οὐδένα ἀφεώρα οὐδὲ προσεῖχέν τινι). (111.11–12)

This last example is analogous to two pairs of phrases already mentioned:

As he was thinking over and saying these things. . . . (100.8)
As he was saying and reflecting on these things. . . . (101.3)
When he had sung and completed this song. . . . (111.1)
When she had completed everything and fluted. . . .
(111.9–10)

The paradigm is particularly illuminating in the latter case, where the
second of the phrases is oddly constructed (ὅτε ἐτέλεσεν . . . πάντας
καὶ αὐλήσασα) and has led to several emendations in the MSS (e.g.,
καταυλήσασα for καὶ αὐλήσασα). We have already seen how oddly
constructed phrases are used to call attention to the peculiar patterns in
the text, and this is clearly another example. That is, we should read
αὐλήσασα as "having fluted," synonymous in its reference with the
phrase ὅτε ἐτέλεσεν πάντας ("when she had completed everything").
Once the paradigm is established by these clear cases, we can see
many more cases where it applies, though its intent is not clear:

They will give glory (δοξάσουσι) to the Father. . . . (110.15)
They gave glory and sang hymns (ἐδόξασαν δὲ καὶ ὕμνησαν).
. . . (110.19)
Her hands signal and suggest (σημαίνουσιν καὶ ὑποδεικ-
νύουσιν). . . . (109.12)
Her fingers suggest (ὑποδεικνύουσιν). . . . (109.13–14)
They will be at that eternal joy (χαράν). . . . (110.10)
They will be in joy and gladness (χαρᾷ καὶ ἀγαλλιάσει). . . .
(110.14)
On her stands and lies (ἐνέστηκε καὶ ἔγκειται). . . . (109.1)
On her head lies (ἔγκειται) the Truth. . . . (109.6)
Her neck lies (ἔγκειται) in the form of steps. (109.11)

Come . . . pray (εὖξαι) over my daughter. . . . (113.9)
. . . that he might pray (εὔξηται) over them. (114.3)
And standing he began to pray and say (εὔχεσθαι καὶ λέγειν).
. . . (114.4)

Two rather odd constructions of similar sort seem to involve extensions of this paradigm:

The joy and gathering . . . the feast which you see today. . . .
(105.3–4)
Her hands signal and suggest the dance of the good eons
announcing. . . . (109.12–13)

In each case the construction is awkward because of the introduction of a third word (ἑορτή and κηρύσσειν) synonymous with the two in the pleonastic construction. In the former case the word also occurs in the nearby context (104.8): "What is this feast (ἑορτή) in this city?" The latter one is a catchword related to Thomas's mission as a "herald (κῆρυξ) announcing the Truth."[3]

This paradigm involves two devices, both of which have been noted already. One is calling attention to an idea by repeating the reference to it. The other is the use of catchword links. It is noteworthy that J. H. Charlesworth has noted both these phenomena in the *Odes of Solomon*, another early Syrian-Christian work.[4]

2.2 The Deliberate Use of Unusual Language and Imagery

In the course of these analyses we have come across many cases where there is a deliberate use of unusual wording, grammatical construction, and imagery. This, plus the well-established fact that there is a good deal going on below the surface of the text, leads to a more systematic treatment of this phenomenon.

We can begin here by simply noticing the most obvious cases where unusual statements lead us to suspect that some deeper meaning is being suggested, without however giving clear indications in themselves as to what that meaning is:

---

[3] See 100.7, 10; 105.5; and 106.10.
[4] Charlesworth, "Paronomasia and Assonance in the Syriac Text of the Odes of Solomon," *Semitics* 1 (1970) 13–15.

He set off for Abban the merchant . . . carrying only his price (τίμημα). For the Lord had given (it) to him saying, "May your status (τιμή) be with you." (103.1–4)

The flutist . . . stood above him fluting at his head for a long time. (108.3–4)

He fixed his attention on no one, but fixed his eyes on the earth, waiting for when he would return (ἀναλύσῃ) from there. (111.12–112.1)

But he did not want to set off (with the king, into the bedroom) because the Lord had not yet been revealed to him there. (113.10–114.2)

Deliberately Ambiguous Phrasing

Turning to the use of specific devices, we have observed that one way of suggesting further meanings is the use of ambiguous phrasing. This has already been noted in the parents' question to the bride (chapter 13), and a similar phenomenon is the deliberate ambiguity as to the character of the woman's attacker (chapter 43). Two cases in chapters 1–10 are also fairly clear in their intent.

Thomas replies to the hostile question as to why he is refusing to eat at the banquet: "I came here for more than food or drink and to fulfill the king's will" (106.7). The "and" makes it unclear whether he is continuing his thought or making a contrast. Both meanings fit the context.[5]

A similar phenomenon shows up in a later passage. Thomas prefaces his curse on the servant who slapped him:

My God will forgive you in (εἰς) the aeon to come but in/to (εἰς) this world (κόσμον) he will show his wonders. (108.9–11)

The parallel construction tends to make one read the second εἰς in the same sense (locative: "in") as the first, but the presence of "he will show" (δείξει) suggests a dative sense. Again both meanings are appropriate in the context.

---

[5] The MS variants show that copyists had difficulty with the phrase. Three have "but" in the place of "and," which still leaves the phrase quite awkward.

Finally, a puzzling construction occurs at the end of the wedding hymn, the ambiguity again due to the use of "and":

> They drank of the wine which made them not thirsty and desirous (literally: which furnished them with not thirsting and desire). (110.18–19)

The passage makes most sense if we read "made them not thirsty or desirous (for more)," an echo of the saying of Jesus in John 4:14 and a parallel to the previous line's "food which had no lack." But the grammatical construction leads more to the sense "gave them not to thirst and gave them desire."[6]

Passages with Several Peculiarities

Moving into more general cases of this phenomenon of the deliberate use of unusual language, there are two passages in particular where a number of unusual features appear interconnected. The first is Thomas's initial refusal to set off for India (100.5–7):

> He did not want to set off, saying he could not nor did he travel (comprehend) because of the weakness of the flesh, and that, being a Hebrew man. . . .
>
> οὐκ ἐβούλετο δὲ ἀπελθεῖν, λέγων μὴ δύνασθαι μήτε χωρεῖν διὰ τὴν ἀσθένειαν τῆς σαρκός, καὶ ὅτι Ἄνθρωπος ὢν Ἑβραῖος. . . .

The first phrase in Thomas's answer is oddly constructed. The next line would make sense if we understand "weakness of the flesh" as "sickness"—a plausible reason for not being able to travel. But in Greek usage we should read a "weakness of the flesh," a phrase properly referring to "human weakness" as opposed to the strength of God or of the spiritually developed person. Taken seriously, this indicates at least that what is spoken of is not Thomas's reason for not "traveling" but for not accepting a spiritually challenging mission. This, in turn, leads us to consider the possibility that χωρεῖν (to travel) is being used here in another sense, "to comprehend" (i.e., a difficult mystery). This would enable us to make sense of the peculiar construction μὴ δύνασθαι μήτε χωρεῖν by noting that it follows the paradigm of the pleonastic constructions analyzed earlier. The meaning "to

---

[6] This particular kind of double meaning also has parallels in the *Odes of Solomon.* See Charlesworth, "Paronomasia," 20–22.

comprehend" is derived from the meaning "to have room for," that is, it refers to spiritual-mental capacity, hence it is capable of a sense synonymous with δύνασθαι (to be able).[7] The second sense of the passage hinted at by these combined peculiarities is then: "He did not want to set off saying he did not have the (mental) strength, nor the capacity to comprehend because of human limitation and that, being a (mere) man. . . ." The second passage has already been mentioned in some detail. It is the scene where Thomas departs for India:

> And he set off to Abban the merchant, carrying with him nothing except only his price. For the Lord had given (it) to him saying, "May your authority be with you, with my grace, wherever you may go." And the apostle caught up with Abban, likewise carrying his equipment onto the boat. And he began to carry (it) on up with him.
>
> And when they had embarked and had sat down, Abban asked the apostle saying, "What work do you know?" And he said. "In wood, ploughs and yokes and scales and boats and oars for boats and masts and pulleys. . . ."

Thomas here sets out carrying only his price (τίμημα) which Jesus refers to as his τιμή (status, worth, authority): "May your τιμή be with you with my grace. . . ." The implication that Thomas carries his price in the place of the customary baggage is taken up in a very puzzling way in the next line: "He caught up with Abban likewise (ἴσως) carrying his baggage (σκεύη)." Again, "likewise" has been suspected by many readers, ancient and modern, as the textual apparatus of Maximilianus Bonnet shows.[8] However, with the growing evidence that peculiar constructions are deliberate, it becomes more obvious that we have to look for other possible ways of explaining these features. Our investigation so far fully supports Bonnet's favoring of the *lectio difficilior* in his printed text.

---

[7] Herman Ljungvik (*Studien zur Sprache der apokryphen Apostelgeschichten* [Uppsala: Lundequistska, 1926] 99) points out that this meaning of χωρεῖν is common in Apocryphal Acts. See also Ign. *Trall.* 5, where it is parallel to νοεῖν. Rom 6:19 has a strikingly similar use of themes: Paul gives his reasons for using metaphors in speaking of high mysteries, ἀνθρώπινον λέγω διὰ τὴν ἀσθένειαν τῆς σαρκὸς ὑμῶν. See also the episode with the colt where Thomas explains why he will not sit on it: "I am weak and feeble (ἀσθενὴς καὶ ἄτονος) for this mystery" (158.11–12).

[8] Bonnet, *Acta*, 2. 2. 103.

The "baggage" (σκεύη) which Abban carries has here a quite clear connection with the "price" which Thomas carries. But σκεύη can also mean "equipment" or "ship's tackle,"[9] which points us to a peculiarity of the passage immediately following this one. As Thomas sits in the boat he talks of making ships and ships' gear, oars and masts and pulleys. The suggested equivalences "price-authority-grace-baggage-ships' gear" are of course very odd and puzzling.[10]

2. 3 Parallels Between Larger Units

We can next examine the parallelisms between larger units in the text, particularly the parallelism between successive scenes.

This parallelism is very clear in the opening scenes, three successive attempts by the Lord to send Thomas to India. In the first scene the parallelism of two lines makes it clear that the result of the casting of lots is looked upon as a divine sending:

> . . . that each might go to the region that fell to him by lot, and
> to the people to whom the Lord sent him. (100.2–3)

The epiphany with its direct command (100.10), and the selling of Thomas (101.7–102.6) are obviously also instances of the Lord's sending.

The banquet scenes preceding the wedding hymn also clearly have a common central focus: they deal with the strained relationship between the heavenly prophet Thomas and the worldly banquet. Thomas is forced to the banquet (104.5–105.10) by a threat and because he is a "foreigner" (i.e., vulnerable). In two gestures that indicate a more specific parallel between two scenes, he refuses to eat (106.5–6) and he ignores the flutist's fluting especially for him (108.6). The guests react to his not eating with a hostile question (106.6–7), and a servant reacts to his ignoring the flutist by hitting him (108.6–7). In the anointing scene (107.2–108.1) he transforms a worldly ceremony into a sacramental ritual, and this scene ends (107.9–11) with an image from Jesus' passion comparing Thomas's position among worldly figures to that of Jesus—an image that is a summary and condensation of the significance of this series of motifs.

---

[9] See LSJ, *s.v.* σκεῦος.

[10] This analysis, like many others in this Chapter, will provide starting points and criteria for the substantive interpretation undertaken in Chaps. 3–6. For parallels to the double entendre involved in the above interpretations of χωρεῖν, τιμή, and σκεύη, see the comments on the *Odes of Solomon* in Charlesworth, "Paronomasia," 17–20.

A more specific parallelism between several of these scenes is indicated by some peculiar language. It is said (108.2) that the flutist "surrounds all and flutes" (περιήρχετο πάντας καὶ ηὔλει) — we would expect περιήρχετο εἰς πάντας ("she goes around to all"). Earlier (104.6 – 7), when Thomas and Abban are entering the city, the "sounds of flutists (αὐλητῶν) and of water-organs and trumpets echoed around them (περιηχοῦσαι αὐτούς)." The general pattern of the parallelism between scenes, the oddity of "surrounded all" and of naming "flutists" (not "flutes") among other instruments, and the phonetic similarity περιηχοῦσαι/περιήρχετο all point to a deliberate linking of these two phrases. The suggestion is that we take "she surrounded all and fluted" according to the model of the pleonastic constructions, with "fluted" synonymous in the context with "surrounded," that is, "she surrounded all with her fluting" just as the "sounds of flutists echoed around" Thomas and Abban.

A third image can be added to this series: in a striking move, Thomas enters the banquet and sits down "in the middle" (ἐν τῷ μέσῳ, 106.1 – 2).[11] Thomas is then "surrounded" by the other guests.[12]

Another striking example of this paralleling of larger units is the structure of the passage immediately following the wedding hymn. It can be looked upon as four small scenes, paralleled by the centering of each on the motif of "looking": (1) the guests "look at" Thomas's changed appearance; (2) the flutist flutes for the others while she "looks and gazes" at Thomas; (3) she finishes her work, sits opposite Thomas and "gazes and stares" at him; and (4) Thomas "was gazing at no one . . . but had his eyes fixed on the earth."

2.4 Allusions to Other Traditions

Another convention of this work that merits mention is that of alluding to other specific traditions.

We have already noted the allusions to Judas's betrayal and to the crowning with thorns. In each of these cases a peculiar feature of the narrative (the name "Judas," the reed) plus several other similarities between the *Acts Thom.* and the respective external tradition established the connection.

Another example here is the allusion to the "doubting Thomas" story (John 20) in the Christ prayer and the narrative immediately preceding it (113.10 – 114.3). At that point a key line from the story

---

[11] Again, several MSS try to soften the language to "in the middle of them (or: of all)."
[12] See a few lines later (106.6): "Those around him (περὶ αὐτὸν) said. . . ."

occurs ("My Lord and my God") as the opening line of the prayer. This could be dismissed by saying that it could easily be a conventional formula. On the other hand: (1) Thomas has the problem here (114.1–2), peculiar in the context, that the "Lord had not yet been revealed to him there"—the same problem as in the other story; (2) the third line (114.6) of the prayer speaks of a "guide and director of those who believe (πιστεύοντας) in him," naming a central issue in the other story; and (3) here, as in John 20, a climax is reached with Thomas's confession.

Several commentators have noticed the similarity between the opening scene in Andrapolis, where Thomas is invited to the wedding, and the parable of the eschatological banquet in Mathew 22. In both stories the fact that a threat accompanies the invitation is a striking departure from what one would normally expect. Added to this we have the pattern described above of suggestions in the narrative preparing for a more explicit presentation in the following speech or prayer: here the theme of the eschatological banquet takes up the final section of the wedding hymn.

One can also mention here the fact that (1) the guests' hostile question (106.6–7: "Why did you come here neither eating nor drinking?") repeats almost verbatim a tradition about John the Baptist (also an ascetic prophet figure) reported in Matt 11:18; (2) as Bornkamm mentions, the story of the flutist (108.1–5; 111.5–11), with its overtones of salvation through sexual attraction, is very similar to the Simon-Helena story;[13] and (3) the story of Thomas's refusal to accept his mission and his eventual forced acceptance (100.4–102.12) closely resembles the Jonah story.

One should mention in this context that these allusions are probably not to other literary texts but to oral traditions (aside, perhaps, from the Jonah story). The *Acts Thom.* often quotes sayings we know from the New Testament, but the formula is always "Jesus said . . ." or "It was said . . ." but never "It is written. . . ."

2.5 Cognates and Assonance

The final conventions with which we must deal are the uses of cognates and assonance to indicate connections. In the case of cognates, we can point to several obvious, if trivial, examples:

---

[13] Bornkamm, *Mythos*, 73–74

He sent announcers to announce (κήρυκας ... κηρύξαι).
(105.5, see 106.10)
The flutist (αὐλήτρια) holding ... the flutes (αὐλούς) ...
fluted (ηὔλει). (108.1–2)
The first maker made (δημιουργὸς ἐδημιούργησεν). ...
(109.11)
They received light (φῶς) ... and were enlightened
(ἐφωτίσθησαν). (110.15–16)

Two cases appear which are of more interest, because the cognates
have somewhat different senses:

They will be for eternity (εἰς τὸν αἰῶνα) at that eternal joy (τὴν
χαρὰν τὴν αἰώνιον) ... that feast at which the eternal ones
(αἰώνιοι) are gathered. (110.9 and 12)
Carrying only his price (τίμημα). ... May your status (τιμή)
be with you. (103.2 and 4)

The case for assonance as a significant device cannot be established
at this point with any certainty. We can only note the many plausible
cases, leaving it for substantive interpretation to provide the decisive
evidence that these are indeed significant.
Some cases are striking because of the juxtaposition of the sounds,
especially so if we keep in mind the ancient practice of reading aloud:

αὕτη ἡ ἑορτὴ ἡ ἐν τῇ πόλει ταύτῃ (104.8)
πανταχοῦ πάντας παρατυχεῖν (105.5)
κλειστάδες ἐν καλάμοις κεκόσμηνται (110.3)
ἀμβροσίαν βρῶσιν (110.17)

Other cases are not so striking, but still somewhat noticeable:

τὸ ἀπαύγασμα ... τὸ γαῦρον ... καταυγάζουσα (109.1–3)
ἀμφιάσονται ... ἀμφότεροι (110.13 and 14)
ἀφῆκεν ... τὰ μέλη. ... ἔλαβον τὰ μέλη. ... εἷς μέλας κύων
(112.3–5)
σμύρνης ... μυρσίναι (110:1 and 2)

The assonance between περιηχοῦσαι and περιήρχετο has already been mentioned. We can also observe that the word for the "blossoms" (ἄνθος) of Thomas's crown is similar to that used for the "thorns" (ἄκανθος) of Jesus' crown in the passion scene to which an allusion is made.

The play on cognates and other similar-sounding words is a well-known trait of semitic literature, and it occurs often in the *Odes of Solomon*. [14]

This brings to a close our preliminary study of compositional devices and organizational paradigms. The following Chapters are based partly on the analysis in these two Chapters; further analysis based on other criteria will show many more cases where the literary structures described above function as appropriate paradigms. The subsequent developments and more substantive interpretaion of the work will support and expand on the analysis of the paradigms accomplished so far.

[14] See Charlesworth, "Paronomasia," 13–23.

3

THOMAS'S TRIP
TO INDIA

The bulk of this Chapter is devoted to a detailed, section-by-section analysis of chapters 1–5 of the *Acts Thom.* The knowledge of literary devices and compositional principles gained in Chapters 1 and 2 is both applied and developed further. Prior to this detailed analysis, however, a final set of preliminary observations should be made, showing that the *Acts Thom.* is made up of many originally separate stories, or short pieces related to traditional themes, now woven together by the redactors.

3.1 The Influence of Traditional Themes and Forms

One of the more obvious characteristics of the *Acts Thom.* is the jerkiness, the lack of smooth flow in the story-telling technique. This is partly due to the frequent interruption of the narrative by speeches. Although I have shown above that there is more relation between these and the narrative context than has been supposed, they clearly introduce completely new themes and have apparently little to do with carrying the narrative action forward. This is often even true of very short comments: Thomas, seeing the dead body of a young man asks (147.5–6), "Lord, is it not because of this that you have led me to come here, to see this temptation?" But nothing in the story carries forward the theme of temptation in any obvious way.

And this abruptness can also be observed in the narrative style even apart from the long monologues. As Bornkamm notes, in the entire first half of *Acts Thom.* (Acts 1–7) "each individual legend has its own point and has no significance for the movement of the whole."[1] Even within individual Acts, the action most often does not proceed smoothly.

The Composition of the Sixth Act

For example, in the Sixth Act (167.4–178.12) a man's hand withers away because he has killed a woman and yet comes to receive the Eucharist. Thomas heals the man's hand (168.21–169.3) and revives the woman (170.11–171.11) who recounts a vision of hell she had when her soul departed her body (171.14–174.11). Thomas makes this an occasion for reminding the crowd of the punishments that await them if they do not convert, and many do (174.12–175.18).

As it stands, the story is particularly unsatisfying to the reader. We would normally expect to hear something of the final condition of the young man cured of the withered hand, and we certainly want to know whether the sinful woman's desire to be delivered from her guilt is granted or not (174.10–11). Instead, we move on to a mass conversion scene (175.18) and then a summary of Thomas's missionary activity (176.5–15).

---

[1] Bornkamm, *Mythos*, 2.

In this passage a process of composition is visible that pervades the *Acts Thom.* and accounts for its abrupt nature. The authors clearly have woven together several traditional narrative themes: punishment, the healing of the young woman, the woman's vision of hell, the mass conversion, and the summary of missionary activity. And in so doing, they give the appearance of not having taken much care to connect and unify them.

The Twelfth and Thirteenth Acts

Another case where it is clear that materials received are imperfectly joined is that of the Twelfth and Thirteenth Acts—though here a different kind of incongruity is shown. Act 13 (259.1–288.2) tells the story of a man who has been a celibate Christian for more than seven years and is being pressured by his father because of his celibacy. Act 12 (245.16–258.13) opens with a variation on the Simon Magus story speaking of one who does not know Thomas's God and wants to barter political influence for a share in his magical power—and the two stories are told of the same man!

These are a few samples of a very general phenomenon that has already been remarked upon by previous researchers. That very many of the stories, story types, and motifs of the *Acts Thom.*, along with those of other Apocryphal Acts, are traditional is the principle point of Rosa Söder's well-received study.[2] Wilhelm Schneemelcher and Knut Schäferdiek rightly draw the comparison to the process of composition of the Synoptic Gospels. In both cases "we have to do with the fixation in writing of a popular tradition . . . one must assume that many passages of the Apocryphal Acts already existed as legends before their fixation in written form."[3] Hence these scholars call for a form- and redaction-critical analysis of the Apocryphal Acts comparable to that done on the Synoptic Gospels.

Part of the focus of the present Chapter is to carry out such a program with reference to chapters 1–10 of the *Acts Thom.* But several more specific observations can be made as to how that methodology is to be applied here, observations based on a few more sample texts from elsewhere in the *Acts Thom.*

---

[2] Söder, *Die apokryphen Apostelgeschichten und die romanhafte Literatur der Antike* (Würzburger Studien zur Altertumswissenschaft 3; Stuttgart: Kohlhammer, 1932).

[3] Schneemelcher and Schäferdiek, "Second and Third Century Acts of Apostles," in *NTApo*, 2. 176.

The Incorporation of Previously Formulated Traditions

In some cases, the evidence points to more or less verbatim incorporation into the *Acts Thom.* of previously formulated traditions. For example, in the previously mentioned summary of missionary activity in the Sixth Act we find two successive sentences that repeat, in different words, a very similar thought that Christ fulfills the scriptures:

> This is Jesus the Christ whom the Scriptures proclaimed, who came and was crucified and after three days was raised from the dead. And secondly ($\delta\epsilon\acute{u}\tau\epsilon\rho ov$) he showed them and explained, beginning from the prophets, the things concerning the Christ, that he must come and that all that had been proclaimed about him must be fulfilled. (176.6–11)

The fact that what is expressed here is a tradition important in early Christian preaching and appears in several similar formulations in the New Testament[4] makes it likely that we are dealing here with the incorporation of two relatively fixed formulations of the same tradition. The passage does not read as though it was composed by a single hand, and this hypothesis also explains the curious "secondly" ($\delta\epsilon\acute{u}\tau\epsilon\rho ov$) that introduces the second formula.

Unusual Combinations of Traditional Motifs

In another case, we seem to have a more free grafting of traditional motifs onto one another, probably not adhering to previous formulations. This seems to be the case in the stories of sexual assaults by demons (the Fifth, Seventh, and Eighth Acts). In both cases, the story begins on this theme, but ends as an account of demon possession and exorcism.

This grafting of different motifs has an even more incongruous result in the Third Act (147.1–156.8). There a young man is caught in sin with a young woman. He is killed by a serpent who is presented as acting both out of jealousy and as an agent of divine justice: he killed him "because he did this on the Lord's Day" (148.4–14). The young man's death, however, is the occasion for presenting a vision of the other life. He saw Jesus, and he reports his experience in the long speech of chapter 34 (comparable to the vision of hell of chapters

---

[4] See Mark 8.31; Acts 3.18; 1 Cor 15.3–4; and Martin Dibelius, *From Tradition to Gospel* (New York: Scribner, 1965) 17–18.

55–57). And this motif is the occasion for presenting the sinful dead man as actually in a position superior to the onlookers, because they are still "in impurities" while he is "gone out of the body" (147.8–11).[5] The combining of motifs has led here to contradictory interpretations of the young man's death.

Narrative Events as Dramatizations of Religious Themes

The preceding examples show how traditional themes or formulations are often incorporated into speeches or narratives in somewhat unusual ways. One further way in which this takes place is that individual events in the narrative are shaped so as to reflect specific religious motifs.

In the Third Act, Thomas does not ultimately kill the serpent by simple fiat, but by having him suck out the poison he injected when he bit and killed the young man. The serpent then bursts and dies (150.3–19). This is not simply an entertaining twist to the story. It is a dramatization of a favorite theme in the *Acts Thom.* As the serpent puts it, "If my father suck out . . . what he has put into creation (evil, poison), then is his end." Likewise in the Fifth Act, when a demon disappears amid fire and smoke, Thomas comments, "This demon has showed nothing strange . . . but his own nature, in which he will be burnt up" (163.17–19; see 164.13 and 189.12).

This same tendency to relate individual narrative events to religious themes is visible also in more conventional examples like the crowd's climbing up on top of things to see Thomas (an occasion for the admonition "lift yourselves up from the earth"). And the Eighth Act has an odd sequence involving the same general phenomenon: a captain traveling in some kind of carriage with Thomas initially has the driver get up and let him drive, but afterwards Thomas asks the captain to get up and sit with him, letting the driver return to his place. The sequence has no apparent function in the narrative except to serve as an occasion for two metaphorical comparisons by the captain, "I ask and pray that I might be worthy to sit at his feet, and I will become his driver on this road, so that he may become my guide on that road that few travel" (185.10–14).

These are all examples, some on a very small scale, of the kind of phenomenon Bornkamm has in mind in his formulation, "The legend is nothing else than a novelistic clothing of a mythological theme."[6] It

---

[5] For the notion of the body as the source of immorality, see esp. 155.10.

[6] Bornkamm, *Mythos*, 23.

is only that we need to expand the formulation to include not only strictly mythical motifs but also common religious metaphors. (A similar enlargement has already been suggested in reference to the themes the speeches use to interpret the narrative.)

All of the examples given so far in this Chapter suggest a partial explanation of the apparently jerky, rambling, and digressive style of the *Acts Thom.* That is, the writers are apparently not sitting down to compose a fresh work in which passages are written specifically to follow each other smoothly. Rather, familiar religious themes are constantly being incorporated, and this is done many times in such a way as to interrupt and distract the reader from whatever central line of thought or narrative development may be present in a given passage.

The result of these observations, as far as reading competence is concerned, is that one must be alert to possible reflections of traditional themes and formulations in the text, even when these seem at first sight to have no particular relevance to the central thread being developed in the context.

3.2 General Observations on Chapters 1 – 10

The remainder of this study will be occupied with a very close analysis of chapters 1 – 10, using the principles discovered in the previous Chapters as guidelines.

Previous Scholarship

Only three previous commentators have treated the narrative sections of these chapters in detail. A. F. J. Klijn contents himself with giving numerous parallels to individual motifs (chiefly from Jewish- and Syrian-Christian sources) and has only sporadic comments on the composition of the piece and the interrelation of elements.[7] R. Reitzenstein begins his treatment by accepting at face value the apparent lack of order in the text.[8] Bornkamm takes the text a little more seriously, but his perspective is somewhat limited by his search to find mythological

---

[7] Klijn, *Acts of Thomas*, 157 – 91.

[8] And Reitzenstein (*Wundererzählungen*, 134 – 50) opens his analysis by remarking on the ineptness of the author: "Side matters are stupidly emphasized, principle ones are carelessly obscured. So even the short description of content which follows will be a kind of reconstruction" (p. 135). He ends by speaking of three different stages of composition, which have further disrupted the text (p. 149).

themes cryptically suggested in the narrative.[9]

Richard Adelbert Lipsius[10] and R. McL. Wilson[11] have given short interpretative summaries of these chapters, and Rosa Söder[12] has made some helpful observations on the story of the wine pourer and its contemporary analogies.

Hence, no study has yet been done that attempts a detailed analysis of the narrative in these chapters as a coherent whole. Particularly, no previous commentators have taken into consideration the organizational paradigms discussed in the preceding Chapters of this work. They have, on the other hand, made many important observations on matters of detail, and these will be discussed in the appropriate places.

Preliminary Form- and Redaction-critical Observations

Turning now to the text itself, it is fairly obvious that these chapters have many of the characteristics just outlined. For example, while there is a central thread being developed both in the story of Thomas's sending and the scenes at the banquet, the action develops in a series of short episodes often with abrupt transitions between them.[13] There is also an anointing scene at the banquet that apparently has little to do with the central theme there of Thomas's relation to the Andrapolitan banqueters. Many of the individual episodes on the other hand are clearly modeled on traditional themes, stories, or story forms otherwise known to us.

One can go further. If one focuses on the individual episodes as separate units and pays attention to their relation to traditional themes and story forms, evidence appears in almost every case for regarding each episode as a previously formulated piece incorporated into what is essentially a new context formed by the joining of many of these previously independent stories. In other words, the previous observations about the influence of traditional themes and materials on the composition of the *Acts Thom.* leads, in the case of these chapters at least, to a properly form-critical analysis of every episode. This includes: (1) a determination of the character of the original material of the piece in question (where possible with the aid of contemporary comparisons),

---

[9] Bornkamm, *Mythos*, 68–74.

[10] Lipsius, *Die apokryphen Apostelgeschichten und Apostellegenden: Ein Beitrag zur altchristlichen Literaturgeschichte* (2 vols.; Braunschweig: Schwetschke, 1883) 1. 250.

[11] Wilson, "The Acts of Thomas," in Werner Foerster, ed., *Gnosis: A Selection of Gnostic Texts* (2 vols.; Oxford: Clarendon, 1972) 1. 337–38.

[12] Söder, *Apostelgeschichten*, 55, 61, 65, and 67.

[13] See 100.8; 101.3; 106.1; 108.1; 109.1; 112.1; 113.7; and 114.4.

and (2) the separating of those elements in each piece which are probably traditional from those which are secondary, redactional additions.

As to the latter issue, one important consideration will be the presence of devices pointed out in Chapters 1 and 2. That is, it is my thesis that the stylistic peculiarities and compositional principles analyzed earlier are in fact for the most part redactional techniques for joining, alterring, and reinterpreting traditional material. Let me outline here some brief indications of the bases on which this thesis rests (to be substantiated further in the course of more detailed analyses).

First, it can be observed in a general way that the devices pointed out in Chapters 1 and 2 are found pervasively throughout the material in chapters 1 – 10, despite the diverse provenance of the traditional material incorporated there. Secondly, devices in the text which single themselves out because of oddity, or for other reasons pointed out above, also frequently operate across the boundaries of individual units to make connections between them—showing that they can only have made their appearance in the text subsequent to the joining together of the various traditional units utilized. Among these devices one can list the following preliminary examples.

The anointing scene diverges from traditional practice at two points ("top of the head," 107.5 – 6; and "teeth," 107.8) in order to link it with images in the wedding hymn where the imagery is also unusual and striking on these points. A third nontraditional element is Thomas's taking the reed in his hand (107.11), a device indicating an allusion to the passion account. Three further divergences from what one would expect draw parallels between the invitation scene (104.5 – 105.12), the initial banquet scene (106.1 – 107.1), and the scene with the flutist (108.1 – 5):

> . . . sounds of flutes and of water organs and trumpets surrounding them. (104.6 – 7)
>
> He lay down in the middle. (106.1 – 2)
>
> She surrounded all and fluted. (108.2)

The last example also involves the pleonastic construction with "and." This construction appears as well in the parallel phrases, "and saying and thinking these things," that link the first epiphany (100.8) with the selling scene (101.3). It appears also in the short introduction to Thomas's interchange with the guests (106.3) to link that scene with the previous one (105.1) via the motif of the "foreigner." The peculiar phrase (100.5 – 6) μὴ δύνασθαι μήτε χωρεῖν ("He did not have the strength nor had he the capacity—did he travel") uses the construction to introduce a second level of meaning into the passage where it occurs. The other passage picked out as involving "price-equipment" appears, on other grounds as well, as a redactional composition almost in its entirety.

Finally, the describing of figures in parallel terms serves to link the interchange with the guests and the invitation scene (105.4–6 and 106.10–107.1) as well as the anointing scene and the flutist episode (107.11–108.1 and 108.1–2).

Redaction-criticism and "Reading Competence"

One final issue that needs to be addressed before proceeding to the analysis of our material concerns the relation of form- and redaction-criticism to our central notion of "reading competence." This relationship can perhaps best be described by pointing to the example of humorously intended signs or notices we find in our own culture which rely on the reader's recognition that some traditional formula is being twisted to some new use. Stores in the United States sometimes announce their policy of not extending credit to customers by posting the notice, "In God We Trust, All Others Must Pay Cash." The reading competence appropriate to such a sign requires precisely an implicit form- and redaction-critical awareness. That is, one needs first to recognize the form of the first part of the notice as a religious motto. And secondly, one needs to understand that a "redactor" is incorporating this religious motto into a composition of an entirely different genre. One who does not perceive these two things will miss the humorous intent of the sign and most likely will also be quite puzzled by its wording. One can also see, however, that someone who had never before encountered the specific motto "In God We Trust" might solve the puzzle if he or she were able by reflection to recognize by its form that this statement is probably a traditional religious motto.

This is essentially our position in relation to the *Acts Thom.* The fact that this work incorporates a good deal of traditional material does not only belong to its history, we should also assume that competent original readers of the work would recognize the traditional material in the text, would also naturally differentiate it in their reading from redactional additions, and would be especially alert and sensitive to new meanings produced by the interplay between traditional and redactional material. This implicit competence of the original readers is what we ourselves must aspire to, and it is what we are trying to gain through explicit form- and redaction-critical analyses.

The most important consequences of recognizing that there are two kinds of material in the text are, first, the recognition that the ultimate meaning of the text is that intended by the redactors and, secondly, that these redactors are not responsible for the wording of every phrase in the text. That is, sometimes the way the text is worded is due simply to the fact that the material involved was worded this way in the tradition which the redactors draw on, and we should not accord the wording any special significance or try to find hidden meanings in it unless redactional work specifically calls attention to it. One further usefulness of form- and redaction-criticism is that in allowing us to recover the traditional material used by the redactors it gives us some clues as to the religio-historical context of the work. It shows us some of the traditions from the surrounding culture which the authors knew and valued and says something about the community to which these redactors belonged. For example, many observations made above imply that some special instruction was necessary on the part of the original community for whom the work was written, in order that it be understood.

It can be remarked in this context that I speak of the "redactors" of the work. The matter is not that certain nor is it crucial to my thesis. I think of several hands at work largely because one can most easily account for an audience capable of reading this work by properly assuming that the kind of reinterpretation of traditions undertaken in it was first of all a living process in a community, the *Acts Thom.* most likely representing a final result of this community work.

This Chapter and those immediately following will attempt to analyze each successive passage of chapters 1–10 from a form- and redaction-critical point of view, to fix the meaning of individual traditional motifs used, and to integrate with these the knowledge of devices derived from Chapters 1 and 2. Many questions of substantive interpretations will have to be passed over in the initial sections. Even some of the differentiation between traditional and redactional material will have to wait until material from later sections can be used to throw light on the earlier ones. Likewise, our grasp of compositional principles will grow as we proceed, particularly in reference to several which are specifically related to individual passages. So although the work at this point takes on the form of a section-by-section commentary, the main thrust is still a cumulative inquiry establishing the nature of reading competence appropriate to the *Acts Thom.* In reality, especially in the earlier sections, we shall be able to establish only part of what this ideally prepared reader should see. We can now begin with the opening scene of the *Acts Thom.*

3.3 The Dividing of the World
Among the Apostles

In the following sections, a translation of the passage under consideration is given with indications of the history of the text as reconstructed
here. Unmarked text indicates traditional material. Italicized text sets
apart redactional alterations or additions. Justification for treating some
of the italicized material as redactional will be given in the discussion
immediately following the extract. At times, however, such
justification will only be found in discussions occurring later in the
study.

> At that time all of us apostles were in Jerusalem, Simon who is
> called Peter, and Andrew his brother, James the son of Zebedee,
> and John his brother, Philip and Bartholomew, Thomas and
> Matthew the tax collector, James the son of Alphaeus and Simon
> the Cananean, and Judas the son of James, and we divided the
> regions of the world, that each of us should go to the territory that
> fell to him by lot, *and to the people to whom the Lord sent him.* By
> lot, then, India fell to *Judas* Thomas, *also called "The Twin."*
> (99.2–100.6)

From a purely literary point of view, the *Acts Thom.* opens with a
scene that is broken off in the middle. We hear of the apostles gathered in Jerusalem to divide up the world "so that each . . . might go to
the region that fell to him by lot." But after Thomas receives his
assignment, the whole scene is forgotten and we are suddenly in the
middle of a different story dealing only with Thomas.

The motif of the twelve apostles' casting lots to divide the world
among themselves is known to us from the Syriac *Didascalia*[14] and the
Martyrdom of Andrew.[15] There is no good reason to suspect literary
dependence in any of these cases, and in all probability we are dealing
with a common oral tradition.

The original context of such traditions is most likely the attempt to
trace the Christian groups in various parts of the world to a common

---

[14] R. Hugh Connolly, *Didascalia Apostolorum: The Syriac Version Translated and Accompanied by the Verona Latin Fragments* (Oxford: Clarendon, 1929) 200.
[15] Bonnet, *Acta*, 2. 1. 46.18.

authoritative source in the group of the twelve apostles. This is precisely the way it is used in the Syriac *Didascalia*: it is the same general motif that led to the ascribing of the teaching in the Didache to the twelve apostles.[16]

This opening of the *Acts Thom.* can be presumed to have had some of these same associations for its ancient readers: what follows has authoritative character derived from its attribution to one of the twelve apostles.[17]

The dividing up of the world among the twelve also has an important association as representing the origins of the Christian mission. This association with origins will prove relevant later when it is shown that the theme of Thomas's sending is related in this work to the myth of the soul's descent.

The phrase, "and to the people to whom the Lord sent him" (100.3), is probably redactional, though it is hard to be sure. It makes the placing of πορευθῇ at the end of the sentence slightly awkward, it interprets the previous phrase by means of parallelism, and it serves to make the casting of lots more explicitly parallel to the Lord's "sending" Thomas in the next two scenes.

If this is so, it implies that the sentence (καὶ διείλαμεν . . . πορευθῇ, 100.1–4) is a traditional formulation to which the redactors make additions.

---

[16] Helmut Koester ("*GNOMAI DIAPHOROI*: The Origin and Nature of Diversification in the History of Early Christianity," in James M. Robinson and Helmut Koester, *Trajectories Through Early Christianity* [Philadelphia: Fortress, 1971] 114–57) has shown that the appeal to the authority of a particular apostle is probably characteristic of several strands of early Christianity, each strand appealing to a different apostle. The tradition of the twelve's dividing up the world among them is perhaps a historicizing recognition of these traditions.

That there was a group who recognized Thomas as the chief among the apostles appears in the *Gos. Thom.* (NHC 2,2) 13: 34.31–35.15 and is perhaps evidenced also in Eus. *Hist. eccl.* 3.1 where Thomas heads the list of the apostles.

Manfred Hornschuh ("The Apostles as Bearers of the Tradition," in *NTApo* 2. 74–84) summarizes the evidence gathered by von Campenhausen and others that the notion of the apostles as guarantors of tradition originates actually in Gnostic circles (probably in imitation of Greek philosophical schools and mystery religions). Both the *Gospel of Thomas* and the *Book of Thomas the Contender* (NHC 2,7) utilize this theme, opening with a declaration that what follows is a secret tradition imparted by Jesus to Thomas. The *Acts Thom.* explicitly mentions "secret sayings" imparted by Jesus to Thomas (164.2–3). Thomas is also presented as an initiate in Christ's mysteries in 156.13–15.

[17] In the Andrapolitan scenes, as in some other sections of the *Acts Thom.*, Thomas is called simply the "apostle," and it is possible that the original stories used that term in a more loose sense and did not specifically have Thomas in mind.

The use of "we" (99.2; 100.2) presents the author as being one of the twelve, a fictional element which is dropped immediately thereafter. The fact that it is dropped, together with the fact that it is a feature of the equivalent scene in the *Didascalia*, may be taken as an indication that it belongs to the redactors' sources.

The apostle list given is almost identical to that in Matt 10.2 – 4. It is not necessary to the context (καὶ διείλαμεν [100.1] could follow directly on Ἱεροσολύμοις, 99.3), and it is the source of some awkwardness as it stands: one expects under the circumstances that the fictional author would single out with which of the apostles listed he is to be identified. This suggests that the apostle list has been inserted into a previously formulated "we" tradition about the division of the world among the twelve, which originally contained no such list (as in the case with the *Didascalia* scene).

The conservatism of the redactors in relation to their sources can also be seen in the fact that Thomas is given no special place in the list. (In the list in the *Martyrdom of Andrew*, Andrew is given such prominence; see Bonnet, *Acta*, 2. 1. 46.19 – 47.7.)

To summarize, the competent reader would see here:
1) a tradition about the dividing up of the world among the twelve;
2) a traditional apostle list interpolated into it, giving emphasis to the sense of being present at the authoritative origins of the Christian mission; and
3) a redactional interpolation making explicit the connection of the lottery results with God's will (a device which parallels this episode with the two to follow).

3.4 The Sending of Thomas to India

But he did not want to set off, saying *that he was not capable nor did he travel* [18] *because of the weakness of the flesh* (διὰ τὴν ἀσθένειαν τῆς σαρκός) *and* that "Being a Hebrew man (καὶ ὅτι ἄνθρωπος ὢν Ἑβραῖος) how shall I be able to go to the Indians to announce the Truth?"

As he was *thinking over and* saying these things, the Savior appeared to him at night and said, "Do not be afraid, Thomas, go to India and announce the Word there. Because my grace is with you."

---

[18] Or: *did not have the strength nor the capacity to understand* (μὴ δύνασθαι μήτε χωρεῖν).

But he did not obey[19] *saying, "Wherever you want to send me—*
send me somewhere else! Because I am not going to India."

The actual story of Thomas's sending follows a general pattern visible
in several biblical passages:[20] a person is given a divine mission which is
initially refused with some remark about its impossibility. God or a
divine being appears with instruction and/or an offer of help after
which the person accepts the mission.[21]

What stands out as incongruous in this context is the selling scene.
The context of the dream-vision requires that Thomas be given some
reason to change his mind. But the story is about a commercial tran-
saction (and verbal trickery) forcing Thomas to go to India having
nothing to do with reasons why he should or should not go. That the
story does not fit the dream-vision frame shows also in the fact that, for
it to work at all, Abban has to be turned into a real-life figure after the
vision is over. Finally, the abruptness with which this scene is introduced is also evidence of its secondary character in this context.

The selling scene is necessary to the Second Act and, we can reason-
ably conclude, was initially part of that story.

According to the typical vocation scheme just described, one expects
Thomas to give in after the second divine commissioning with its offer
of help. In this light, Thomas's second refusal, striking in its direct-
ness, is probably a redactional addition to provide an occasion for the
selling scene. It is of course possible, but less likely, that the refusal is
original in which case the selling scene replaces some other kind of
divine intervention.

What we are left with is an initial sending of Thomas by the casting
of lots, an initial refusal, an epiphany, and an acceptance
(102.10–103.1). That we are dealing at least partially with a previously
formulated tradition shows in the sign of secondary reworking visible in
the scene of Thomas's initial refusal. There Thomas actually gives two
completely separate reasons for not accepting the mission: (1) sickness
and the resultant inability to travel, and (2) the problem of being a
foreigner in India. The two reasons are juxtaposed rather than
integrated, and they are introduced by different grammatical constructions (λέγων with the infinitive, and with ὅτι).

---

[19] Or: *was not persuaded* (οὐκ ἐπείθετο).
[20] As noted by Klijn, *Acts of Thomas*, 160.
[21] See Exod 3–4; Judg 6.11–14; Jer 1.4–6; and Acts 18.5–8.

The pleonastic construction involved in μὴ δύνασθαι μήτε χωρεῖν is characteristic of the redactors. The second answer (minus ἄνθρωπος) is therefore the original one. One can see here how the redactional process works, drawing μὴ δύνασθαι ("not capable") by association from πῶς δύναμαι ("how can I," 100.7), and χωρεῖν (to travel) from the general idea of travel inherent in the situation.

This also shows that a mission to a very foreign country was involved in the original story, this being the original reason for the refusal.

In general, this vocation story belongs to the category of biographical legends originating as edifying stories of ideal figures. This story in particular probably belongs to a group of stories about a legendary trip of the apostle Thomas to India. There is no reliable historical evidence for such a trip, and it seems quite likely that the whole theme is modeled on the popular legends about Alexander the Great and about the god Dionysos:[22] their "triumphs" in the exotic land of India are the model of Thomas's struggle and victory in converting Indian royalty in the Second Act and in the Seventh through the Thirteenth Acts.

The use of δύνασθαι as synonymous with χωρεῖν (= νοεῖν) is specifically Gnostic, "power" having to do in that context with spiritual-mental advancement accompanying gnosis.[23] The thought that understanding is the issue at stake is continued in two pleonasms, "saying and thinking over these things" (ταῦτα αὐτοῦ λέγοντος καὶ διαλογιζομένου/ἐνθυμουμένου, 100.8 and 101.3). That is, contrary to the general context, these represent Thomas as "thinking over" his problem in an internal dialogue. This reinterpretation along noetic lines makes it likely that the redactors see a double meaning also in οὐκ ἐπείθετο (100.11): "He did not obey" and "He was not persuaded."

Introducing the *Acts Thom.* in this way makes it a close parallel to the Hermetic tractate *Poimandres* which opens with the scene of someone "thinking over" a problem of understanding, followed there also by a vision (*Corp. Herm.* 1.1–3).

We may summarize these results, from the point of view of the competent reader:

1) The core is a biographical legend, a vocation story. It recounts how Thomas was sent to a foreign and exotic India and initially refused because the extreme foreignness of India made the mission seem

---

[22] See K.-H. Roloff, "Dionysos," *Lexicon der Alten Welt* (Zürich/Stuttgart: Artemis, 1965) 757.

[23] See, for example, *Corp. Herm.* 1.27.

impossible. He was won over, in a conventional way, by a personal visitation from Jesus and a promise of divine aid.

2) The traditional theme of the prophet's reluctance for his mission is now, by redactional work, overlaid by a conventional Gnostic literary opening, puzzlement over a difficult mystery. This redactional theme is introduced by two peculiar passages (μὴ δύνασθαι . . . διὰ τὴν ἀσθένειαν τῆς σαρκός and διαλογιζομένου καὶ λέγοντος) and elaborated on in that the spiritual incapacity to understand the mystery is related to (fallen) existence in the body, the "weakness of the flesh." The redactional theme overrides the conventional one and induces the reader to understand the theme of the prophet's reluctance as a metaphor whose ultimate referent is the redactional theme, the incapacity for understanding.

3) The combined motif of Thomas's recalcitrance and his lack of spiritual capacity is underlined by Thomas's direct refusal of Jesus' command, a striking departure from the conventional vocation-story schema. The double character of the motif is continued by the double sense of οὐκ ἐπείθετο.

To summarize the argument methodologically, two peculiarities (μὴ δύνασθαι . . . ἀσθένειαν τῆς σαρκός and διαλογιζομένου καὶ λέγοντος) draw attention to themselves as redactional additions. Taken together they also evoke a traditional Gnostic motif, an introductory scene where someone is struggling with a problem. The mode of introducing the theme also follows the same pattern in both cases: the same phrase conveys both conventional meanings consistent with the surface reading of the story and, construed more strictly and according to special conventions, new meanings incongruous with the surface reading. This is what leads to the understanding of the conventional, surface readings as a provisional, metaphorical level of the text whose real referents lie on the level of the new redactional theme. This pattern will be repeated often in the sections to come.

3.5 The Selling Scene

As he was *thinking over and* saying these things the Savior appeared to him at night and said, "Do not be afraid, Thomas, go to India and preach the Word there. Because my grace is with you."

But he did not obey, saying, "Wherever you want to send me—send me somewhere else! Because I am not going to India."

And as he was saying and reflecting on these things, there happened to be there a merchant coming from India, whose name was Abban, who had been sent by the king Gundaphorous *and had received a command from him* to buy and bring back to him a craftsman. So the Lord saw him walking in the marketplace at midday and said to him, "Do you want to buy a craftsman?" And he said to him, "Yes." And the Lord said, "I have a servant, a craftsman, and I want to sell him." And when he had said this, he pointed out Thomas to him far off. And he agreed with him on three pounds of uncoined silver *and wrote a deed of sale, saying, "I Jesus, son of Joseph the craftsman, agree to sell my servant, Judas by name, to you Abban, merchant of Gundaphorous, king of the Indians."* And when the sale was complete, the Savior took *Judas, who is also* Thomas, and led him to Abban the merchant. And when he saw him, Abban said to him, *"Is this your master (δεσπότης)?"* And the apostle answered and said, "Yes, he is my Lord (κύριος). And he said, "I bought you from him." And the apostle was silent.*

The next day early in the morning, *having prayed and* entreated the Lord, the apostle said, "I go wherever you will, Lord Jesus, your will be done."

The selling scene does not fit in the context of a dream vision, but it is necessary for the Second Act in order to get Thomas to India as a carpenter-slave. We may assume then that it was originally the beginning of that story, and it was transferred here when the present introductory scenes were constructed and joined to the rest of the legends. As it stands now, it gives the sending of Thomas an air similar to that of the Jonah story, and it is probably an allusion to that tradition.

 The present exchange between Thomas and Abban in the boat ("What work do you know") clearly pertains also to the Second Act where it is repeated (125.1–2). It was probably originally part of the selling scene but without the references to boat building. Its most natural place would be before the sale since Abban is inquiring about the skills of his prospective slave.

On the other hand, the question Abban asks Thomas in the present selling scene ("Is this your master?") is superfluous from a conventional point of view. This suggests that this ending is redactional.

The mention of Jesus as "son of Joseph the craftsman" and the naming of Thomas as "Judas" have already been seen to be literary devices of the redactors. There is some likelihood that the entire passage about the contract is not original since it is not necessary.

The statement that he *"had been sent* by king Gundaphorous and *had received orders* from him to buy" (101.5) is somewhat tautologous and serves to compare Abban to Thomas.

To summarize from the point of view of the competent reader:
1) The conventional scheme of prophetic call, reluctance, epiphany, and acceptance is now interrupted in the final step by Thomas's strikingly direct refusal. The reader recognizes that the beginning of a different story about Thomas's sending to India is interpolated into the narrative at this point, introduced as a parallel to the previous epiphany scene by a parallel introduction, "As he was saying and reflecting on these things. . . ." With its focus on the selling and the slavery theme, this scene presents Thomas's sending as similar to that of Jonah: the reluctant, disobedient prophet is forcibly sent on his way.
2) The selling account has been altered in several ways. Abban is introduced in such a way as to parallel his mission with that of Thomas. The apostle is named "Judas" in the deed of sale to remind the reader of Judas's selling Jesus. Furthermore, connection is made between Thomas and Jesus via the "craftsman" motif. Finally, new interchange between Thomas and Abban is added which implies that, in addition to being forced on his way by being sold, Thomas is tricked by a play on words into verbal acceptance of his metamorphosis into a slave.
3) The selling scene is now presented as a continuation of the vision-epiphany occurring during the night. The retention of Thomas's willing submission ("Your will be done") from the first vocation story, now placed after the selling scene, leaves a puzzle for the reader. Is there an implication that Thomas's being forced into India by being sold, as well as his having been influenced by a vision, have been made into something that convinces Thomas to go? Or, to go further, does it in some way solve Thomas's problem of understanding as presented in the initial sending scene?

3.6 Thomas's Departure

And *he set off* to Abban the merchant, carrying with him nothing at all *except only his price* ($\tau i\mu\eta\mu\alpha$). *For the Lord had given it to him saying, "May your authority* ($\tau\iota\mu\dot\eta$) *be with you, with my grace, wherever you may set off for." And the apostle caught up with Abban, likewise carrying his baggage*[24] *onto the boat. And he began also to carry it on up with him.*

---

[24] Or: *equipment* ($\sigma\kappa\epsilon\dot\nu\eta$).

And when they had embarked on the boat and had sat down, Abban asked the apostle, "What work do you know?" And he said, "In wood: plows and yokes and balances *and boats, and oars for boats and masts and pulleys.* And in stone: pillars and temples and royal palaces." And Abban the merchant said to him, "Yes, we have need of that kind of craftsman."

And they began to sail. They had a friendly wind, and they sailed *willingly* (προθύμως) until they came to *Peoplecity* (Andrapolis), *a royal city.* (103.1 – 104.4)

The scene of Thomas's joining Abban is a continuation of the selling scene. The same can probably be said of the sea journey.[25]

The motif that Thomas carried no baggage may also belong to the original story. It is probably an ascetic development of the tradition preserved in Matt 10:9 – 10.[26]

The rest of the scene is entirely redactional, as has already been shown on stylistic grounds in Chapter 2. In light of the tendency of the redactors toward word play, noted in the case of χωρεῖν and ἀσθένειαν τῆς σαρκός above, it seems likely that προθύμως (104.3) refers secondarily to Thomas's final "willingness" to go on his journey after the initial refusals.

In the present version Thomas and Abban do not end up in India but in "Andrapolis." This is plainly a redactional introduction to a series of episodes that have been interposed between the selling scene and sea journey and the arrival in India.[27] In the light of general word coinage elsewhere in the *Acts Thom.*, R. McL. Wilson is undoubtedly right to see Andrapolis as a coined word, "Mancity."[28] A "royal city" (πόλις βασιλική) is of course likewise redactional and draws attention to the role of the Andrapolitan king in the next scenes.

The competent reader will notice here, then:
1) There is a complex chain of connections "price-authority-grace-baggage-equipment-ship's gear." Additionally, one notices that conferring authority (τιμή) on Thomas is a partial answer to his original

---

[25] Klijn (*Acts of Thomas*, 163) notices the difficulty presented by the notion of a sea journey from Jerusalem to India. This may be an indication that the original story was envisaged as occurring on the Persian Gulf, or on the Euphrates. Or it may simply show the composers' disregard of realistic geography.

[26] See also the *Martydrom of Andrew*: "(He went) carrying nothing but only the name of . . . Jesus" (Bonnet, *Acta* 2. 1. 47.12 – 13).

[27] See Bornkamm, *Mythos*, 3.

[28] Wilson, "Acts of Thomas," 338. As Klijn (*Acts of Thomas*, 164) notes, attempts to locate a real town corresponding to Andrapolis (or the *Sandaruk* of the Syriac text) have failed.

fear of the vulnerable position of a foreigner in a strange country. Likewise one observes that the "grace" offered in the earlier epiphany (100.10–11) is now being conferred and that the redactors again underline Thomas's present willingness to go, in contrast to his initial reluctance.

2) Thomas talks of boat building as he sits in a boat.

3) "Peoplecity" in place of the traditional India gives the first indication in the text so far that Thomas's journey and his destination are of an allegorical nature.

The narrative section dealing with the wedding feasts consists of a number of episodes. On the surface, what they have in common is the context to which they belong: invitation, food, entertainment, and anointing. All are customary at Syrian wedding feasts[29] and to these belongs also the particular genre of a part of the wedding hymn. The same features, plus also the crown of blossoms, belong to the context of the Greek symposium[30] and it is not unlikely that this setting is also in the background here.

These episodes, except for the anointing scene, also have in common the presentation of the tension between the divinely sent Thomas and the "worldly" activities at the wedding banquet. The gist of the story is that he is forced to go to the wedding, but he refuses to participate by eating or listening to the music. He is then attacked for these reasons, but he is finally vindicated by a miraculous punishment of one of his attackers with his vindication producing some conversions. This general story line, however, is very much complicated not only by the seemingly irrelevant anointing scene and the wedding hymn, but also by many narrative details and allusions.

3.7 The Invitation Scene

And getting out of the boat, they entered the city. And behold, *the sounds of flutists and of water organs, and* trumpets (φωναὶ αὐλητῶν καὶ ὑδραύλεων καὶ σάλπιγγες) echoing around them! And the apostle asked, saying "What is this feast *in this city?"* And those who were there said, *"The gods have led you here also to enjoy a banquet* (ἵνα εὐωχηθῆς) *in this city. Because* the king has an only

---

[29] See Klijn, *Acts of Thomas,* 166–68.
[30] See Walter Hatto Gross, *"Symposion" Der Kleine Pauly: Lexicon der Antike* (5 vols.; Munich: Druckenmüller, 1964–75) 5. 449–50.

daughter and is now giving her to a husband in marriage. It is for the wedding, the *joy and* gathering, *the feast* which you see today. And *the king* has sent out heralds to announce everywhere that all are to attend the wedding, rich and poor, slaves and free, foreigners and citizens. And if anyone makes excuses and does not attend the wedding he will be answerable to the king." *But when Abban heard this he said to the apostle, "Let us set off then, too, so that we give no offence to the king, especially since we are foreigners." And he said, "Let us set off."* And when they had unpacked *at the foreigners' house* (ξενοδοχείῳ) *and had rested a little, they set off* to the wedding. (104.5 – 105.12)

The composition of the invitation scene shows some incongruities. On the one hand, it opens with a rather joyful scene and speaks of the gods' (i.e., Jesus') bringing them there to enjoy a banquet (105.1). On the other hand, it closes with a threat: Thomas as a vulnerable foreigner is forced to go to the wedding.

Several details reinforce this initial impression of incongruities:

1) The answer in 105.1 ("The gods have led you here also") is not really addressed to Thomas's question. It is clearly a redactional addition linking this passage to the earlier motif of Thomas's divine sending.

2) The phrase in 104.6 ("sounds of flutes and of water organs, and trumpets") is grammatically awkward, pairing two genitives (αὐλητῶν καὶ ὑδραύλεων) with a nominative (σάλπιγγες).

3) These two peculiarities go with another incongruous feature: the sounds that surround Thomas are given two different explanations. He is first told that what he sees is "joy and gathering . . . feasting" (105.3 – 4). Then reference is made to the heralds (105.5), an explanation of the trumpets Thomas has heard. These are not sounds of feasting, but of the proclamation-threat. The remark, "The gods have brought you," is clearly redactional. We recognize "joy and gathering . . . feasting" as redactional on stylistic grounds.

The indication is that we are dealing with some original formulations concerning heralds and the invitation-threat. It has been secondarily reworked to include references to feasting as well.

The threat accompanying the wedding invitation is of course unusual even in the original story, and this is apparently part of what has led Bornkamm[31] and Klijn[32] to suggest the parallelism to the parable of the

[31] *Mythos*, 29 n. 2.
[32] *Acts of Thomas*, 165.

wedding feast in Matthew 22. However, they ignore the incongruity this produces over against the next episode where the "stranger" motif pits the divinely sent Thomas against the worldly banquet guests. In the light of this latter passage at least, the invitation comes from a worldly, not a divine figure.

It is difficult to tell whether the "foreigner" motif (105.11) belongs to the original story, or whether it is a redactional addition to link this episode with other passages. For our present purposes, it is enough to show that the implied interpretation this gives to the text is in accord with traditions visible elsewhere in the *Acts Thom.* and which therefore can be presumed to be familiar to the original readers.

The *Acts Thom.* actually has another story about a woman being forced to go to a wedding (Seventh Act), but there is no mention there that she has religious objections, and it is unclear whether the motif originates in a religious context or not. A closer parallel, though not having to do specifically with a wedding, is the story of Vazan in the Thirteenth Act. Harrassed by his father for his celibacy, he is pressured toward a life of wordliness as opposed to (Christian) asceticism. Additionally, there is the story immediately following this one where Thomas is attacked for not eating. Finally, one should also consider the story of the wine pourer, in its original as well as in its present form, where the slap is motivated by Thomas's refusal to participate in the banquet. All these stories are reminiscent of narratives found in Daniel and the Maccabaean literature, except that here the social pressure is not directed at Jewish religious beliefs and practices but against asceticism.

The original reader would have seen the invitation-threat in this light, and the parallelism is not so much to Matthew 22 as to Daniel 3 where one also finds trumpets proclaiming an order felt to be antireligious (idolatry in that case). It is likely that the original story was constructed with this parallel in mind as well.

On the other hand, the references to feasting are in direct contrast to this invitation-threat motif. Most explicitly, Jesus is represented as bringing Thomas to feast in this city (105.1). In this respect of course, the story in Matthew 22 is very apropos: Thomas is to come to the wedding under divine command. (Thus the threat in 105.7–8 belongs with this interpretation as well.)

This of course sounds contradictory. Some precedent was established for this peculiar kind of composition in the earlier analysis of the twofold interpretation of the young man's death in the Third Act. It is only later argumentation, however, that will provide a plausible explanation of this peculiarity. We may anticipate that explanation briefly here. The unity of this scene, as well as those immediately subsequent, is experiential. What is unequivocal is Thomas's experience (and the reader's vicarious experience) of a banquet that he encounters as something that feels foreign and coercive. From the theological point of view of the redactors, this experience as such is ambivalent because this foreign feeling is a property of both divine perfection and of the ungodly (later: demonic) world.

This interpretation, which can only be fully substantiated later, should be kept in mind through the following scenes, each of which continues this feature of ambivalence.

In summary, what the competent reader would see here is:

1) An invitation-threat is interpreted both as a divine command to attend a heavenly banquet (echoing Matthew 22) and as an harassment by an oppressive antireligious (anti-ascetic) tyrant (echoing Daniel 3). The latter motif belongs in the context of (ascetic) culture hero stories. The former belongs in that of parables of the kingdom and as such implies that the "king" here allegorically represents God. The story is based on a previously formulated piece, of which this passage contains only a segment, the beginning. Very likely it once had as a part of its immediate continuation the scene of Thomas's (Jesus') preaching to the couple about celibacy in their bridal chamber (116.9–118.10). On the one hand that scene needs some such introduction as this, and on the other it provides a fitting follow-up: the ascetic apostle turns the tables on the tyrant.

2) The reader will notice some continuations of parallels to the opening scenes: Thomas is again being coerced to go ("set off") somewhere he would rather not, "led" also in this case partly by the Lord. The "foreigner" motif is carried over, too. Thomas's fears of being in a vulnerable position in a strange land are beginning to be realized. In the context of the allusion to Daniel 3, "foreigner" begins to have religious connotations, a suggestion which will be further developed and emphasized in later scenes.

3) One may here make some preliminary observations substantiated only later. "Set off" ($\dot{\alpha}\pi\epsilon\lambda\theta\epsilon\hat{\iota}\nu$) is repeated several times in the redactional exchange between Thomas and Abban (105.9, 11, 12). This passage is clearly an addition belonging to the stage at which the stories were joined. It begins to suggest a parallel between the various destinations of Thomas's (allegorical) "journeys." Earlier he did not want to "set off" for India (100.5–6), then he "set off" to join Abban going to India (103.1). And later he will be reluctant to "set off" into the bridal chamber with the king (113.10–114.1). This suggestion is supported by the assonance of the redactional

phrase αὕτη ἡ ἑορτὴ ἡ ἐν τῇ πόλει ταύτῃ ("this feast in this city"), tending to connect in the reader's mind "city" and "feast." "Flutists" also stand out here and will draw attention later to the parallel between Thomas's reception upon entering the city and his reception at the banquet by the woman flutist.

4) The short passage about the inn shows two catchwords used in the redactional presentation ("set off" and "foreigner's house," 105.12), drawing attention also to some possible special significance for the "resting," an important religious theme in the *Acts Thom.*

3.8 The Interchange with the Guests

And when the apostle saw that they were all lying down at table, he also lay down, in the middle. And all were looking at him as one who was a foreigner and had come from a different country (ἀλλοδαπῆς γῆς). And Abban the merchant, since he was a master, sat down in a different place (ἄλλον τόπον).

As they were eating and drinking, the apostle tasted nothing. So those around him said to him, "Why did you come here neither eating nor drinking?" And he answered them saying, "I come here for something greater than food or drink and to fulfill the king's will. Because the heralds announce the king's matters, and whoever does not listen to the heralds will be liable to the king's judgment."

Thomas's interchange with the guests (106.1–107.1) has marks of an apophthegm,[33] centered on the contrast between the divine mission of an ascetic apostle and worldly banqueting.[34]

It is possible that the apophthegm here was constructed specifically for this context as an episode belonging to the original story of an ascetic apostle forced to come to a wedding. In this case, we must still assume some redactional alteration to produce the ambivalent phrasing of καὶ ἵνα τὸ θέλημα . . . τελέσω so that it can refer both to fulfilling Jesus' will (a reference to "Your will be done," 103.1) and that of the Andrapolitan king.

However, it seems much more likely that we are dealing with a previously formulated apophthegm secondarily reworked. The prevalence of such a phenomenon in the history of the surrounding episodes itself makes this likely. The main additional argument is the appearance of

---

[33] On the form of apophthegm, with examples, see Rudolf Bultmann, *History of the Synoptic Tradition* (New York: Harper & Row, 1963) 39.

[34] Asceticism in regard to food is a common motif in the *Acts Thom.* See, e.g., chapters 20 and 29.

the lines, "Why did you come here neither eating nor drinking?" and "I came here for more than food or drink." The latter especially sounds more like a formula related to an ascetic life than a specific reference to one particular gesture at this banquet. And in fact, it is verbally identical to a tradition (minus ἐνθάδε, present here) preserved in Matt 11:18 about John the baptist, also an ascetic.

Secondly, one could point to the fact that Thomas's answers consist really of two answers, unintegrated, and do not fit the context very well. The first, "to fulfill the king's will," is not a specific enough contrast to eating and drinking. The second is no direct contrast at all.[35] (Probably, then, only the first half of Thomas's original answer is preserved here.)

Assuming that the previous episode of the invitation is meant to recall Matthew 22, then "Why did you come here neither eating not drinking?" (τί ἦλθες ἐνθάδε μήτε ἐσθίων μήτε πίνων) is very likely seen as recalling Matt 22:12: "Why did you come here not having a wedding garment" (πῶς εἰσῆλθες ὧδε μὴ ἔχων ἔνδυμα γάμου)? That is, the ambivalent interpretation of the wedding feast and Thomas's relation to it is carried into this scene as well, as it is in subsequent scenes.

In any case, the preceding redactional references to feasting (esp. εὐωχηθῆς, 105.1) operate to connect the previous scene to this one, thus deliberately carrying over the theme of the divine (as well as worldly) feast into this episode suggesting that Thomas's refusal is in part reprehensible.

In contrast to the apophthegm proper, the brief introduction (106.1–4) to this scene appears entirely redactional. Thomas's reclining "in the middle" is a link to the "surrounding" motif of 104.6–7 and 108.2, continued also by the image of Thomas surrounded by guests who are staring at him. The phrase about Thomas as a foreigner is a pleonasm and serves to link this scene to the previous one. The removal of Abban from the scene plainly belongs to the present joining of all these scenes as one continuous narrative.

As the story stands, it is impossible to tell whether the staring of the guests is curiosity, welcoming, or something else. The connection with

---

[35] Klijn (*Acts of Thomas*, 166) and Bornkamm (*Mythos*, 70) both see a reference here to John 4:34: "My food is to do the will of him who sent me." This is a good example of the kind of punch line that would be appropriate here. But, this is also representative of how Klijn and Bornkamm are satisfied with suggesting the general gist of meaning for a passage without really explaining the wording as it stands. Why is the present wording different from John 4:34?

their hostile question in the apophthegm suggests hostility. But one might posit that it is also linked to their staring in admiration in 111.2–3.

The ambivalent presentation of the banquet given here and elsewhere in the context suggests that the lack of clear interpretation given to the staring is deliberate. It is meant to be seen as both welcoming (like the flutist's fluting) and hostile (like the question and the servant's slap).

The main thread of the apophthegm pits the heaven-sent apostle against the worldly guests. In the light of this theme in the immediate context, and of the general uses of the foreigner theme in the *Acts Thom.*,[36] it is clear that "foreigner" here has a double reference. It refers both to Thomas's traveling away from his homeland, and to the fact that, as a divinely sent apostle, he is a foreigner in this world.

By implication this scene generalizes the elements presented: the worldly banquet becomes a representation of the world as such to which Thomas comes as a "heavenly" Hebrew. The allegorical nature of Thomas's journey is becoming clearer.

To summarize, what the competent reader would see here is:

1) There is an apophthegm in defense of the ascetic life, whose sense is now modified both by internal additions and alterations and by the setting in which it is placed. Both these factors are managed so that this scene, like the last one, presents two contrasting interpretations of the wedding banquet.

2) One interpretation is in accord with the point of the original apophthegm. It continues the negative interpretation of the banquet implied in the previous scene's allusion to Daniel 3. Thomas is a heaven-sent prophet, "foreign" to this worldly scene and surrounded by hostile residents of the world pressuring him to comply with their customs. A secondary meaning of Thomas's reply indicates that his forced agreement to attend the banquet does not imply that he is under orders to this foreign king. He counters threat with threat. He also is a "king's herald" backed up by divine power.

3) The other interpretation implies a critique of the original apophthegm and its ascetic hero. Thomas is likened to the man in the wedding banquet parable who comes in without a garment. The stance of the ascetic prophet is presented as a foolish refusal to participate in the divine banquet where he is being welcomed. So his words about "those who do not listen to the heralds" apply ironically to himself. The reader will also recognize here an echo of the theme

---

[36] See Bornkamm, *Mythos*, 11.

of Thomas's recalcitrant attitude toward his "journey" in the initial scenes.[37]

4) "Foreigner" both refers to the situation of Thomas as a Hebrew in a foreign country and evokes the conventional theme of the heaven-sent prophet who is a foreigner in this world. This employs the device of interpenetrating, overlaid motifs noted in the analysis of the initial sending scene. It also contributes to the reader's grasp of Thomas's journey as an allegorical one.

3. 9 The Anointing Scene

And after they were eating and drinking, and crowns and oils were brought, each took oil, and *one* anointed *his eyes, another his beard* (γένειον), *another other* parts of his body. But the apostle anointed *the top* (κορυφὴν) *of* his head, smeared a little on his nostrils, dropped some in his ears, touched his *teeth*, and smeared carefully the area around his heart. And the crown which was brought, woven of myrtle and other blossoms, he took and placed on his head, and *he took* a reed-branch in his hand *and held it.*[38]

As all commentators have seen, the anointing and crowning scene (107.2–108.1) is partly modeled on sacramental practice. This shows most of all in the anointing of the organs of the senses (eyes, ears, nose, and mouth). This practice would be out of place in a merely secular anointing after meals.

The intent here, as most commentators agree, is to show Thomas transforming a secular practice into a religious one. The implied genre this episode belongs to is, so far as I can see, a purely literary one.[39] It seems to have some parallel in the passage (145.17–146.3) where Thomas replies to a request for food by blessing and distributing bread and oil and herbs and salt.[40]

---

[37] This double intention will become more clear further on. Here it can be pointed out that chap. 79 contains a diatribe against the very kind of ascetic apostle who seems to be the hero of the *Acts Thom.* This holds even though the complaint there is against hypocrisy rather than against asceticism as such.

[38] In this case there was no established traditional material with which the redactors worked. They merely draw on several ideas traditionally converted with sacramental practice. Italics here indicate ideas specifically added by the redactors.

[39] Though, of course, it has its roots in the common practice of basing ritual usage on everyday usages, this notion is still alive in the *Acts Thom.*, as is shown by the enumeration of the properties of oil in 266.10–267.5.

[40] Oil is clearly meant to be sacramental here, which means bread probably is also. This may be an attempt to combine a sacramental reference with one referring to

The details of the anointing are somewhat puzzling. The description here differs from that given elsewhere in the *Acts Thom.* where simply pouring oil on the head is the norm (142.4–5; 239.25). The closest parallel I have been able to find is the baptismal rite commented on by Moses bar Kepha (ca. 900 CE). There is an anointing of the organs of sense, "forehead . . . heart . . . joints."[41]

The "top of the head" and "teeth" are examples of redactional technique linking the passage to the wedding hymn. About the latter, especially, there can be no doubt that it is due to the redactors' alteration of a reference to lips (or, less likely, the tongue), which one would expect representing the sense of taste.

If we take seriously that an anointing of the five senses is taking place, it is impossible to ignore the fact that Thomas anoints only three (hearing, smell, and taste), the guests anoint a fourth (sight), and the traditional fifth (touch) is apparently missing.

This is very odd. Thomas certainly transforms a secular practice into a religious one. But, contrary to Bornkamm[42] and Reitzenstein,[43] there is not really a contrast between Thomas and the guests on this score. They apparently complement each other instead.

A similar complication probably also shows in the fact that, as Lipsius[44] mentions, Thomas does accept the oil despite the fact that it is as much a part of the worldly banquet as the food he rejects. The redactors actually seem to play up this parallel between the food and the oil. The same phrase (δειπνησάντων οὖν αὐτῶν) introduces both this scene and the previous one, which one tends to take in the same sense despite the fact that the first clearly means "while they were eating," while as in the latter case it should be more naturally understood as "after they had eaten."

The anointing of the head and heart and "other parts of the body" can possibly be accounted for as sacramental practice. "Chin" (γένειον) is somewhat more difficult.

Thomas's ascetic diet of "bread, salt, and water" (131.7; 217.8–9). See also the description of "bread, oil, and water" as Thomas's "magical implements" (261.14–18).

[41] K. A. Aytoun, "The Mystery of Baptism by Moses bar Kepha Compared with the Odes of Solomon," in Jacob Vellian, ed., *Studies on Syrian Baptismal Rites* (The Syrian Churches Series 6; Kottayam: C. M. S., 1973) 14. Reitzenstein (*The Hellenistic Mystery-Religions: Their Basic Ideas and Significance* [Pittsburgh: Pickwick, 1978] 45) mentions anointing of the senses (with blood) in the Phrygian mysteries.

[42] *Mythos*, 69.

[43] *Wundererzählungen*, 135.

[44] *Apostelgeschichten*, 250.

My suggestion is that γένειον is intended as double entendre. The reader is actually supposed to read it as a derivative of γεννᾶν, that is, as γέννειον, a reference to the sex organs, representative of the (otherwise missing) sense of touch, a very natural association in a milieu where sex is the sense-pleasure par excellence.[45]

That the redactors of the *Acts Thom.* coin words like this seems most evident from the strange Βαβύρινθος in the Hymn of the Pearl (223.4), a combination of Λαβύρινθος (222.7) and Βαβυλῶν (223.5).

The crowning is probably based on the customs of the Greek symposium, possibly with some basis in sacramental practice as well.[46] Care is taken in the composition of the scene to link the oil and the crown, both by the introduction of "crowns and oils" together at the beginning and by the repetition of προσενεχθέντος (107.3 and 9–10), and possibly also by the placing of both on the top of the head.

The holding of the reed has no basis in either secular or sacramental practice.[47] It is a device to evoke the image of the mocked king Jesus, implying also a comparison of the passion scene with Thomas's situation here.

We may summarize our observations:

1) This passage in its entirety is a literary creation of the redactors, based on secular customs, sacramental practices, and an image from the passion account.

2) There is a continuation of the earlier contrast between Thomas's conduct and the worldly activity at the banquet. Also continued, however, is the interpretation of the banquet as a divine offering, presented here by paralleling the oils and crowns with the food. What now complicates the picture is the fact that the guests share the sacramental anointing with Thomas.

---

[45] In the anointing rituals I was able to consult, hands seem most often to represent the sense of touch. The navel is however sometimes mentioned, and, as C. Ruch ("Extrême Onction du Iᵉʳ au IXᵉ Siècle," *DThC* 5 [1913] 1982) mentions, this is very likely a modification, for modesty's sake, of an anointing of the genitals. Until very recently there was an optional anointing of the loins in the Roman Catholic Church, but the earliest documentary evidence I could find for this is the "Decree for the Armenians" in 1493. See DS, 336.

[46] A baptismal hymn of Ephraim mentions "crowns . . . set on your heads" (NPNF 13, 283).

[47] Reitzenstein (*Wundererzählungen*, 138) gives no reference or argumentation for his interpretation that Thomas "in addition to the crown also takes the branch and stands there meditating" as a sign that he is about to sing. Klijn's attempt (*Acts of Thomas*, 167) to connect this feature to the custom of bridegrooms holding a myrtle branch ignores the wording of the text here.

3) The final image captures the implied ambivalence about the banquet perfectly: by evoking the parallel image of Jesus' passion, the joyful blossom crown still represents, together with the reed, the persecution Thomas is subject to in Andrapolis.

3.10 The Flutist

> And the flutist, holding the flutes *in her hand went around all* and fluted. And when she came to the place where the apostle was, she stood *above* him fluting *at his head* for a long time. *This flutist was Hebrew by race.* (108.1–5)
>
> And moving away from him she fluted for the others, but she often looked away and looked at him. Because she loved him very much, *as being a man of her own race. And* he was in appearance more beautiful than all who were there. And when the flutist had completed everything *and had fluted*, she. . . . (111.6–10)
>
> . . . broke her flutes and threw them down, and went and sat at the apostle's feet. . . . (113.1–2)

As the episode with the flutist now stands, her conversion is represented as partly motivated by Thomas's hymn and by the miraculous punishment of the wine pourer. But these motivations are merely juxtaposed, not integrated with each other or with the motives internal to her story.

Her story is largely told in two blocks (108.1–5 and 111.5–11). Two features still visible suggest that these blocks were continuous narrative at a previous stage, only now split up by intervening material. First of all, the phrase "moving away from him" (111.6) is somewhat incongruous in its present context, where there is no mention of her previous nearness to Thomas. It does make sense, however, as a continuation of 108.4. The flutist is going around to all the guests, stops for a long time for Thomas, then moves away from him and continues around. The material that now intervenes obscures this connection. These same remarks apply, with less certainty, to the clause (111.9–10), "when she had completed . . . everything ($\pi\acute{\alpha}\nu\tau\alpha\varsigma$)," which seems to refer to the earlier clause (108.2), "she went around to all ($\pi\acute{\alpha}\nu\tau\alpha\varsigma$)." Secondly, even leaving out the hymn and the miracle, the flutist is still given two separate reasons for being attracted to Thomas: (1) they are compatriots, "Hebrews" (108.5), and (2) Thomas is "beautiful above all those present there" (111.8–9).

Both motifs have a clearly religious intent, "Hebrews" being obviously allegorical. "Hebrews," however, is not a common allegorical theme in the *Acts Thom.*, and seems, therefore, to depend on the present position of this piece in the larger context, that is, its link with Thomas's identifying himself as a "Hebrew man" in 100.7.

"Beauty" (κάλλος, also ὡραῖος as here), however, is a specifically religious theme in the *Acts Thom.*, applied several times to Jesus (154.12; 237.15; 258.8; and 272.2). In 154.12–14 it is a motive for attraction to Jesus, making the convert desirous of (κατεπιθύμιος) and in love with him: "And (his beauty) will prevent you from leaving (him)." This theme also goes well with the sexual overtones of this story.[48] Hebrew kinship does not. Hence, the indication is that the latter motif is redactional.

So Bornkamm is right about the genre of this story: it is of the type in which a mythical theme is dramatized in the form of a legend. He is also right in seeing a relation of this story to the Simon-Helena legend, which likewise represents the saving of a prostitute by her sexual attraction to a heavenly redeemer figure.[49] The original story did not, however, go so far as the Simon-Helena legend and represent a sacred marriage between Thomas and the flutist.

In its original form this was a conversion story dramatizing the mythical motif of divine beauty (embodied in the apostle as a semidivine figure) and its ability to save souls out of their degraded state ("prostitutes") by its irresistible attraction.[50]

This genre assumes a rather restricted audience, one already familiar with the motifs being dramatized and also with the genre as such. This must be presupposed in order that the story make sense without the burdensome attention to detail which is necessary for us to uncover its meaning.

This genre, then, is not suited to public propaganda of any sort, neither does it instruct. It is meant rather to portray, in an emotionally involving form, thoughts already familiar to the readers. The story form that it utilizes is, then, similar to liturgy in that it invites a meditative, experiential participation in the ideas and attitudes it incorporates and, for the properly prepared reader, actualizes.

---

[48] Women entertainers were generally prostitutes, as both Klijn (*Acts of Thomas*, 167) and Wilson ("Acts of Thomas," 250) point out apropos to this passage.

[49] Bornkamm, *Mythos*, 72–73. There is a suggestion in the latter part of the *Acts Thom.* (212.3–9) that Thomas lures away other mens' wives on this basis, although there this theme comes only as a complaint by Thomas's enemies.

[50] We must, of course, assume a somewhat different ending to the original story than we have at present. Perhaps the flutist once (111.10) sat at Thomas's feet with some statement of her recognition of him as a savior. See the dividing of the world by the apostles, the invitation scene, and the ascetic apophthegm, also broken off after the beginning.

The genre is in a somewhat different category than those studied so far, and this is true for two reasons. First of all, the story is metaphorical throughout. It is not at all intended to build up the figure of the real-life apostle as hero or θεῖος ἀνήρ, as are many other stories here and elsewhere in the *Acts Thom.*[51] Thomas's "beauty," the degraded state of the flutist-prostitute, and the sexual attraction are all meant to be representative of aspects of a religious experience potentially affecting everyone.

In this respect, the genre of this story lies close to the genre of the *Acts Thom.* as a whole.[52] As such it helps provide evidence as to the milieu, with its particular assumptions and predispositions, in which the *Acts Thom.* itself was originally received and read.

The Opening Section of the Flutist Story (108.1–5)

As to the small section of the flutist story at hand, it has obviously been reworked by the redactors to a considerable degree.

The first sentence has been specially worded. The flutist is now "holding in her hand the flutes," paralleling the immediately prior description of Thomas holding in his hand a reed-branch. Additionally, the original probably read "she went around *to* all" (περιήρχετο εἰς πάντας) and is now altered to leave out the εἰς, making the image here more explicitly parallel to the two preceding "surrounding" images.

The intention here is fairly plain: it continues the tendency of the redactors to highlight parallels between each scene of this section (beginning with 104.5). This paralleling is also the purpose of the striking image of the flutist "playing at his head" (i.e., this belongs with "top of the head" in the anointing scene). The same is true of "she stood above him."

By implication, then, the flutist now becomes part of the divine-worldly banquet, as is evident in any case in 108.6, which continues the ascetic motif precisely by having Thomas ignore her fluting.[53]

---

[51] The myth behind this story was apparently acted out in fairly literal fashion by Simon and Helena—if we can believe the Church Fathers. The redactors of the *Acts Thom.* avoid any such suggestion and attack such literalizing of this theme in the diatribe in chap. 79.

[52] This has already been shown to some extent, insofar as the reference to Matthew 22 in the invitation scene implies an allegorical interpretation of the king and the banquet. And the use of the "foreigner" motif in the introduction to the ascetic apophthegm also interprets "Hebrew," and by implication the banquet, allegorically.

[53] Reitzenstein (*Wundererzählungen*, 135) followed by Bornkamm (*Mythos*, 70) thinks that Thomas's ignoring the flutist is a sign that his senses have been suspended as a

The statement that the flutist is Hebrew is also redactional. It injects into the story the motif of divine kinship, common in the *Acts Thom.*[54] This kinship motif is in accord with the original intent of the story to present Thomas as saving a lost soul by the attraction his presence has for her. It adds to the original story the explicit theme that she is in some sense herself a "heavenly" figure out of place in this worldly scene. This, of course, is in direct contrast to her position as part of the worldly banquet that Thomas rejects, another very clear example of the ambivalent meaning of elements in this banquet scene.

By the principles of my general hypothesis, the ancient "competent" readers were probably familiar with the story of the flutist in its earlier form. They would recognize this piece as the beginning of that story, altered now in the following ways:

1) Her fluting is made parallel to the previous ambivalent "surrounding" images, the "sounds of flutists . . . and trumpets" inviting-threatening Thomas, and the staring welcoming-hostile guests. The original themes of the story are expanded on by these parallels and continue the ambivalent interpretation of the banquet. On the one hand she is a fallen and now a worldly figure whose seductiveness is part of the ungodliness that the heaven-sent Thomas rejects. On the other hand her attention to Thomas represents a recognition of him as a savior, an invitation (using a sexual metaphor), and a welcoming to the divine banquet. The ambivalent meaning of the flutist is underlined by its being paralleled with the image of Thomas holding the reed.

2) The larger context and the following line about Thomas's ignoring the flutist emphasizes her position as part of the banquet that is foreign to Thomas. The redactional addition that she is "Hebrew" emphasizes her kinship with Thomas (a motif probably already implicit in the original story). The use of this theme here, as well as the genre of the original, make the allegorical character of the "foreigner" theme very clear.

The presentation of the flutist as both foreign and kin to Thomas is a very clear example of a deliberate pattern that can now be seen to be less obviously suggested in previous scenes: the guests, on the one

---

result of the anointing. This rests on an imagined (not directly attested) connection between the mention of ecstatic suspension of the senses in the *Corpus Hermeticum* with an anointing of the senses in the mysteries. It also ignores the parallelism of the scenes here, which the analysis above has shown to be a pervasive characteristic of the redactional joining of these episodes.

[54]See 151.17; 156.17; and 161.11. This theme is related to the theme of God's "own" in John's Gospel and that of "divine sparks" rescued by the redeemer in Gnosticism.

hand, are worldly figures hostile to the ascetic Thomas and, on the other hand, they share his sacramental anointing. And the fluitist "surrounds" all the guests as well as Thomas. Abban is, on the one hand, a foreigner with Thomas and, on the other hand, it is emphasized that he sits in "another place" (ἄλλον τόπον—a phrase that is underlined by the presence of ἀλλοδαπῆς . . . γῆς in the previous line).

3.11 The Wine Pourer

> *The apostle was looking away at the ground, and* one of the wine pourers *stretched out his hand and* slapped him. And the apostle raised his eyes and turned to the one who *struck* (τύψαντι) him and said, "My God will forgive you this wrong in the age to come, but *to* (or: *in*) this world he will show his wonders. And I shall soon see the hand that *struck* me being dragged by dogs." (108.6–12)
>
> And *that* wine pourer *who had slapped him* went down to the spring to draw water. And *there happened to be there a lion, and he killed him and left him lying in the area, having torn apart his members* (τὰ μέλη). *And right away dogs took his members, among whom one black* (μέλας) dog, took hold of his right hand in his mouth, and brought it into the banquet area. And seeing this all were upset, asking who it was among them who had left. And when it became clear that the hand was that of the wine pourer who had struck the apostle the flutist broke her flutes and threw them down and went and sat at the apostle's feet saying, *"This man is either a god or an apostle of God. Because I heard him saying to the wine pourer in Hebrew, 'I will soon see the hand that struck me being dragged by dogs.' This is what you have seen. Just as he said, so it happened."*
> And *some* believed *her,* others did not. (112.1–113.7)

In the story of the wine pourer, there is only one indication of reworking visible at this stage that would show it to be an incorporation of previously existing material. If the story were composed specifically for this context, one would expect that the idea of the Hebrew curse would be introduced at the very beginning of the story when the curse is spoken. It comes much later, and it appears as a surprise since one originally assumes that Thomas's words were intelligible to the servant (as they were earlier to the guests). The "Hebrew" curse is thus easily identified as a redactional addition.

Besides this, it can be remarked that: (1) this story does not need the setting here or in any of the other episodes to make its point; (2) it is told in two large blocks rather than woven into the rest of the material; and (3) it clearly belongs to a category of stories well known outside the *Acts Thom.*[55] It seems almost certain, as with the preceding episodes, that it had a prior existence outside the *Acts Thom.* and has been incorporated here by the redactors.

At present, the servant's slap is motivated by Thomas's ignoring the flutist, that is, it is a worldly attack on the ascetic Thomas, a scene parallel to the ascetic apophthegm (106.5 – 107.1).

The original story obviously had a different beginning. The fact that a wine pourer is mentioned suggests that the original motivation was the refusal of wine.[56]

So the original story here, as Söder states, belongs to the category of "mission-aretalogy," propaganda for the (probably ascetic) apostle as a representative of God. It combines the motif that punishment is visited upon those who show disrespect for figures connected with the divine and the motif of the divine efficacy of the apostle's curse. (See Jesus' curse in Mark 11:13.) She cites several Old Testament passages (esp. 3 Kgs 21:19, 23; 22:38) to show that the dogs which appear in this story are a special element of disgrace.[57]

Thomas's curse is specifically on the hand that slapped him, and this is probably based on the theme of the punishment fits the crime.[58] In this light it may be asked whether the original story had a more literal fulfillment of Thomas's curse, such as the dog's biting off the servant's hand rather than his being killed by a lion.[59] The only redactional modification of the opening section of this episode (108.6 – 13) easily discerned at this stage is the ambivalent construction εἰς τὸν κόσμον τοῦτον (in/to this cosmos) which, in its secondary meaning, is an explicit reference to the allegorical meaning of the banquet as cosmos.

In the light of the paralleling of the scenes and of the use of "hands" already as a linking image, it appears likely, even at this stage, that "stretching out his hand" (108.7) is an intentional paralleling of this scene with the previous two.

---

[55] See Söder, *Apostelgeschichten*, 55.

[56] In 230.16 wine is contrasted with water, the drink of the ascetic (131.7).

[57] Söder, *Apostelgeschichten*, above n. 55.

[58] See the hell vision (171.14 – 176.11) which speaks explicitly of this theme. I suspect the withering of the man's hands in chap. 51 was also originally due to touching the Eucharist unworthily. Söder, ibid., cites the Armenian text of the *Acts Thom.* as telling of the withering of the hands of those who want to stone Thomas.

[59] Augustine cites this story as one showing an excessively cruel punishment for a simple slap. He knew of it because of his association with the Manichaeans who held the *Acts Thom.* in high regard; see C. Faustum 22.79. Klijn's idea (*Acts of Thomas*, 168) that Thomas's statement about forgiveness means that this punishment is actually expiation has no justification in Thomas's words and goes against the plain sense of the story.

The ambivalence in overall interpretation in this section is not carried forward here in any obvious way visible at this stage of our
investigation.[60] The sense of the scene as it can be seen at this point is
therefore fairly plain, and so a summary of the impression it conveys
will be postponed until other complicating features can be made clear.

3.12 Summary

The story up to now manifests a common thread: it is about an
apostle-prophet figure in a series of different kinds of encounters with
the world of his mission field. The surface of the general story line
itself invites us to make connections between various elements belonging to a single category.

I have been using the term "worldly" as a category to which belong
the feasting in the city, the banquet, the invitation-threat, the guests
and their hostile question, the seductive flutist and her fluting, and the
hostile wine pourer and his attack on Thomas. Over against these
worldly elements we have the apostle, his attitudes and his experience:
he feels vulnerable and coerced, he refuses to participate, he meets
hostility with threats of divine punishment for those who do not respect
him, and he receives recognition as a savior.

So even the surface of the narrative, due to the way the redactors
juxtapose traditional materials, begins to show a certain deliberate pattern of organization. It uses images that are enough alike to invite us
to think of them under a single general category. Yet they represent
very diverse aspects of this classification. They do not, for example,
simply repeat in various ways the theme of the hostility between
worldliness and the prophet.

This is an important factor in our reading of this text. It has to do
with what appears at first as simply disjointedness, discontinuity, and
diffuseness: we look in vain for a single train of thought or narrative
development carried out in all the individual episodes and details.

Our perception of this feature of the *Acts Thom.* changes consider-
ably if we regard it as the result of a deliberate attempt to gather
together and present in story form the many facets of the prophet-
world relationship as this theme had been developed in tradition.

That we are correct in reading the text in this way shows in the way
the redactors use particular devices to further it. The clearest examples
here are the parallel images. The three "surrounding" images are an

---

[60]Later it will be shown that it is actually intended and indicated by a play on the
meaning of τύπτειν.

attempt to bring together in the reader's mind three different aspects of the prophet's reception in the world: (1) the music surrounding Thomas upon entering the city represents the welcoming invitation the prophet receives, as well as the coercion to participate in worldly affairs; (2) the guests who surround Thomas and stare at him represent recognition of him as being different, and it portrays the additional pressure that he conform and take part in their activities; and (3) the fluting which surrounds Thomas represents worldly entertainment and seductive temptation to sin as well as recognition of him by a lost soul as a savior and kinsman. The three images related to the "hand" add (4) the humiliation and persecution of the prophet by worldlings (represented by the crown and reed), and (5) the hostile attack on the prophet (the servant's slap).

This device of presenting multiple facets of a single theme is pursued in a more complex and unusual way when, in several cases, contradictory facets of the theme are presented, often within a single image. Here we have: (1) the allusion of the invitation scene to both Matthew 22 and Daniel 3 (making the wedding feast both a divine and an irreligious affair); (2) Thomas's blossom crown, both a symbol of joy and celebration and an allusion to Jesus' passion; and (3) the figure of the flutist, both worldly and heavenly ("Hebrew"), both seducing Thomas and recognizing him as savior.

The device just described is in effect a new organizational paradigm. It requires that the reader regard the diversity of currents in the text as deliberate rather than merely a product of diffuseness on the part of the authors. We have to keep in mind several complicating elements in the story so far, though we cannot yet know for certain how they are to be integrated into the rest of our interpretation.

The first of these complicating elements is the allegorical nature of Thomas's journey. The use of the motifs "foreigner" and "Hebrew" in the Andrapolitan scenes seems to merge deliberately the literal fact that Thomas is away from his homeland with the metaphorical motif that the prophet and his "kin" whom he comes to save are foreigners in this world. This in turn gives a cosmic and mythical dimension both to my interpretative category "worldly" and to Thomas's journey. That the initial scenes about the sending and the journey and the later scenes at the banquet are to be linked this way becomes apparent in the fact that Thomas ends up not in India, but in "Peoplecity." Additionally, the catchword "set off" (ἀπελθεῖν) draws a parallel between Thomas's setting off to India and his setting off for the banquet. Finally, the invitation speaks of Jesus' (the "gods'") leading Thomas to this city.

The idea is that Thomas's mission field, India-Andrapolis, represents the earthly realm to which Thomas travels beginning from his homeland, the heavenly, Hebrew realm. One thinks of the so-called Gnostic redeemer myth which is presented in the Christ prayer soon to follow. There is also the (Platonic) myth of the descent of the soul, which is actually incorporated in the Gnostic myth in that there the redeemer comes to lead souls back to their common homeland. This motif is suggested here by the figure of the Hebrew flutist. All these features suggest that the whole story and its central theme of the prophet-world relationship must be interpreted within a mythical frame of reference.

However, several features mentioned above, chiefly the allusion of the invitation scene to the divine banquet of Matthew 22, present a different train of thought which goes directly against the conventional associations of the prophet-world confrontations presented in the narrative. That is, they present the earthly realm Thomas comes into as having a divine character, and his ascetic stance toward it shows up as foolish and disobedient.

This train of thought is supported by parallels between the opening scenes and those at the banquet. In both cases Thomas is reluctant to "set off" and is forced to go. The line, "The gods have led you here to enjoy a banquet in this city" (105.1), confirms the reader in perceiving that, by one line of interpretation, it is Jesus in both cases who is sending-forcing Thomas into the worldly realm. The foolish prophet Jonah's refusing the Lord because of his Hebrew superiority is an appropriate image not only in the sending scenes, but in the banquet scenes where Thomas refuses the foreign food.

The observation can be made in this context that sacramental thinking prominent in other sections of the *Acts Thom.* would consider the oil of Thomas's anointing as both earthly and a medium of divine grace—a thought that neatly links the two ideas that the banquet is somehow both earthly and divine.

Finally, we ought not forget a theme prominent in the early scenes, the presentation of Thomas's difficulty about traveling as a (Gnostic) difficulty in understanding. This draws our attention all the more now that we have seen the allegorical nature of Thomas's journey. We do not yet have sufficient additional information to integrate this theme into our interpretation. For that we need to pursue our investigation further by taking up the wedding hymn.

4

THE WEDDING HYMN

The wedding hymn analyzed in this Chapter is one of the more well-known parts of the *Acts Thom.*, having been studied by a number of scholars. The analysis here differs in two major respects from previous interpretations. First, as in the above treatment of the narrative, it recognizes two layers of material: compositions inherited from tradition and redactional additions and alterations. Following the principles established in Chapter 1, some of this redactional reworking can be seen as an attempt to establish links between the hymn and the preceding narrative. Secondly, it asserts that the mythical figure who is the hymn's central subject is closer to the shekinah of Jewish mysticism than to the typical Gnostic Sophia whom many have seen here. This praise of the shekinah as God's earthly presence represents a climax of one of the two conflicting narrative strands just mentioned which sees India and the Andrapolitan banquet as a "worldly" but also a divine realm which Thomas is entering.

4.1 History of Research

The wedding hymn which Thomas sings immediately following his cursing of the servant has been the subject of much discussion among scholars. Six major studies[1] have been devoted to it, and several other works have proposed interpretations and observations on individual points that will also enter our discussion.

Most of the discussion has centered on the identity of the woman who is the principle subject of the hymn and the numerous difficulties presented by the unusual imagery in the text. Many have wanted to identify the woman with the mythical "Sophia-Achamoth" whose fall and redemption is a favorite subject of many Gnostic writings.[2] This thesis causes problems in explaining why what is said in the hymn is not more exactly and explicitly in accord with what is said of the Gnostic Sophia elsewhere.

The opinions of previous scholars on many individual points will be discussed as they come up in this commentary. Here a brief overview of the previous writings on the hymn can be given to show their general character and tendencies and to place this work in relation to them.

The connection with the Sophia myth was first proposed by Thilo in 1823 in a detailed commentary on the hymn that contains many acute observations on details as well as comparisons with a very broad range of contemporary literature (primarily reports of Gnostic doctrine in the Church Fathers). This is still by far the most detailed commentary and the one that tries most to come to grips with all the problems of both content and form. On the other hand Thilo is very direct in confessing that the form of the hymn remains in many places a puzzle to him. He attributes this to the fact that its author was a heretic (a *poeta male sanus*) who should not be expected to make sense.[3]

Many later commentators essentially follow Thilo's interpretation, differing in some points of detail, extending and making more precise the religio-historical background of the various motifs. Erwin Preuschen pays special attention to the Gnostic reports closest to the particular combination of motifs in the hymn, those concerning the Ophites. He also lays stress on the relation of the woman here (as the

---

[1] Joannes Carolus Thilo, *Acta S. Thomae Apostoli* (Lipsiae: Vogelli, 1823) 121–51; Lipsius, *Apostelgeschichten*, 301–11; G. Hoffmann, "Zwei Hymnen der Thomasakten," *ZNW* 4 (1903) 273–309; Erwin Preuschen, *Zwei gnostische Hymnen* (Giessen: Töpelmann, 1904) 28–44; Bornkamm, *Mythos*, 82–89; see also idem, "The Acts of Thomas" in *NTApo*, 2. 425–41; Klijn, *Acts of Thomas*, 168–79.

[2] See Jonas, *Gnostic Religion*, 176–99.

[3] Thilo, *Acta*, 135.

Gnostic Sophia) to the feminine deity in whom belief was widespread in the semitic world.[4] And he calls attention to a study of modern Syrian wedding feasts and wedding hymns by the ethnographer J. G. Wetzstein[5] as shedding some light on this hymn. Bornkamm is concerned primarily with the discrepancies between the wedding hymn and the Sophia myth. He ends by opting for some combination of the pagan Mother-Goddess with the Gnostic Sophia so that she here becomes a savior.[6]

G. Hoffmann compares the Greek text of the hymn with the Syriac, interspersing interpretative comments amid his comparisons. He follows Thilo and Lipsius in general, though he does not agree with the Sophia thesis. He thinks the woman of the hymn represents the soul as bride of Christ.[7]

Klijn's commentary on the hymn consists mainly of the citation of numerous possible parallels, leaning heavily again on Jewish- and Syrian-Christian, and here also on Manichaean, sources. He implicitly rejects the Gnostic Sophia thesis preferring to see here the Sophia of the Wisdom of Solomon and Sirach, with a common connection to the semitic goddess as well.[8]

As to the less-extended studies, Wilhelm Bousset proposed that there are many Manichaean additions to the *Acts Thom.*, among them the final section of this hymn. His view of the body of the hymn is unique in that he thinks the mythic imagery in the text was originally no more than poetic expressions exalting the bride. The Manichaean addition, he thinks, implies a Manichaean reinterpretation of the whole.[9]

Reitzenstein has very few comments on details of the hymn. In his interpretation the apostle was originally the representative of a god who was about to take the god's place in a sacred marriage with the bride. The hymn was originally a half-sensual, half-mystic praise of the bride by her divine bridegroom. It has been reworked by Syrian-ascetic, and later by Christian editors. There is nothing specifically Gnostic about it.[10]

---

[4] Preuschen, *Hymnen*, 29.
[5] Wetzstein, "Die syrische Dreschtafel," *Zeitschrift für Ethnologie* 5 (1873) 270–302.
[6] Bornkamm, *Mythos*, 84.
[7] Hoffmann, "Zwei Hymnen," 295.
[8] Klijn, *Acts of Thomas*, 169, 178.
[9] Bousset, "Manichäisches in den Thomasakten," *ZNW* 18 (1917) 1–39.
[10] Reitzenstein, *Wundererzählungen*, 134–50.

Finally, Gershom Scholem has made some passing comments on this hymn in his work on the origins of the Kabbalistic tradition. He pointed out that several features of the hymn are better explained against this background than against that of the specifically Gnostic Sophia myth.[11]

The present study is dependent on previous works for many points of detail. It does, however, start from a different perspective. First of all, it places primary emphasis on the problem of explaining systematically the form of the text as we have it, and, secondly, it operates informed by a knowledge of many basic organizational paradigms of the redactors of the *Acts Thom.* visible elsewhere which are in evidence in this hymn as well. Detailed explanations of the literary organization of the hymn will enable us to fix the meaning of individual motifs according to their use in the context, and this will give us the control necessary to decide on issues of comparability with contemporary material, heretofore the source of so much controversy.

One additional point should be made here. From the perspective of this study, there should be a distinction made between an investigation of the nature of reading competence in relation to this material and an investigation of the history of the ideas or motifs connected with it. The two are interrelated, but distinct. Focus on reading competence means that comparisons with contemporary material are relevant insofar as they shed essential light on the associations one must bring to the text in order to understand it as it was intended. The history of how these associations developed or of their historical relation to other motifs and association complexes is only of indirect concern to this study.

In what follows, we shall attempt a section-by-section explanation of the hymn, following divisions that will be established as we proceed. A summary assessment will follow, as well as a discussion of the proper religio-historical background for the hymn and the woman in it.

On the surface, the hymn comes rather abruptly with little apparent sequential connection with the narrative action, and it introduces many entirely new themes. This serves as initial justification for treating it as a unit by itself. Full treatment of its relation to the narrative context will come in Chapter 5.

---

[11] Scholem, *Ursprung*, 81–85.

4.2 Section 1: 108.12–109.4

And saying these things he began to sing and say this song:
The maiden is the Daughter of Light.
On her lies and rests the proud radiance of kings.
And her appearance is lovely,
Shining with bright beauty.
Her clothes are like spring blossoms,
Outpourings of good smells are given out from them.

The "Daughter of Light" here is a clearly mythical figure. "Light," as all are agreed, stands here as a name for the divinity. Following upon this, ἀπαύγασμα (radiance) represents manifestations of this divinity radiating from her presence.[12] Given this fact, "shining with bright beauty" (φαιδρῷ κάλλει καταυγάζουσα) continues the reference to the divine radiating from her, this time in connection with her beauty. Note also the assonance connecting these words: ἀπαύγασμα ... γαῦρον ... καταυγάζουσα. The first and last words here are also cognate.

The description of her scented clothing continues this reference to the woman's presence as a manifestation of the divine through the repetition of words with "radiating" connotations: ἀποφορά ... διαδί-δοται, an intended link with καταυγάζουσα. The same configuration is found in the description of the bridal chamber (109.14–110.1): φωτεινός ... ἀποφοράν ... διαπνέων ... ἀναδιδούς.[13] The structure of the section implied in this analysis suggests that it may have been composed as a religious interpretation of a fragment of a secular song. That is, the original song may have said:

The woman is the daughter [of the king?].
Her appearance is lovely;
Her clothes are like spring blossoms.

The religious interpretation has simply altered the first line to "Daughter of Light," then added lines alternating with the original ones to continue the theme that the woman's radiant beauty is a

[12] Thilo (*Acta*, 132) cites Wis 7:26 in support of this where Wisdom is called the ἀπαύγασμα φωτὸς ἀιδίου. For ἀπαύγασμα as a manifestation of the divine, see also Heb 1:7 and *1 Clem.* 36.

[13] For scents as an image of divine manifestations, see Klijn (*Acts of Thomas*, 170) who cites Ephraim, ". . . a portion of that aroma which blows through the Good (God)," as well as *Manich. Psalm* 118.29, "What smell is there . . . like thy fragrant smell?" See also Iren. *Adv. haer.* 1.21.3.

manifestation of the divine. On this hypothesis, the supposed reworking took place at a stage prior to the present redactions.

Admittedly, we cannot be certain that this is the actual history of the
text. Even if it is not, however, it does throw into relief both the
structure of the passage and the fact that it basically uses the ways in
which this beautiful woman impresses those around her as images of
the divine manifesting itself through the mythical figure the woman
represents.

4.3 Section 2: 109.5–14

And on top of her head (κορυφῇ) the king is established,
Feeding with his ambrosia those established on him.
And on her head lies the Truth,
And she manifests joy with her feet.
Her mouth is open, fittingly (πρεπόντως) for her,
Thirty-two are those who sing *her* hymns.
Her tongue is like the curtain of the door,
Which is shaken by those going in.
Her neck *lies in the form* of steps,
Which the First Maker made.
Her two hands signal *and suggest*
Announcing the dance of the good eons.
And her fingers suggest the gates of the city.

The image of the king seated "on top of her head." does not follow the
themes or the structure outlined above, and this marks 109.5 as the
beginning, literarily at least, of a new section. It also begins the mention of specific parts of the body which is a basic feature of the structure of 109.5–14. The description of the bridal chamber, a new topic,
begins with 109.14. This provides some initial justification for analyzing 109.5–14 as a unit.

Relation of This Piece to Traditional Wedding Songs

Thilo already noticed the similarity of some of the images in this section to those in two similar praises of the bride in the Song of
Solomon.[14] As mentioned above, the ethnographer J. G. Wetzstein in
1873 published an account of modern Syrian wedding feasts he had
attended. He gives a copy of a song similarly based on a description of

---

[14] Thilo, *Acta*, 137.

the different parts of the bride's body. The genre, he says, is called a *wasf*.[15] Klijn also notes the similarity to Song Sol 4:1–5 and 7:1–5 and adds 1QapGen 21.2–8.[16] More recently Wolfram Herrmann has published a study of many examples of this genre based on recent finds of material including a section of a Sumerian hymn from 2,000 BCE and the description of Sarah in the *Genesis Apocryphon* from Qumran Cave 1. He assumes it was a common form in both religious and secular contexts throughout the ancient Near East. All the parts of the body mentioned in the wedding hymn in the *Acts Thom.* (head, mouth, teeth, neck, hands, and fingers) are mentioned in one or more of the examples he cites, except for the tongue.[17] It seems fairly certain that this section of the wedding hymn is structured along lines of a genre familiar to the original readers of the *Acts Thom.*, probably already in both secular and religious contexts. In this light, the fact that the bride is here assumed to be dancing is not so strange as it might appear. The Song of Solomon begins a similar song (7:1) with the mention that the woman is dancing, and Wetzstein mentions that the bride "often does a little dance to show off her bridal costume."[18]

The striking difference between this hymn and all the other examples (including the religious ones) is the complete departure from images highlighting the real beauty and attractiveness of the bride represented by the images of the king seated "on top of her head" (109.5) and her neck's being like stairs (109.10–11). This most of all points to the necessity of some kind of allegorical interpretation of the images used as comparisons.

Esoteric References in the Original Piece and Their Origin

This section is also the part of the hymn which has the most obviously esoteric references, the "first demiurge" and the "eons," and these will serve as a starting point for the interpretation here, for reasons that will become clear as we proceed.

---

[15] Wetzstein, "Dreschtafel," 288.

[16] Klijn, *Acts of Thomas*, 171.

[17] Herrmann ("Gedanken zur Geschichte des altorientalischen Beschreibungsliedes," *ZAW* 75 [1963] 176–97) also notes more specifically that mentions of the parts of the body are mostly interwoven in these songs with images to which they are compared: "[her mouth] . . . is a lotus blossom." One also finds images of how attractive they are to her lover (in whose place the singer puts himself): "My [glance] takes her hair for bait in a trap that has been set" (p. 179).

[18] Wetzstein, "Dreschtafel," 292.

"Eons" as hypostases is typical of Gnostic usage. In Gnosticism this is a general name for various mythical figures intermediary between God and the visible world.[19] The "First Demiurge" is likewise Gnostic (borrowed from Platonism) and is used in the same context to distinguish the highest God from intermediary creators.[20]

The statement that "thirty-two are those who sing her hymns" has troubled many commentators. Preuschen wants to ignore it as hopelessly corrupt.[21] Thilo makes the accurate observation that the basic image is that of the bride's thirty-two teeth. This is undoubtedly, as he notes, what MS C represents with its addition of λευκημονοῦντες ἄγγελοι. He cites the description of the woman's teeth in Song Sol 4:12.[22]

In this context one can see that the "thirty-two" probably also represent an esoteric reference to some mythical beings whose identity was familiar to the original readers but difficult for us to determine. The proximity of "eons" makes one think of the "thirty eons" of Valentinian gnosis, though the number is not exact.[23]

Another esoteric reference in the context helps us a good deal with this problem: βαθμοί (steps) was used in the Greek philosophical schools, the mysteries, and in Gnosticism to refer to initiation grades.[24] This meaning is supported here both by the esoteric context in general and by the mention in the preceding line of "those going in." In the light of the woman's role as manifestor of the divine, it is clear that "those going in" do so for some kind of contact with the divine.[25]

There is a context in which each of the features mentioned has a natural place: the traditions preserved in the protokabbalistic *Sepher Yezirah*.[26] It speaks (1.1) of "thirty-two paths" by which God created

---

[19] See Jonas, *Gnostic Religion*, 51–52.

[20] See *Exc. Theod.* 47 and *Corp. Herm.* 1.9.

[21] Preuschen, *Hymnen*, 41.

[22] Thilo, *Acta*, 136. Hoffmann ("Zwei Hymnen," 299) follows Thilo in these observations. Herrmann ("Gedanken," 182) notes the same motif in a seventh-century Egyptian love song.

[23] Thilo, *Acta*, above n. 22; Klijn, *Acts of Thomas*, 171; Lipsius, *Apostelgeschichten*, 305–6; and Hoffman, "Zwei Hymnen," above n. 22.

[24] See BAG, *s.v.* βαθμός, and *Disc. 8–9* (NHC 6,6) 52.13.

[25] Lipsius (*Apostelgeschichten*, 306) agrees here: "[Her neck is] a staircase that leads to the upper region of the Light." He appeals to the *Acts of Philip* (Bonnet, *Acta*, 2. 2. 70.6), where βαθμός is also used in connection with the image of the cross as a ladder to heaven.

[26] I am using the term "protokabbalistic" to refer to material reflecting the transition in Jewish mysticism from early Merkabah mysticism to the fully developed Kabbalistic thought of the medieval *Zohar*.

the world. These are also the means by which, through meditation, one achieves union with God (1.3; 6.10)—this is presumably why they are called "paths." Scholem has shown that these thirty-two paths are directly related to Gnostic "eons."[27] That is, assuming this as a background, the "thirty-two" = the "steps" (paths) = the "eons." In this light, the whole passage becomes a projection of tradition about the "thirty-two paths" onto the description of a woman's body (modelled on the conventional *wasf*).

The use of protokabbalistic traditions as background for this section receives added support in the use of the love songs in the Song of Solomon by protokabbalistic circles as a basis for the description of the parts of the "body of the shekinah" (i.e., the manifestation of God), a tradition known as the *Shiʾur Komah.*

Note finally that the woman here, as in some sense containing the "thirty-two eons," stands closer to the Gnostic idea of the Pleroma, the realm of the Eons altogether, than to the normal Gnostic figure of Sophia: "She includes in herself the realm of the Eons," and "(her) body is an image of the realm of the Pleroma."[28] In this respect also we find a close parallel in the protokabbalistic tradition. In the *Bahir* (§ 43) the shekinah is not only (like the Gnostic Sophia) the last of the emanations of God, she is also the summation, the "receptacle" of all the other emanations.

The above comments serve as some initial justification for seeing this passage against the background of protokabbalistic speculation. The arguments are derived mostly from the researches of Scholem, who has shown that the traditions preserved in the *Sepher Yeẓirah*, in the *Bahir*, and in the tradition of the *Shiʾur Komah* are contemporary with early Gnosticism with which they show close relationships. He has suggested that there is some close relation of the wedding hymn in the *Acts Thom.* to these traditions, though he was unable to push this suggestion very far.[29]

This thesis needs, of course, more justification than is given here. I shall treat the entire matter at the end of this Chapter where I shall discuss further Scholem's evidence for dating the traditions in question, other contacts between them and the *Acts Thom.* (especially this

---

[27] Scholem, *Ursprung*, 61–75.

[28] Bornkamm, *Mythos*, 82–83.

[29] Gershom G. Scholem, *Jewish Gnosticism, Merkabah Mysticism, and Talmudic Tradition* (New York: The Jewish Theological Seminary of America, 1965) 36–42; idem, *Major Trends*, 1–79; idem, *Ursprung*, 15–174; idem, "Bahir, Sefer ha-," *EncJud* 4. 96–101; idem, "Shiʾur Komah," *EncJud* 14. 1417–19; and idem, "Yeẓirah, Sefer," *EncJud* 16. 782–88.

hymn), and the relation of this thesis to the rival one that the woman here finds her closest counterpart in the Gnostic Sophia.

Assuming this Jewish tradition as the background for the section, the following interpretations can be given for specific details.

A) Her mouth is open fittingly ($\pi\rho\epsilon\pi\acute{o}\nu\tau\omega\varsigma$) for her.

It is difficult to see how an open mouth would enhance the woman's beauty (it is clear from what follows that wide open is meant). Therefore, the reference must be to the fact that it is "fitting" that one who manifests Truth should have her mouth open in speech. Hoffmann agrees here: "Her mouth is open, and this befits her, because she speaks pure praises with it."[30]

B) Thirty-two are those who sing *her* hymns.

The author has in mind that the woman is opening her mouth in song. The visual image of the thirty-two beautiful teeth[31] puts him in mind of the thirty-two eons which are the prime manifestations of God. Her singing is attributed to them.

One would not expect, however, on this interpretation, that the thirty-two singing for the woman are also praising her ($\tau\alpha\acute{v}\tau\eta\nu$ $\acute{v}\mu\nu\circ\lambda\circ\gamma\circ\hat{v}\nu\tau\epsilon\varsigma$). On this basis, one can surmise that "her" ($\tau\alpha\acute{v}\tau\eta\nu$) was added by the redactors when the hymn was put together and they looked upon her as an object of attention in her own right.[32]

C) *Her tongue is like the curtain of the door which is shaken by those going in.*

The next line I regard as redactional, for reasons which can only be made fully clear later. One pivotal point for my interpretation can be discussed here, the meaning of $\acute{\epsilon}\kappa\tau\iota\nu\acute{\alpha}\sigma\sigma\epsilon\iota\nu$.

Lipsius comments, "Her tongue is like the curtain, which is opened (shaken) for those going in, a symbolic expression of the thought that

---

[30] Hoffmann, "Zwei Hymnen," 298; see also Lipsius, *Apostelgeschichten*, 305. This interpretation also receives some support from Herrmann, "Gedanken," 187. On the basis of Sumerian parallels, word morphology, and the reading of the LXX, he suggests "Your speech [rather than 'your mouth'] is lovely" for Song Sol 4:3. He cites also 2:14: "Your voice is lovely." Following his thesis, it is quite possible that references to the women's pleasant speech are customary in this genre.

[31] See Song Sol 4:2; and Herrmann, "Gedanken," 182.

[32] This is in partial agreement with Lipsius: "In the original . . . the 32 praise the primal Father through the mouth of Sophia" (*Apostelgeschichten*, 306).

the knowledge of the truth, which her tongue proclaims, lets the gnostics enter into the realm of light above, as through a curtain."[33] Wilson is presumably following this interpretation when he gives "swept aside" for ἐκτινάσσεται.[34]

However Lipsius himself gives the proper meaning "shaken" for ἐκτινάσσεται in his parentheses. At this point the inconsistency shows up. "Shaken" is not really the same as "open," as Lipsius tries to explain.[35] And on the other hand, if the tongue represents something proclaiming the "knowledge of Truth," it is not proper to say that it is "swept aside" to allow people to enter into the Truth.[36]

In my view, Lipsius is basically right in his understanding of ἐκτινάσσειν as "shaken" and his (implicit) interpretation of this shaking as a reference to the tongue moving in song. M. R. James apparently has a similar understanding with his "waving to and fro."[37] Speaking on the grounds of the realistic basis of the image (people going through a curtained doorway) the most natural interpretation is that the curtain is being shaken by those going in (dative of agent). This implies, on the level of the image, that the woman's song is in some sense caused by "those going in."

The fact that the tongue is singing here, when the previous line has pictured the teeth as singing, serves as some preliminary justification for regarding this line as redactional. The duplication makes it awkward, and on the other hand, exhibits a technique which can be shown to be redactional elsewhere.[38]

D) Her neck *lies in the form* of steps which the First Maker made.

Thilo rightly sees that the apparently familiar image of the neck as a tower (Song Sol 4:4 and 7:4) partly occasions the "steps" motif here.[39]

---

[33] Ibid.

[34] Wilson, "Acts of Thomas," 345.

[35] Lipsius, *Apostelgeschichten*, above n. 32.

[36] Add to this the fact that "swept aside" is not an attested meaning for ἐκτινάσσειν, and it is hard to manage as an image referring to the tongue here. See LSJ, *s.v.* ἐκτινάσσω.

[37] James, ed., *The Apocryphal New Testament* (Oxford: Clarendon, 1924) 367.

[38] Note also that this line has nothing specific to do with the *Sepher Yeẓirah* traditions, nor is the "tongue" one of the body parts attested in other extant examples of the *waṣf*.

[39] Thilo, *Acta*, 137; Klijn (*Acts of Thomas*, 172) agrees.

"Lies (ἔγκειται) in the form (εἰς τύπον)[40] of steps" is odd. "Lies" must be a redactional catchword link to the pleonasm in the first line of the hymn (ἐνέστηκε καὶ ἔγκειται).

E) Her two hands signal *and suggest announcing* the dance
   of the good eons.

This line represents the movements of the (dancing) woman's hands as an image of the dance of the (thirty-two) eons, implicitly relating these figures to the traditional "dance of the cosmos."[41] This probably relates to the idea expressed in the *Sepher Yeẓirah* (2.2) and the Marcosian tradition (Iren. *Adv. haer.* 1.14.1–4) that it is the different combinations and permutations of the basic elements (here the "dance of the [thirty-two] eons") that constitutes the ongoing process which is the universe.

Thilo asserts that the hands are "pointing" to the dancing stars, and most translators have followed him in this. However, his interpretation is based on a mistaken reading of the next line, as I shall show below.[42] Beyond this, the idea that the hands themselves are representing the dance is supported by the fact that the woman herself is clearly dancing, as the fact that "she manifests joy with her feet" shows. The image of her feet dancing while her hands point steadily to the heavens is not so plausible.

The construction σημαίνουσιν καὶ ὑποδεικνύουσιν ... κηρύσσοντες (signal and suggest ... announcing) is an extended pleonastic construction. This line is obviously connected to the next by ὑποδεικνύουσιν. The word κηρύσσοντες is a link to a repeated theme in the narrative (100.7, 10; 105.5; 106.10–107.1). Therefore, σημαίνουσιν can be taken as the original.

These lines are the core of this section. That the last line is redactional already appears partially in the use of the pleonasm with ὑποδεικνύουσιν and the presence of πόλις (city) as the main allegorical image—which is not specifically related to the *Sepher Yeẓirah* tradition

---

[40] The phrase εἰς τύπον will be treated below, 5.2.
[41] See, e.g., Plato *Tim.* 40c and *Epin.* 982e. The peculiar line in the *Acts of John* τῷ δὲ ὅλων ᾧ χορεύειν ὑπάρχει (Lipsius *Acta* 1. 198.6) has to do with this same theme.
[42] Thilo, *Acta*, 138.

but does form a link with the narrative's "Peoplecity."[43]

F) *She shows forth joy with her feet.*

This line (which occurs near the beginning of this section, 109.7) is not specifically related to the *Sepher Yeẓirah* tradition, and it is slightly out of place. All examples of a *wasf* given by Herrmann[44] move consistently either up or down the woman's body, whereas here "feet" precedes "mouth." It is also focused on "joy" as what is signified, a catchword in 110.10 and 14 and a member of a pleonastic construction in 105.3–4.[45] Therefore, it is probably also redactional.

G) On top of her head the king is established, *feeding with his ambrosia those established on him.*
And on her head lies the Truth.

First of all, it can be said with some confidence that "feeding with his ambrosia those established on him"[46] is redactional. The image of the king seated on the woman with others seated on him departs drastically from the general style of this section (109.1–14) which nowhere else contains such a visually complicated image. The only passage comparable is the other redactional one that portrays both the teeth and the tongue singing.

On the other hand, the reference to the king's feeding people with ambrosia fits easily into the paradigm of recurrent motifs, here forming a link both to the "king's banquet" of the narrative and to the final section of the hymn where "ambrosial food" is also given out by the "Father."

The statement that the "king is seated (ἵδρυται) on her" has caused problems for many commentators.[47] Paying attention to the wording, ἱδρύειν means "to sit" with the connotation of "to be established."[48]

---

[43] In the narrative, πόλις is repeated at 104.4, 5, 8; and 105.1.

[44] Herrmann, "Gedanken," 176–97.

[45] Its conjunction with "gathering" in 105.3–4 is possibly another connection, the dancing feet here compared to the feet of those gathering there.

[46] Preuschen (*Hymnen*, 10) emends "on him" (ἐπ'αὐτόν) to "under him" (ὑπ'αὐτόν), but it hardly helps in this respect.

[47] Klijn (*Acts of Thomas*, 170) thinks of a crown, on the basis of parallels in the *Odes of Solomon* (1:1–2; 5:12; and 9:8). Heinrich Schlier (*Christus und die Kirche im Epheserbrief* [Tübingen: Mohr-Siebeck, 1930] 57–58) supposes that the king is the head and the woman is his body (as in Eph 5:23–24). Schlier's opinion is based on the Syriac version and an emendation of the Greek.

[48] None of the attestations in LSJ (*s.v.* ἱδρύω) or BAG (*s.v.* ἱδρύω) mean simply "lie upon" in a general sense.

In accordance with this Preuschen[49] and Bousset[50] read "enthroned upon." This reading is supported (a) by the general background in Jewish mystical thought I have shown for this section as a whole—the "throne" motif stands at the origin of this tradition[51] related specifically, as is the shekinah, to the manifest aspect of God (also called there "king")—and (b) by the redactional play on the meanings of ἰδρύειν. As both Klijn[52] and M. R. James[53] rightly interpret, τοὺς ἐπ᾽ αὐτὸν ἰδρυμένους means "those established upon him," according to a manner of speech used in the LXX and the New Testament (e.g., "established in righteousness," Isa 54:14).[54] This suggests that ἵδρυται has a similar meaning in the first phrase, that is, the king is "established" on the woman as on a throne. It is clear then that at least the redactors understood the first image to be that of a king enthroned.[55]

"On her head lies the Truth" can be shown to be redactional in that (a) it is somewhat awkward in the context, being a doublet to the "king seated on the top of the head;" (b) "truth" is a theme linking this passage to 110.20; and (c) "lies" (ἔγκειται) is a redactional catchword linking this passage with 109.1 and 11.

Schlier correctly notes that the parallelism implies an identity between "king" and "Truth."[56]

Most likely then, the only nonredactional part of this section is "On her head the king is established." Its naming of a part of the body (κορυφή) and its general lack of compatibility with 109.1–4, justify us in regarding it as an original part of the second section (109.5–14) probably coming immediately before "Her mouth is open. . . ."[57]

[49] *Hymnen*, 41.

[50] "Manichäisches," 22.

[51] See *Seph. Yeẓ.* 1.3.

[52] *Acts of Thomas*, 170.

[53] James, ed., *The Apocryphal New Testament* (Oxford: Clarendon, 1924) 367.

[54] See also "established in understanding" (Prov 24:3), "established in God" (Ps 70:6), and "established in Truth" (2 Pet 1:12).

[55] As Thilo (*Acta*, 135) mentions, the omission of αὐτῆς after κορυφῇ is conspicuous. In view of the redactional use of paronomasia, it is not unlikely that the omission is redactional, bringing out the similarity κόρη / κορυφή. Therefore, what should echo in the reader's mind secondarily is ἐν τῇ κόρῃ ἵδρυται ὁ βασιλεύς, bringing out even more clearly that she is on his throne.

[56] Schlier, *Christus*, 58.

[57] The difficulty presented by the fact that, unlike the rest of the section, the part of the body itself is not the immediate basis of an image can perhaps be explained on the assumption that the author has explicitly in mind Song Sol 7:6: "The king is caught in her hair." The original meaning of this line may have been that the attractiveness of the woman's hair "captures" her lover, called a "king" in 1:4. For a similar image of the hair as a "trap," see Herrmann, "Gedanken," 179. The composers of the piece here,

Sections 1 and 2 Together

Some remarks can now be made on the light these observations shed on the first section of the hymn (109.1–4) and on the relation of these two sections to each other.

It is fairly clear that "on her lies and rests (ἐνέστηκε καὶ ἔγκειται) the proud radiance of kings" contains a familiar redactional pleonasm with a catchword link both to "her neck lies (ἔγκειται) in the form of steps" and "on her head lies (ἔγκειται) the Truth." There are a series of connected images in the text related to the "head" motifs beginning with the anointing scene ("He anointed the top of his head"), the flutist scene ("She stood above him fluting at his head"), and the hymn references just mentioned ("On top of her head the king is established . . . on her head lies the Truth"). Hence in the redactional version of the hymn we should read ἦ ἐνέστηκε καὶ ἔγκειται as "on her (above her, on her head) lies and rests." The original probably meant "*in* her rests. . . ." This is more in accord with the rest of the section which speaks of light radiating from her. The word most likely added by the redactors is ἐνέστηκε, to match ἔστη ἐπάνω αὐτοῦ ([the flutist] stood above him, 108.3).

It seems likely that the "radiance of kings" is also a redactional addition to link this line with "on top of her head the king is established." "Kings" complicates the imagery a bit as it stands (God is already represented as "Light," and "Shining" refers to this light motif). This use of the plural, I suspect, is a redactional trait. In this context, we can note the "aliens" (ἀλλότριοι) which refers to the mythical Enemy (161.1) and the "gods" (θεοί) which refers to Jesus (115.1).

The first two sections of the hymn literarily follow a different structure. The first uses the image of the beautiful woman's appearance as a basis for speaking of divine radiance emanating from her. The second is based on the enumeration of body parts of the traditional *wasf*. The two may easily have been joined prior to their use by the redactors, or it may be that the structural division reflects their originating independently of each other. In either case the new redactional interpretation of the first line functions as a familiar device to link the two sections by a common motif ("on top of the head").

It is clear that even if the two pieces have independent origins, they arise in the same milieu. The genre and use of imagery is the same. And the idea that the woman radiates the divine presence is in perfect

---

using common midrashic technique, saw the difficulty of this passage as an opportunity for reading a favorite idea of their own into it.

accord with the Jewish notion of the shekinah, the subject of the second section. (This is not a theme traditionally associated with the Gnostic Sophia.)

In accord with this we can now make out some general lines of interpretation for these first two sections of the hymn describing the woman. She represents the shekinah: God's manifest aspect, God's presence in the world. The figure of the woman is used as a fundamental image into which are injected many favorite motifs of protokabbalistic thought: God is "Light," a "king," the ultimate "Truth." She is his "daughter," his throne—radiating his divine presence as beauty, as scents, as song. She is the sum of the universe, the pleroma, containing the thirty-two archetypal principles ("eons") that underlie all of reality, who "sing" through her (and, redactionally, to her and for her). A redactional line speaks of "those entering her" enlarging on the traditional theme that the thirty-two archetypes she contains are also initiatory "steps" (βαθμοί) for those seeking God.

The thought that the woman represents the shekinah begins to suggest the relationship of the hymn to the narrative. In our analysis of the preceding episodes we saw a train of thought which portrayed the worldly banquet, representing the earthly realm in general, as a divine feast. The suggestion is clear that the hymn is carrying forward this train of thought by introducing a theme, shekinah, related precisely to God's presence in the world. The redactors specifically relate the banquet and the woman by speaking of the king's "feeding people with ambrosia" while seated on her as his throne. The thought of the woman, and hence the banquet, as the place where one can be initiated implies another furtherance of the criticism of Thomas's ascetic stance. Participation in the banquet would actually mean contact with the divine.

4.4 Section 3: 109.14–110.3

And her bedroom is bright (φωτεινός)
Breathing forth (διαπνέων) outpourings (ἀποφοράν) from balsam and every spice
And giving out (ἀναδιδούς) a sweet smell of myrrh and herbs.
And inside are strewn myrtle and very many blossoms.
But the barred doors (κλειστάδες) are decorated with reeds.

The description of the bridal chamber is almost completely made up of motifs and catchwords that link this passage to other sections of the hymn and to the narrative. Most of the catchwords are connected to the description of the bride in 109.1–4:

φωτεινός and φῶς ... ἀπαύγασμα ... φαιδρός ... καταυγάζουσα
ἀνθέων and ἄνθεσιν
ἀποφορά ... ἀναδιδούς and ἀποφορά ... διαδίδοται
ὀσμὴν ἡδεῖαν ... ἡδυπνόων and εὐωδία.

Three catchwords also link this section to the image of the crowned Thomas holding the reed (107.9–108.1): myrtle, blossom, and reed.

We may note finally that the description here speaks of both the outside (109.14–110.1) and inside (110.2) of the chamber, as the earlier sections speak of the outer appearance of the bride but also of "those going in" (109.10).

Given the general thesis that motif and catchword recurrences are redactional techniques to establish connections both inside the hymn and between narrative and hymn, it seems best to assume that this entire section is a redactional construction. To suppose that it is a previously separate piece would involve either very many coincidences in catchwords and motifs or very extensive revision. It is also somewhat difficult to imagine what point this section has in itself that would enable it to stand alone. It is very different stylistically than the previous and following sections, so it is not to be read as originally joined to them.

The redactional composition is, however, based on a traditional theme. Thilo mentions a sacramental rite of the Marcosians known as the "bridal chamber" (Iren. *Adv. haer.* 1.21.3),[58] and now we also have in the newly found *Gospel of Philip* (NHC 2,3) a Gnostic text full of references to this theme, also in conjunction with a sacramental rite. "The bridal chamber that fails not you have received" is a reference to baptism in a hymn by Ephraim.[59]

As has already been suggested, the meaning of the bridal chamber in the hymn is fixed primarily by the parallelism drawn between it and the figure of the woman earlier in the hymn. In the light of the earlier (redactional) mention of "those going in" the woman for initiation (109.10), the implied significance of the "bridal chamber" here is not far removed from these traditions.[60] The statement later in the *Acts*

---

[58] Thilo, *Acta*, 141.

[59] NPNF, 13. 283.

[60] There are actually several further points of contact: *Exc. Theod.* 68 speaks of a "child of the man and the bridal chamber" implying the equivalence bride = bridal chamber. *Exeg. Soul* (NHC 2,6) 132.13 reads: "(The soul) purified herself in the bridal chamber, she filled it with perfume." We have seen that the woman represents something similar to the Gnostic Pleroma. The bridal chamber is explicitly identified with the Pleroma in

Thom. (118.8–10) concerning the eschaton, "You will be bridesmaids coming into that bridal chamber full of immortality and light," connects also with these traditions and is probably a direct reference to this passage.

The fact that the "barred doors are decorated with reeds" (αἱ κλεισταδες ἐν καλάμοις κεκόσμηνται) has troubled both ancient copyists and modern commentators,[61] mostly because of the word κλεισταδες which is unattested elsewhere in Greek literature, but also because of the unusual use of "reeds" as decoration.

It is clear that the redactors engage in word play, and it is only a small step to coining words. Morphologically, κλεισταδες is derived from κλείω / κλείς, following a pattern visible also, for example, in θυσταδες (sacrificing priests) from θύω / θυσία. The connection with κλείς suggests the meaning of "bars" or other devices for locking the door of the chamber. This word is most likely a link to τοὺς ἐγκεκλεισμένους in the Christ prayer (115.6). "Reeds" (καλάμοι) is clearly a catchword link to the "reed" held by Thomas in the narrative (107.11–108.1). Finally, one should note the assonance of σμύρνη and μυρσίνη.[62]

4.5 Section 4: 110.3–9

Her bridegrooms are surrounding her,
Whose number is seven,
Whom she herself has chosen.
And her bridesmaids are seven,
Who dance before her.
Twelve in number are those who serve *before* her
And are subject to her,
Having their gaze *and vision* (σκοπὸν καὶ θέαμα)
    toward the bridegroom,
That by *the vision* (θέαμα) *of* him they might be enlightened.

Iren. *Adv. haer.* 7.1, and this may also be the significance of the Manichaean Psalm quoted by Bornkamm ("Acts of Thomas," 433): "I would dwell in thy eons, thy bridal chambers of light." Finally, the position of this piece in the hymn may suggest that we are still dealing with the description of the bride's body, the bridal chamber representing her womb. This has a parallel in Iren. *Adv. haer.* 1.13.3: "Receive in thy bridal chamber the seed of light."

[61] See Bonnet's textual notes.

[62] The construction μυρσίναι καὶ ἀνθέων seems ungrammatical, and, following my hypothesis, is probably deliberately so. It is, however, the one case of an odd phrasing in these chapters for which I can think of no explanation.

The description of the bride's attendants is clearly separate from what goes before. Further, it is striking that the awaited arrival of the bridegroom described here is never actually mentioned. His function of "enlightening" (110.9) also is incongruous with 110.15, which ascribes the imparting of light to the "Father of All" whom the couple (ἀμφότεροι, 110.14) are praising. Finally, "they will be with him" (σὺν αὐτῷ ἔσονται, 110.10) strikingly leaves out any mention of the bride and instead speaks only of the attendants who are joining the bridegroom—an indication that "with him" at that point is a redactional attempt to link that section to this one, though they were previously separate.

All these features indicate that this section is also a previously independent piece incorporated into this hymn by the redactors. All are agreed that the "seven" and the "twelve" mentioned here are a reference to the planets and the signs of the zodiac. But the double group of seven has troubled commentators, as has the mention of "seven bridegrooms."[63]

On the other hand, the construction of parallel lines is seen to be a common redactional technique in this work, as is the use of unusual images. Following these criteria, the whole first line here singles itself out as redactional.

This is supported by two other features:
1) "Those serving before her and subject to her" (110.7–8) is a familiar pleonastic construction. The first member is linked to the seven dancing *bridesmaids* by the repetition of "before her." The second member refers to the seven *bridegrooms* "whom she herself chose," that is, the latter phrase describes a reversal of the expected roles of bride and bridegroom, and the mention that they are "subject to her" is another reference to this same relationship.
2) This suggested linking of the two groups of seven by pleonasm is carried out also by the ungrammatical change of the gender of the article in 110.5 and 6 (αἱ παράνυμφοι ... οἵ ... χορεύουσιν). The redactors in both these passages present a verbal merging of the two groups of seven (and the twelve), a literary feature repeated further on when ἀμφότεροι (110.14) presents a literary merging of the

---

[63] Preuschen (*Hymnen*, 41–42) wants to explain the double group of seven as referring to the seven planets and the seven tutelary spirits of the planets mentioned in Orig. *Cels.* 6.31, but this is a conjecture. His parallel text does not itself make a distinction between planets and spirits. Thilo (*Acta*, 142) wants to emend νυμφίοι (bridegrooms) to παρανυμφίοι. But, the latter properly refer to "friends of the bridegroom"—what are they doing surrounding the bride?

couple with the attendants. This adds some weight to the supposition that it was the redactors themselves who introduced the extra group of seven in the first place.

Finally, "gaze and vision ($\theta \acute{\epsilon} \alpha \mu \alpha$)" is a pleonasm connecting this phrase to the following, "by the vision ($\theta \epsilon \acute{\alpha} \mu \alpha \tau o \varsigma$) of him." This is already reason to suspect that both occurrences of $\theta \acute{\epsilon} \alpha \mu \alpha$ here are redactional. Thus in the pleonasm it functions to weave the new theme into the inherited material. In the context, $\sigma \kappa o \pi \acute{o} \varsigma$ is normal and therefore original.

The word $\theta \acute{\epsilon} \alpha \mu \alpha$ links this section and the parallel phrase in the hymn's last section (110.16): "They were enlightened in the vision ($\theta \acute{\epsilon} \alpha$)." The word $\theta \acute{\epsilon} \alpha$ (vision) can be associated with $\theta \epsilon \acute{\alpha}$ (goddess) and thus has a secondary reference to the "Mother of Wisdom" as the goddess-consort of the "Father." There is also a probable link with $\theta \acute{\epsilon} \alpha \mu \alpha$ in 109.2–3 where the woman (shekinah) is the manifest aspect of the "Father."

The interpretation of the redactors is that the attendants are enlightened actually by the bride and bridegroom together—the bride being the "appearance" (manifestation) of the bridegroom. This follows the sense of 109.10 where people "go in" the bride for initiation. This is recalled more literally by the later statement, "They were enlightened in ($\grave{\epsilon} \nu$) the vision-goddess" (110.16).

Returning now to the piece as it existed previously, it spoke of a bridal figure surrounded by seven bridesmaids and twelve dancers watching for the arrival of a bridegroom who would enlighten them. The natural interpretation of the bride here is that she represents the earth, surrounded by the planets and the zodiac.[64]

Given all of this, the natural interpretation of the bridegroom is that he represents the dawning sun. The original author had in mind the earth at night surrounded by the planets and constellations "waiting for" the sunrise which will enlighten all. The original probably spoke of the bride as well as the attendants being enlightened.[65]

"Seven" and "twelve," like the "thirty-two" (109.7–14), play an important role in the *Sepher Yeẓirah* (2.1; 4.1–7; and 5.1–4) where they are also related to the planets and the zodiac. Their primary significance, however, is the same as that of the "thirty-two." They are

---

[64] Bornkamm (*Mythos*, 84) states that she is the moon. But this ignores the fact that for the ancients the moon was itself one of the seven planets while the earth was not.

[65] For "sunrise" in connection with the divine light in the *Acts Thom.*, see $\phi \omega \nu \grave{\eta} \; \grave{\alpha} \nu \alpha \tau \epsilon \acute{\iota} \lambda \alpha \sigma \alpha$ (164.11) and $\grave{\epsilon} \pi \acute{\epsilon} \phi \alpha \nu \sigma \epsilon \nu$ (151.11). See also the *Acts of John*, Lipsius *Acta* 1. 180.25. The motif is, of course, common elsewhere as well.

he first creations of God which serve as the basic structures of the
universe, the means by which everything else was created. In this light
here is probably an intended connection between περιεστοιχισμένην
(surrounded, 110.3) and στοιχεῖα (elements). As Scholem notes,
ᵛesôd is the equivalent of στοιχεῖα, and it is applied in the *Sepher
Yezirah* to the elements by which God made the world.[66] The word
ⲥⲧⲟⲓⲭⲉⲓⲁ is used later in the *Acts Thom.* (279.6) to refer to the traditional Greek "four elements."

This coincidence of 110.3–9 with the *Sepher Yezirah*, their common
use of the planets and the zodiac, and the presence of two earlier passages in the same genre add up to a great likelihood that this passage
also has its original milieu in protokabbalistic mysticism. The theme
there that closely approximates the intention here is that of the "lower
shekinah" (*Bahir* § 90), a personification of the world ("earth") far
from God's presence.[67] A favorite title for the shekinah in the *Bahir* is
also the "Bride," a motif implicit here, too.

The genre of the original piece is very similar to that of the pieces
found in 109.1–4, 5, and 7–14, so it would be well to treat them here
together. (The remaining two sections represent a somewhat different
genre.) Thus, the three traditional pieces in the first part of the hymn
read roughly as follows:

1) The woman is the Daughter of the Light,
   In whom lies proud shining,
   And her appearance is lovely,
   Shining with bright beauty.
   Her clothes are like spring blossoms,
   Outpourings of good smells are given out from them.

2) On top of her head the king is established.
   Her mouth is open, befitting her,
   Thirty-two are those who sing hymns.
   Her neck is like the steps which the First Maker made,
   Her two hands represent the dance of the good eons.

3) Her bridesmaids surround her,
   Whose number is seven.
   Twelve are they who dance before her,
   (All) having their gaze toward the bridegroom
   That by him they might be enlightened.

---

[66] Scholem, *Ursprung*, 37 n. 46.

[67] It is in this aspect that the shekinah does resemble the "fallen Sophia" of Gnostic
speculation. One of the titles of Sophia is γῆ (earth); see Iren. *Adv. haer.* 1.1.5.3.

The imaginative style of each follows the same pattern: a natural image is used as a basis for presenting specific religious ideas.

In the first, the radiant presence of the beautiful woman is the basis for presenting the shekinah as the manifestation of the divine. In the second, the traditional wedding song describing the bride's beautiful body (*wasf*) is the basis for presenting the concept of the thirty-two divine "eons" which underlie the created world, manifest the divine there, and are the "steps" which lead one to God. The third takes the image of the earth at night surrounded by the planets and constellations, waiting for the sunrise. It uses this as a basis for presenting the theme of the lower shekinah, waiting with all the fundamental elements of the world for the eschatological (or mystical) dawn of the divine light upon creation.

These three pieces may have existed together at a previous stage. However, the fact that in the first the woman radiates divine light already, while in the third she awaits enlightenment, probably means they were originally conceived separately.

The genre of these pieces is not unlike that outlined above in relation to the story of the flutist. The genre of these three, like that one, is allegorical and esoteric. Both are a concrete presentation and experiential actualization of ideas presumed to be familiar to the reader, presented for meditation rather than instruction or persuasion.

In more modern times, we would call the original pieces in the hymn poetry. This is a close approximation of the genre here in that they are probably composed to be meditated upon. However, religious poetry written simply to be read is fairly rare in the ancient world. Liturgy and liturgical hymns seem a more normal *Sitz im Leben* for the kind of creations represented here. They are probably hymn fragments, or verses of hymns.

4.6 Section 5: 110.9–15

And they will be with him for eternity
At that eternal joy,
And they will be at that wedding at which the great ones
    are gathered,
And they will remain at the banquet of which the eternal ones
    are counted worthy,
And they will put on royal clothing,
And will dress in bright robes,
And they will *both* be in *joy and* great gladness,
And they will give glory to the Father of the All.

Following the mention of waiting for the bridegroom we expect to hear of his arrival, and it is somewhat surprising when we are instead taken to the wedding feast itself. It has already been noted that "with him" puts the attendants in the place we would normally expect the bride to be.

These two features show that the wedding banquet section is not an original part of the previous piece—"with him" shows up as a redactional attempt to unite the two. On the other hand, 110.9 stylistically begins a new section. The change of tense there and the new themes (closer to the Old Testament wisdom literature than the rest) suggest that the stylistic break is also an indication of the original independence of these pieces from one another.

This section shows some unique vocabulary: the "great ones" ($\mu\epsilon\gamma\iota$-$\sigma\tau\hat{\alpha}\nu\epsilon\varsigma$), the "eternal ones" ($\alpha\iota\dot{\omega}\nu\iota o\iota$), and "Father of the All" ($\pi\alpha\tau\acute{\epsilon}\rho\alpha$ $\tau\hat{\omega}\nu$ $\ddot{o}\lambda\omega\nu$) are not common themes elsewhere in the *Acts Thom.*[68] The title $\pi\alpha\tau\acute{\eta}\rho$ $\tau\hat{\omega}\nu$ $\ddot{o}\lambda\omega\nu$ is Gnostic.[69] The use of the other two suggests that they are also esoteric. Like the "thirty-two" and the "eons" of 109.7–14 they are mentioned as though their names alone are sufficient to give away their identity to the reader. Klijn[70] and Bornkamm[71] cite Manichaean usage of $\mu\epsilon\gamma\iota\sigma\tau\hat{\alpha}\nu\epsilon\varsigma$ referring to heavenly beings. In the light of other parallels in the hymn to Jewish mystical literature, one might think of the use of *śar* (prince), frequently used in the Hekaloth literature to refer to angels. Lipsius[72] and Thilo[73] connect the $\alpha\iota\dot{\omega}\nu\iota o\iota$ with the Gnostic "eons," and in view of the word play with cognates in the *Acts Thom.* and the earlier occurrence (109.13) of "eons" ($\alpha\iota\hat{\omega}\nu\epsilon\varsigma$), it seems most likely that the redactors, at any rate, made this connection. It is even quite plausible that $\alpha\iota\dot{\omega}\nu\iota o\iota$ is a redactional modification of $\alpha\iota\hat{\omega}\nu\epsilon\varsigma$, particularly in view of the redactional word play on $\alpha\iota\dot{\omega}\nu/\alpha\iota\dot{\omega}\nu\iota o\iota$ in the first line. These terms have led all commentators to see here some version of the heavenly wedding feast common in both Jewish and Christian circles.[74] This connection and their uniqueness in the *Acts Thom.* provides some

---

[68] There is one occurrence of $\mu\epsilon\gamma\iota\sigma\tau\hat{\alpha}\nu\epsilon\varsigma$ in the Hymn of the Pearl (220.22); the others are not listed in Bonnet, *Acta*, 2. 2, index, *s.v.*

[69] See *Exc. Theod.* 33; Iren. *Adv. haer.* 1.13.3.and 1.21.3.

[70] *Acts of Thomas*, 175.

[71] "Acts of Thomas," 433.

[72] *Apostelgeschichten*, 308.

[73] *Acta*, 149.

[74] See references in Klijn, *Acts of Thomas*, above n. 70.

initial evidence that this, too, is an originally independent piece secondarily woven into the hymn. This is supported by indications of secondary reworking.

It has already been mentioned that ἀμφότεροι in this section causes some difficulty. In the context of a wedding, this word most naturally refers to the couple, yet the implied subject of the plural verbs has been the bride's attendants.

One might suppose that ἀμφότεροι is a part of the original piece and only became incongruous when it was added on to the hymn. Against this, however, it can be said that the general tenor of the piece is to picture what a marvelous thing it is to be at the feast because there one is mingling with the great. The mention of the couple in this context is incongruous: one does not normally speak of the wedding couple as being privileged to mingle with dignitaries who are their guests.

So a better explanation for ἀμφότεροι here is that it reflects the redactors' intention of verbally merging the figures of the bride, bridegroom, and attendants.

The line "They will put on royal clothing and will dress in bright robes" closely resembles the motifs of 109.1–4: there is both (a) the equation of "king" ("royal") with "light" ("bright") which is also implied here by the parallelism and (b) the association of clothing with divinity ("royalty"). The motifs seem to be original in 109.1–4, which suggests they are secondary here for the purpose of drawing a parallel between the banquet and the woman, a tendency observable in all the other sections so far. This is supported by the facts that (a) this line interrupts the stylistic device of parallel sentence structure of this section (ἔσονται εἰς . . . ἔσονται ἐν . . . παραμενοῦσιν τῇ . . . ἐν . . . ἔσονται), and (b) it is also something of an interruption in the thought.

The expression "in joy and gladness" as a pleonasm bears the familiar mark of the redactors. "They will be . . . at that eternal joy" (110.10) uses "joy" (χαρά) in an unusual, concrete sense, and this reflects the usage in the redactional narrative phrase the "joy and gathering you see today" (105.3–4). This line (110.10) also contains a word play on cognates: εἰς τὸν αἰῶνα . . . εἰς . . . τὴν χαρὰν τὴν αἰώνιον.

When combined, these features suggest that this entire first line of the section (καὶ εἰς τὸν αἰῶνα . . . τὴν αἰώνιον) is redactional and that the pleonasm "joy and gladness" shows the redactional addition of joy to further connect this first line to what follows.

Here in this section, therefore, we have the clearest case of the redactors' technique of adding lines parallel to those of their inherited material. Both the first line and the middle line about clothing are such additions.

We have already noted three such cases in other sections: (1) "On her head lies the truth" (109.6–7); (2) the line about the tongue shaken by those going in which juxtaposed the singing tongue to the singing teeth (109.9–10); and (3) the line about the seven bridegrooms juxtaposed to the seven bridesmaids (110.3–6). We shall meet one more, the receiving of light parallel to the receiving of food (110.15–17). In each case, there is other evidence that would incline one to see the line as redactional work. Taken together, especially with the lines in this wedding banquet section, they mutually support the thesis that adding parallel lines is a major redactional technique in the work of combining and reinterpreting the original pieces.

The genre of the original piece here and its milieu of origin is not easy to fix given the small amount of surviving material and the widespread use of the motif it contains.

The point seems to be that the figures spoken of as the subjects of the sentences will be privileged to mingle with heavenly beings at a common feast, implied to have been given by the "Father of the All." The fact that it is a wedding feast seems not very important, unless we understand that fellowship of the meal is meant as a kind of participation in a mythical divine marriage.

Some such idea as this actually seems to be reflected in *Exc. Theod.* 63 and 64: "Then comes the wedding feast common to all the saved, until all became equal and recognize one another . . . and at the same time as the Mother receives her bridegroom, each of them, too, receives his bridegroom."

If we take seriously the parallelism of the lines, the redactors equate this mingling with the great ones with "putting on the royal robes" which clothe the woman in 109.1–4. That is, it is equivalent to "going in" the woman of 109.7–14 and being initiated by the manifestations of the divine that she incorporates.

The redactors take the banquet to be an image equivalent to the woman: for them it expresses the same ideas in a different guise. This may well be in close accord with the original intention of the piece. If we understand αἰώνιοι as a reference to (or modification of) αἰῶνες, the scene may well be an image of the gathering of all energies in the Pleroma. This would also be the referent of the "Father of the *All.*" We have already noted that the woman of 109.1–14 represents something like the Pleroma, as does the bridal chamber.

The Hermetic tractate *Poimandres* has a piece with a very similar point coming at the end of the long instructional vision: "He comes to the eighth Nature . . . and sings to the Father with the Beings. Those who are there are glad at his arrival, and having become like them . . . they (all) go toward the Father . . . and they give themselves over to the powers and, becoming powers, they merge in God" (*Corp. Herm.* 1.26). The *Acts Thom.*, of course, stops short of the complete mystical union pictured in *Poimandres*, but otherwise the ideas seem to be the same.

This certainly gives the sense of the piece here as the redactors intended it, and it is most likely the sense of the original as well.

Given the redactors' usual respect for their sources, we should probably take the future tense as original here. There seems to be no other apparent reason for the change of tenses. The past or present would do here as well as the future. It has been generally noted that this gives the scene an eschatological flavor.

Assuming that this is an originally separate piece, the tense probably also has something to say about the genre. The future tense is rare in the hymns of the *Acts Thom.* Myths as such are spoken in the past or present tense, and reports of visions are as well. One might imagine instructions for visionary experiences spoken in the future tense, but the third person plural seems out of place in that context.

In view of these considerations, the original material perhaps owes something to the genre peculiar to apocalyptic, the foretelling of the state of things in the eschaton. In this case, the third person plural may well be an indication that collective, cosmic eschatology is what the author(s) had in mind, the final destiny of all the saved souls. The themes here are Gnostic, cast in this apocalyptic form.[75]

Concretely, the original piece here was the ending of a hymn which presented eschatological events for the hope and encouragement of the (Gnostic) faithful. It read:

> And they will be at that wedding at which the great ones
>   are gathered,
> And they will remain at the feasting of which the eons
>   are accounted worthy,
> And they will be in great gladness,
> And they will give glory to the Father of the All.

---

[75] For other examples of these two movements' influencing each other, see Philip Vielhauer, "Apocalyptic," in *NTApo*, 2. 599.

4.7 Section 6: 110.15–20

Whose proud light they received,
And were enlightened in the vision (or: *Goddess*) *of their master,*
Whose ambrosial food they received, having no lack.
And they drank of the wine which made them not thirsty
   and desirous,
And they *gave glory and* sang hymns *with the Living Spirit*
To the *Father of Truth and the* Mother of Wisdom (σοφία).

As it stands now, the last section of the hymn continues the theme of the banquet. As was mentioned earlier, however, the change of tense is a clue that this was not originally part of the previous piece.[76]

This section actually makes no mention of a wedding. The reception of marvelous food is described (110.17) in a way that bears close resemblance to the wording found in two wisdom hymns: "Come eat my bread and drink the wine I have prepared for you" (Prov 9:5), and "They who eat me will hunger for more and they who drink me will thirst for more" (Sir 24:21).[77] Both these passages are concerned with the tradition about the "banquet" Wisdom provides for the seekers.

These close parallels are an argument in favor of the thesis that these lines also come from a previously formulated ("Wisdom banquet") tradition. This argument is supported by the following:

1) "Sophia" is present in the next line but occurs nowhere else in the *Acts Thom.* as a person.
2) The *Acts Thom.* elsewhere consistently expresses a negative attitude toward wine.[78]
3) "Made them not thirsty and desirous" (μὴ δίψαν ... παρέχοντος καὶ ἐπιθυμίαν) is a type of ambivalent construction also found in 106.9 ("... and to fulfill the king's will"). Just as in 106.9, it is likely that the present wording represents a secondary addition or alteration of a previous formulation (which either omitted ἐπιθυμίαν entirely or read μήτε ἐπιθυμίαν).[79]

---

[76] See also Bornkamm, *Mythos*, 88.

[77] The saying is reversed here, as it is in John 4:14, but the similarity of the motif is still evidence of contact.

[78] See 191.15–16; 192.9–10; and 230.16–17. Klijn (*Acts of Thomas*, 177) notes this tendency in connection with the fact that "wine" is not mentioned here in the Syriac.

[79] Klijn (*Acts of Thomas*, 176) points out the fact that ἀπουσία normally means "absence" and is thus odd in this context. Its meaning seems clear from the parallel with μὴ δίψαν ... παρέχοντος, i.e., it is perfect food. I have no explanation for this usage, perhaps it does mean here simply "lack" as all translators apparently assume.

To speak further of redactional additions, the mention of "receiving light" departs from the banquet imagery. "Proud light" (φῶς γαῦρον) is a repetition of two words at the beginning of the hymn (109.1–2) where they are original. The next line ("And they were enlightened . . .") depends on the first, and is also a close parallel to 110.9, ". . . that by the vision of him they might be enlightened."[80]

All these features suggest that these lines (110.15 and 16) are redactional, joined here by the familiar redactional techniques of parallelism and catchword repetition: "they received" (ἐδέξαντο).

The last line of the hymn contains some puzzles that have caused much conjecture on the part of the commentators:

1) It presents a divine couple, the "Father of Truth" and the "Mother of Wisdom," whom it apparently places on equal footing (a suggestion reinforced by the general context of a wedding). This is rare in contemporary Jewish, Christian, and Gnostic literature.[81] The closest parallel is in the *Acts Thom.* itself (157.16–17) where we find a similar formula at the end of a hymn to Christ, "We sing to you and your invisible Father and your Holy Spirit, and the Mother of all creation." The "Mother of Wisdom" also causes difficulties to those who want to see the bride of the hymn as representing "Sophia."

2) The "Living Spirit" is a title that occurs nowhere else in the *Acts Thom.* One should note also that the phrasing here is ambiguous, perhaps deliberately so. Is the Spirit one of those praising or an object of praise along with the Father and Mother? The "Spirit" is of course common in the *Acts Thom.* as in contemporary literature.[82] It occurs most often in the *Acts Thom.* in the traditional form, "Holy Spirit," either alone[83] or in the formula, "Father, Son, and Holy Spirit."[84]

Bousset attempts a solution by appealing to Manichaeism, where the "Living Spirit" is a title well attested; a "Father of Greatness" and a "Mother of Life" are also to be observed.[85] On this basis, he treats the

---

[80] Its inclusion of δεσπότης can be seen as a plausible connection with Abban the "master" (106.3–4).

[81] In Epiph. *Pan.* 31.5, a divine pair produces the first man, but there the "Mother" is clearly subordinated to the Father.

[82] It is often interpreted in Gnostic literature as a name for "Sophia," causing more problems with the "Mother of Wisdom."

[83] See 143.2; 168.20; 239.14; 246.13; 266.5–6; and 284.12.

[84] It occurs in this form seven times; see Bonnet, *Acta*, 2. 2, index, *s.v.* πατήρ, υἱός, and πνεῦμα.

[85] Bousset, "Manichäisches," 10; Bornkamm (*Mythos*, 88) concurs. See Geo Widengren, *Mani and Manichaeism* (London: Weidenfeld and Nicolson, 1965) 48–52.

hymn as having undergone editing by Manichaeans; Bornkamm thinks the ending of the hymn (110.15-20) is a Manichaean addition.[86]

But on the other hand, this argument is weak, depending almost entirely on the coincidence of the title "Living Spirit." The Manichaean parallels to "Father" and "Mother" are no closer than Gnostic ones. And given the analysis of style and composition developed in this study, there are other much more plausible ways of accounting for the formula.

It has already been mentioned that "Sophia" here most likely derives from the previous formulation of this section—it is directly related to the "Sophia" of wisdom literature.

In my hypothesis, both this section and the previous one originally ended by speaking of divine praises (they were both probably originally endings of other hymns). The motif of singing to the Father and the Mother is easily accounted for as arising out of the conflation of these two traditions. We should also note Wetzstein's report of the Syrian wedding custom of enthroning the bride and bridegroom and singing to them as king and queen.[87] Finally, "Father of Truth" is plausibly accounted for as a catchword related to 109.6-7, "On her head lies the Truth."

It is, of course, hard to miss the looser connection of this formula to the traditional "Father, Son, and Holy Spirit" found often in the *Acts Thom.* Playing on traditional formulae is visible elsewhere in the *Acts Thom.*[88] It is very likely that this is going on here as well.

Concerning the ambivalent phrasing and unusual title involved in "with the living Spirit," it is plausible to assume, in light of the derivations given for the other two titles here, that "living Spirit" is a novel creation. Additionally, "living" is a title attributed elsewhere in the *Acts Thom.* both to Jesus (237.16; 284.8) and to the "heavenly water" (in the epiklesis, 168.15).

The statement "They were enlightened by the vision of their master" is parallel to an earlier phrase, "through the vision of him they might be enlightened" (110.9). Grounds were presented earlier for seeing a double meaning in θέα. Here it refers to the woman as a "vision" (manifestation) of the Father-Master and as his "Goddess"

---

[86] Bornkamm, *Mythos*, above n. 85.

[87] Wetzstein, "Dreschtafel," 288-91.

[88] Reitzenstein (*Wundererzählungen*, 137) observes that Thomas departs from the bedroom with a slightly altered traditional formula, "The Lord will be with you"—and immediately Jesus appears. Note also redactional reinterpretation of the traditional formula, "My grace is with you," will be noted below (6.6).

or consort. The parallelism, the play on words, and the awkwardness of the phrase "enlightened *in* the vision" mark this line as redactional. It continues the redactional attempt to make all the images of the hymn parallel—all of them images of the place where one meets the divine.

We may assume that this section is built on a fragment of an older formulation, ". . . whose (Wisdom's) ambrosial food they received, having no lack, and they drank of the wine which left them no thirst or desire, and they sang hymns to Wisdom." It was probably the ending of a hymn, speaking of the wisdom which (hypotasized, divine) Wisdom gives as a banquet. The motifs stand close to the Old Testament wisdom tradition.

4.8 Summary

We can now give a summary of the discussion of the wedding hymn so far, indicating what in the hymn is traditional, what is redactional, and what can be learned about the redactors' intentions.

The competent reader would see here basically: (1) three hymn fragments of a common genre (a natural image as a basis for religious themes); (2) two hymn endings; and (3) a redactional composition based on the traditional theme of the bridal chamber as a place where one contacts God.

These basic units of the hymn have been linked together by redactional additions or alterations:

1) The first and second sections (109.1–14) are linked by the "top of the head" and the "king" motifs and by the catchword "lies" (ἔγκειται).
2) The third section (109.14–110.3) is linked to the first by numerous references to radiant scents and to light and blossoms.
3) The fourth section (110.9–15) is linked to the first by the motif of divine clothing and to the second by the motifs of joy and eons (αἰῶνες / αἰώνιοι).[89]
4) The final section is linked to the first by the catchwords "light" and "proud." Assuming that recurrent motifs are especially to be expected linking the first and last sections of hymns in the *Acts Thom.*, we note that there is also a connection between the king in the first section and the Father-Master of the last. This is

---

[89] The fourth section is probably linked to the third via the motif of the dance of the ²ons-stars, but this is due to a juxtaposition of previous material rather than alteration. Γhe theme of enlightening through/in the vision-Goddess also links the fourth and sixth ²ections.

strengthened by the equation of king with truth in the second section and with the "Father of Truth" in the last. The last section is also linked to the second by the divine banquet motif (strenghtened by the catchword "ambrosia") and to the fourth by the parallel phrases "they were (might be) enlightened in (through) the Goddess-vision."

These connections generally have a substantive as well as a formal function. They emphasize the parallelism of the various images in the hymn: all represent a figure (the woman) or places (the bedroom, the eschatological wedding banquet, the wisdom banquet) which are means of God's self-revelation and offers gifts to people. This thought was already present in the inherited materials in their original milieux, and the redactors have emphasized it. Besides the parallels drawn between the sections, we can mention in this regard especially: (1) "On her head the king is established *feeding with his ambrosia those established on him*" (109.5–6); (2) "Her tongue is like the curtain of the door, shaken by those *going in*" (109.9–10); (3) the bedroom composition; and (4) the alterations indicating that one is enlightened through/in the woman as vision-Goddess (110.9, 16).

There are several lines added to the original pieces by the redactors using basically two techniques to integrate them into the inherited material: parallelism and catchwords (often with pleonasms).

Connections between the hymn and the narrative will be treated principally in Chapter 5. Besides these, the principle unsolved problems about the hymn are the following:

1) We remain puzzled concerning the intent of the redactional line "Her tongue is like the curtain of the door which is shaken by those going in" (109.9–10) and the line about the seven bridegrooms (110.3–5).

2) A problem remains concerning the relation between the bride and bridegroom on the one hand, and the "Father of Truth" and the "Mother of Wisdom" on the other. It is clear that the latter pair are thought of as different from the former: the couple ($\dot{\alpha}\mu\phi\acute{o}\tau\epsilon\rho o\iota$, 110.14) are among those who sing hymns to the Father and Mother. On the other hand they have parallel functions. Both the bride-groom and the Father are bringers of enlightenment (110.8–9, 15–16). The bride and the Mother are both manifestations ($\theta\acute{\epsilon}\alpha\mu\alpha/\theta\epsilon\dot{\alpha}$) through whom enlightenment comes (110.9, 16).

4.9 The Religio-historical Background of the Original Material of the Hymn

The foregoing interpretation of the wedding hymn postulates that the proper religio-historical background of the material in the first, second, and fourth sections of the hymn is the protokabbalistic tradition as evidenced in the *Sepher Yezirah*, the *Bahir*, and the tradition called the *Shiʾur Komah*. It remains here to give a more systematic treatment and substantiation of the historical question involved here.

The most important issue is the dating of the protokabbalistic tradition itself. The earliest historical mention of the *Bahir* comes from the twelfth century in France. The oldest written account of the ideas related to the *Shiʾur Komah* is a tenth-century document. The *Sepher Yezirah* has been dated by scholars as late as the sixth century. The thesis proposed here, that the traditions in question existed early enough to influence the *Acts Thom.*, rests chiefly on the researches of Scholem who actually suggested such a relationship.[90] His arguments can be summarized as follows.

The principle point is the close parallelism between many motifs in these protokabbalistic works and early Gnostic sources. These include such specific ideas as the double nature of Sophia, corresponding to the shekinah in the *Bahir*,[91] the existence of intermediary semidivine beings ("eons" in Gnosticism, *middôt* in the Jewish writings),[92] and the letters of the alphabet as the prime constituents of the "body" of the world (a connection between the Marcosion report in Iren. *Adv. haer.* 1.14.2 and the *Shiʾur Komah*).[93]

Scholem has gathered many more parallelisms in motifs.[94] When combined, they present a strong case for a connection between the two movements. In addition, he points out that it is unlikely that there was a sudden interest on the part of early medieval Judaism in the reading and utilization of old Gnostic texts and that many of these Gnostic motifs and ideas were certainly heretical by postsecond-century standards of orthodoxy—yet the texts in question show no consciousness of

---

[90] Scholem, above n. 29.
[91] Scholem, *Ursprung*, 80–85.
[92] Ibid., 61–75.
[93] See Scholem, *Jewish Gnosticism*, 36–37.
[94] Scholem, *Ursprung*, 59–85.

being at odds with accepted norms. His conclusion is that these traditions originated in the same era as Gnosticism and in milieux close to it
culturally.[95]

Proceeding now more specifically to the contents of these materials
and their relation to the wedding hymn of the *Acts Thom.*, Scholem
dates the basic ideas of the *Shiʾur Komah* in the second century.[96] This
tradition speaks of the "body of the shekinah" relating the various
parts of this body to the twenty-two letters of the Hebrew alphabet.
This speculation is explicitly related to the descriptions of the woman's
body in Song Sol 4 and 7. That is, it is an extension of, and an elaboration on, the same *wasf* form which lies behind the second section of
the wedding hymn.[97]

The *Sepher Yeẓirah* seems to be a conflation of two traditions, one in
accordance with the *Shiʾur Komah* picturing the world as made up of
the twenty-two letters of the alphabet (1.2–9), and another making ten
sepārîm the basic constituents of the world (2–6). The conflation of
these two ideas is what produces the thirty-two *middôt* referred to in the
Bahir. It breaks down the alphabet into a group of seven related to the
planets, a group of twelve related to the zodiacal signs (see *Acts Thom.*
110.5–8), and a group of three related to the elements of fire, water,
and air (§§ 3, 4, and 5). The *Sepher Yeẓirah* gives several other associations to each of the thirty-two *middôt* and recommends that the reader
study these closely (1.3) saying that such study brought Abraham to
intimacy with God (6.10). This corresponds to the representation in
Acts Thom. (109.8–13) of the thirty-two eons as the "steps" by which
one ascends to God. Scholem states, "The idea-world of the *Sepher
Yeẓirah* matches that of Palestine or its immediate surroundings in the
second or third century."[98]

The *Bahir* is longer and more complex than the other two bodies of
material. It consists of many small paragraphs recording sayings of
various rabbis, allegorical interpretations of scripture, and parables on
allegorical themes.[99] It apparently consists of a collection of many

---

[95] Scholem, "Bahir, Sefer ha-," *EncJud* 4. 100; and idem, *Ursprung*, 58–59. It is well
known, on the other side, that Gnostics frequently drew on Jewish traditions.

[96] Scholem, *Jewish Gnosticism*, 42.

[97] Scholem (*Jewish Gnosticism*, 38–40) argues for the early date for the *Shiʾur Komah*
on the basis of Oen's report that speculation on the Song of Solomon was one of the esoteric subjects forbidden to Jews of his time—along with the more well-known prohibition
related to the creation account and the chariot passage in Ezekiel.

[98] Scholem, *Ursprung*, 24.

[99] The following citations are based on Gershom Scholem, *Das Buch Bahir* (Leipzig:
Drugulin, 1923).

different traditions which it leaves unharmonized on many points.[100] Scholem's thesis is that the book as we have it shows medieval editing and additions, but much of its material originated in milieux close to Gnosticism.[101]

The importance of this book in relation to the wedding hymn is that several of its sections focus on the figure of the shekinah (see esp. §§ 116–23), sometimes also called "Wisdom" (§§ 44, 90, 97), the "king's daughter" (§§ 36, 43, 44, 52, 62), the "Queen" (§ 90), or the "Bride" (§§ 104, 124, 137). She has an "upper" and a "lower" manifestation. In the latter she is the last of God's emanations. She is closely connected with the earthly realm, the farthest removed from God. On the other hand, her function is to manifest God's presence in this realm (§ 116). This follows the widespread notion of the shekinah, the manifest aspect of God, the presence of God on earth, as distinct from God's transcendent and intangible presence in heaven.[102]

Two quotations will give a more specific notion about how this theme is treated in the *Bahir* (§ 116):

> There is a shekinah below, as there is a shekinah above. What is this shekinah? Say that it is the Light which emanated from the First Light. It surrounds everything . . . And what is its function here? It is like a king, who has seven sons . . . He said to them, "Dwell one upon the other." Then the one who dwelt lowest said, "I do not want to dwell lowest, and I do not want to be so far from you." He said to them, "I am daily with you." . . . and so it is said, "The whole earth is full of your glory." And why did he dwell under them? To protect them and give them a foundation.

In section 90, the same biblical quotation is taken up:

> What does it mean, "The whole earth is full of your Glory?" This is that "Earth" which was made on the first day, and it corresponds to the Land of Israel above, and it is "full of God's glory." What is that? It is Wisdom . . . What is "God's glory?" . . . The matter is like a king, in whose room was the queen . . . and they had sons. They came . . . and said to him, "Where is our Mother?" And he answered them, "You cannot see her yet." Then they said, "Praise be to her, wherever she is."

---

[100] See Scholem, *Ursprung*, 44–52.

[101] Scholem (*Ursprung*, 35–36) points out that medieval authors say it arrived in France from Palestine, and he adds (p. 52) that internal evidence of acquaintance with Palestinian flora and customs confirms this.

[102] See Scholem, "Shekinah," *EncJud* 14 (1972) 1349–54.

Scholem comments on these passages (drawing also on others):[103]

> She is on the one hand the Queen, who remains invisible, and
> after whom the king's sons seek. On the other hand she is the
> Daughter of the King himself, who has taken up her dwelling in
> the world, thought of as a world of darkness, although she herself
> stems from the "Form of Light."

Many of the features of the shekinah in the *Bahir* resemble those of
the Gnostic Sophia, particularly her double character ("upper" and
"lower") and, in her "lower" aspect, her connection with the earth as
a realm far from God.[104] These resemblances form part of Scholem's
argument for an early date for the traditions of the *Bahir*.[105]

The importance of connecting the woman of the wedding hymn in
the *Acts Thom.* with the shekinah of *Bahir*, over against the Gnostic
Sophia, lies in the several ways in which the attributes of the former
are different from those of the latter. And the principle issue here is
whether or not we are to read the wedding hymn against the background of the Gnostic myth of the fall and redemption of Sophia, a
prominent feature in Gnostic accounts of Sophia but absent from
descriptions of the shekinah in the *Bahir*.[106] This myth has influenced
many previous commentaries on the hymn, beginning with Thilo's.[107]
Since there is very little in the hymn itself that suggests such a myth,[108]
the reason for this kind of interpretation is apparently that the Gnostic
Sophia has seemed to be the only candidate for the obviously esoteric
tradition referred to by the "Daughter of Light."

But, given the probability of an early date for the traditions in the
Bahir established by Scholem, it can now be pointed out that the shekinah figure there, of whom no fall is mentioned, provides a closer analogy to the woman of the hymn than does Sophia of the Gnostic myth.

This has already been suggested to some extent by Scholem who, in
making his case for the connection between the shekinah of the *Bahir*
and the Gnostic Sophia, places special emphasis on the resemblances

---

[103] Scholem, *Ursprung*, 84.

[104] See Jonas, *Gnostic Religion*, 176–99.

[105] Scholem, *Ursprung*, 123.

[106] See Scholem, *Ursprung*, above n. 103.

[107] Thilo, *Acta*, 121–51. Preuschen (*Hymnen*, 40) is perhaps the most extreme example.
He sees the hymn as relating "how the Mother, the Holy Spirit, resolves upon the
redemption of Sophia and the freeing of the light that has been banished in matter, and
sends Christ as savior."

[108] Bornkamm (*Mythos*, 83) recognizes this.

between the lore about the shekinah and what is said of the Daughter
of Light in the wedding hymn of the *Acts Thom.* He appeals to three
principle correspondences: (1) the motif of the "thirty-two" who "sing
her hymns" (109.8); (2) the fact that her function is to manifest the
presence of God (esp. 109.1–14); and (3) her probable role as a
representative of the created world.[109]

In the last respect, she is not so different from the Gnostic Sophia.[110]
As to being one who manifests the presence of God, this motif occurs
in relation to the Gnostic Sophia,[111] though it does not generally
receive the emphasis there that it has in the wedding hymn and in the
Bahir.

Scholem remarks on the fact that the myth of the fall is missing in
the *Bahir* and on the fact that the presence of the shekinah on earth is
explained by the fact that her role is to manifest God's presence there.
This is in accord with the role of the Daughter of Light in the first part
of the wedding hymn, as Scholem points out:[112]

> It is in any case important for the Jewish conception of the Bahir
> that it is the vocation of the Daughter to be at work and to rule in
> the world below . . . She is the one "taken from the Good One,"
> the one who was taken from the good and hidden Light and given
> to this our world as its "*Midda*" . . . This Daugther is "the shining
> that was taken from the First Light," just as in the wedding hymn
> of the *Acts Thom.* it is said "the shining of kings is in her."

Aside from the lack of the fall myth, it is the mention of the
"thirty-two" in the wedding hymn that provides the most convincing
evidence of a connection between the wedding hymn and the *Bahir.* As
several commentators mention, the number has no correspondences in
Gnostic texts (twenty-eight or thirty eons is the usual number).[113] Not
only does the number correspond to the tradition in the *Bahir,* the
thirty-two eons have the same relation to the woman in the hymn as
the thirty-two *middôt* have to the shekinah in the *Bahir.* Bornkamm

---

[109]Scholem, *Ursprung,* 83–85. For the latter observation he points out F. C. Baur's
assessment of the woman in the hymn: "She seems to me in general the queen and protectress of the created visible world, and seems to represent this world itself in its various
aspects" (*Das manichäische Religionssystem,* [Göttingen: Vandenhoeck & Ruprecht, 1928]
225). Baur's opinion is strikingly in accord with the interpretation proposed here.

[110] See Jonas, *Gnostic Religion,* 176.

[111] See George W. MacRae, "The Jewish Background of the Gnostic Sophia Myth,"
NovT 12 (1970) 90.

[112]Scholem, *Ursprung,* 84–85.

[113] See Thilo, *Acta,* 136; and Klijn, *Acts of Thomas,* 171.

notes, "The woman [of the hymn] includes in herself the realm of the eons."[114] In the *Bahir* the shekinah is the "receptacle" of the thirty-two *middôt* (§§ 43, 52, 97). In Gnosticism, Sophia is sometimes the last of the eons as the shekinah is in the *Bahir*, but there is no mention that she includes them in herself.

These then are Scholem's three principle arguments for a connection between the shekinah sections of the *Bahir* and the wedding hymn in the *Acts Thom.* Scholem's chief interest in drawing these comparisons is the dating of the traditions in the *Bahir.* His conclusion is then "that oriental sources from the world of gnosis have influenced the symbolism of the *Bahir*, or else that the shekinah fragments of the *Bahir* themselves belong to a stratum of such sources."[115]

Scholem seems to give a certain priority to Gnostic sources, and speaks of the shekinah lore in the *Bahir* as a "Judaizing" of Gnostic thought about Sophia.[116] He apparently has in mind the monistic views of the *Bahir* (connected with the lack of a fall myth) over against the dualism of the Gnostics.

Two observations can be made that would actually strengthen Scholem's case for an early dating of the *Bahir* traditions, obviating at the same time the necessity of supposing that the shekinah of the *Bahir* is a copy of the Gnostic Sophia.

First of all, the way in which ideas are expressed in the wedding hymn of the *Acts Thom.* assumes that the reader is familiar with the identity of the "Daughter of Light," particularly in reference to her relation to the thirty-two eons-steps. It seems clear that some of the ideas specific to the *Bahir*'s shekinah antedate the hymn.

Secondly, a good case can be made that the *Bahir*'s shekinah is a direct development of the figure of Sophia in the Wisdom of Solomon. Many of the ideas connected with the shekinah in the *Bahir* are actually present in that earlier work. She has two aspects, a heavenly one in which she is the "companion of God's throne" (9:4; see 8:3) and an earthly one in which she "pervades all things" (7:24; see 1:7 and 8:1). And it is her function to reveal God's mysteries to people (7:21). Also one can note that the *Bahir* speaks of the "thirty-two ways of wisdom" (§ 67) and also makes mention of wisdom as God's gift to Solomon (§ 2; see Wis 8 and 9).

---

[114] Bornkamm, *Mythos*, 83.
[115] Scholem, *Ursprung*, 85.
[116] Ibid.

Recently there have been persuasive attempts to interpret the Gnostic Sophia figure herself as a development of the Sophia of the Jewish wisdom tradition. And it is noteworthy that the chief obstacle here is the lack of the myth of the fall.[117] In other words it seems likely that the shekinah figure of the *Bahir* rather than being a Judaizing of a Gnostic Sophia is a parallel, but monistic, development of the Sophia of the Wisdom of Solomon. The wedding hymn of the *Acts Thom.*, with its connections both to the Wisdom of Solomon[118] and to the *Bahir*, serves as a good connecting link.

One slight qualification of this thesis must be made in relation to the fourth section of the hymn (110.3–9) which pictures the woman-bride as the earth surrounded by the planets waiting for enlightenment. Here we do have the motif that the woman is originally in darkness waiting for the divine light, which departs from both the presentation of Sophia in the Wisdom of Solomon and from that of the *Bahir*'s shekinah. While this does not necessarily reflect the full dualistic view of Gnostic sources, it does perhaps approach it. And this may be connected with the fact that the bedroom section of the hymn (109.14–110.3) has no parallels in the wisdom tradition of the *Bahir*.[119] It does have a parallel in the reports of Marcosian Gnosticism which also shows some affinity to the *Sepher Yezirah* and has a fall myth.

Closer determination of the interrelations of these traditions must await further research. One more issue can be treated here, and that is the relation of the redactors of the *Acts Thom.* to the traditions they have utilized in the wedding hymn.

It can be said that the *Acts Thom.* in general lacks the explicit interest in the elaborate cosmogonies of which the Sophia myth is a prominent part in many Gnostic sources. Along with this it can be said that, at least in chapters 1–10, they show a monistic theology. These features they share with their sources (and with the Wisdom of Solomon and the *Bahir*).

On the other hand, there are a number of figures mentioned in the inherited material of the hymn who are not mentioned again in the *Acts*

---

[117] See George W. MacRae, "The Jewish Background of the Gnostic Sophia Myth," *NovT* 12 (1970) 98–101.

[118] Also note the verbal connection between the description of Wisdom in Wis 7:26: ἀπαύγασμα . . . φωτὸς ἀιδίου ("radiance of the Eternal Light") and in *Acts Thom.* 109.1–2: τοῦ φωτὸς θυγάτηρ, ᾗ . . . ἔγκειται τὸ ἀπαύγασμα ("daughter of Light, on whom radiance lies").

[119] Both do, though, employ erotic imagery, Wis 8:2 and *Bahir* § 2.

Thom.:[120] the "first demiurge" (109.11); the "eons" (109.13); "Sophia" (110.20). And the "great ones" (μεγιστᾶνες, 110.11) occurs only once more, in the Hymn of the Pearl (220.22). It seems likely that the redactors are drawing on traditions other than those current in their community, though they may have figured in its past. The material in the wedding hymn is also probably from a different source than the narrative material used in these Acts. (It is noteworthy that there is no mention of Christ and nothing is specifically Christian about the hymn.)

---

[120]This information is based on Bonnet, *Acta*, 2. 2, index, *s.v.* and a cursory reading of the *Acts Thom.* It may not be complete, though Bonnet usually lists the major occurrences of special themes like these.

5

THE IMPLICATIONS OF
THE FOREGOING ANALYSES

This Chapter departs from the detailed, section-by-section analysis of the *Acts Thom.* pursued in Chapters 3 and 4. Drawing on many of the results of these earlier analyses, it pieces together a coherent picture of the redactors' presentation so far as it can be understood at this point: its main concerns, its leading themes, and its imaginative style. The chief focus of the discussion is the theme of Thomas's transforming "initiation" which overcomes his previous resistance and leads him to see the world as a manifestation of God's presence. A comparison with Gnostic (Ophite) material makes this interpretation plausible. The Chapter closes with a discussion of how the thought here relates generally to Hans Jonas's conception of Gnostic thought in which alienation from the world plays a central role.

5.1 The Double Presentation of the "World"

It was remarked earlier that the shekinah theme in the hymn carries forward the narrative motif of the world as a divine offering. The fact that, as we now see, the banquet in the hymn is a parallel image to that of the woman-shekinah makes clear the relation between the narrative banquet and the hymn banquet. The latter takes up the positive strand of redactional interpretation of the narrative banquet, and both represent the world as a divine offering. There is then a positive relation between these two banquets, not just a contrasting one as might initially be suspected.

It is in light of this kind of correlation of narrative and hymnic images that many of the catchword and motif correspondences between narrative and hymn are undoubtedly to be understood. These can be briefly listed here, beginning with those involving the narrative invitation scene (104.5–105.12).

The redactors represent Thomas's entrance into the city as an entrance into feasting. They also have the Andrapolitans tell Thomas, "You, too, have the gods brought that you might enjoy a banquet in this city" (105.1). Finally, the redactors add pleonastically "joy" and "feast" to the "gathering" in their sources (105.3–4). It is clear that these are catchword connections to "joy" and "banquet" that are parallel to each other in the hymn (110.10, 12) and probably, as well, to "her feet show forth joy" (109.7). Another such catchword recurrence involves Thomas's crown (parallel to the oil) "woven of myrtle and other blossoms" (107.10) and the blossoms to which the woman's clothes are compared in the hymn (109.3–4). See also the "myrtle and blossoms" in her bedroom (110.2). Finally, note that a king is the giver of the banquet both in the narrative and the hymn (105.2–4; 109.5–6; 110.16–19; and see the redactional addition, "king's city," 104.4).

We have also seen how the principle redactional reworking in the hymn has to do with the presentation of the woman-bedroom-banquet motifs as places where God is manifested, places where one meets God and receives gifts. Understanding that these are images of the world as a medium of the divine presence, the anointing scene now appears much more organically connected to its context than was previously suspected. According to sacramental thinking, prominent elsewhere in the *Acts Thom.* (168.15; 230.18–19; and 266.11), the oil itself is a material (worldly) element that is at the same time a medium of divine grace.

A final motif connection between the narrative and hymn needs some discussion here. It involves two hymn lines: "Her fingers suggest the gates of the city" (109.13–14) and "The barred doors (κλειστά-δες) are decorated with reeds" (110.3). Both these lines are redactional. The latter is particularly strange as an image, and it also puzzlingly recalls the reed Thomas holds in the narrative (107.11–108.1) as an allusion to the passion of Jesus. What this suggests is that the redactors want to inject into the hymn, in at least a token way, the motif of opposition, of painfulness and difficulty, which is the other side of the theme "world" as it appears in the narrative. The bridal chamber, like the woman and the banquet, represents "world" as a divine offering, but the way "into" it is through "barred doors" (κλειστάδες) decorated with the reeds of suffering. Thus the double presentation of the category "world" that characterizes the redactional presentation in the narrative is injected in a small way into the hymn as well.

This interpretation sheds light on the last lines (109.13–14) of the previous section of the hymn, "Her fingers suggest the gates of the city" (πύλας τῆς πόλεως). As Thilo has noted, "city" here represents the heavenly city,[1] but it refers as well, to "Peoplecity," the world which is also a "king's (God's) city" (104.4), a theme parallel to that of the banquet. "Suggest" (ὑποδεικνύουσιν) is most naturally taken as synonymous with "represent" (ἔοικεν, 109.9–10). The easiest way to have fingers represent city gates is to spread two of them apart in a V-shape. This image, in turn, resembles the V-shaped flutes of the flutist, and these are paralleled with Thomas's reed in the narrative.

The connection of this series of images is supported by the parallelism of the hymn lines involved: the point of each is somewhat extraneous to the section where it occurs, and the fact that both occur at the end of their respective sections and mention entrances (doors-gates) tends to make their connection to each other stronger than their connection to their immediate context.

So, symbols which signify oppression for Thomas in the narrative (reed-flutes), in the hymn stand at the entrance to the "world" as a heavenly city.[2] This interpretation will be supported by comparative

---

[1] Thilo, *Acta*, 138.

[2] As will be shown later in more detail, the Christ prayer also shows a compositional pattern similar to this. The dominant theme there presents a mythicized version of the negative evaluation of "world" in the narrative: it is "Hades . . . the prison of darkness" dominated by the enemy and his rulers (115.1–7). And yet there also the middle section of the prayer (114.10–17) presents the opposite theme: "You (Christ) are in all things . . . lying upon all your works, manifesting in the energies of all."

material below, where "gates" (πύλαι) refer to the gates guarded by hostile "rulers" barring a person's way in an initiation.

What will occupy our attention in the rest of this Chapter is the implications of the above remarks particularly in relation to the double, seemingly contradictory, presentation of the banquet-world by the redactors. The foregoing observations have shed new light on this feature of the text, and the state of the case can now be summarized.

On the surface, the banquet narrative is principally concerned with the relation of and interaction between the heaven-sent apostle and the worldly (ungodly) wedding feast and those present there. The redactors have also arranged the material and added elements to suggest in addition that the entrance of Thomas into the banquet and his dealings there are meant as an allegorical representation of the myth of the descent of a heavenly figure to the earthly realm.

It has been apparent all along that there is tension between these ideas and an opposite strand of redactional thought that the banquet is a divine offering and Thomas is stubborn and foolish to refuse it. Analysis of the principle redactional trend in the wedding hymn (the world-shekinah as a place where one contacts God) and the parallels between the hymn and the narrative now increases the impression of the tension. What this analysis suggests is that the elements presenting the banquet in a positive light belong to an allegorical scheme. They implicitly represent Thomas not as a superior reedemer figure come to the ungodly earth, but as one who needs enlightening, like a candidate for initiation who enters into the world for this purpose.

A puzzle remains as to the kind of logic or literary imagination that could let these two seemingly contradictory allegories overlap in such a way. And this is connected to another problem, unmentioned so far. The banquet episodes represent increasing tension between Thomas and the Andrapolitans. Thomas refuses to have anything to do with their banquet, allegorically representing the world. Then suddenly, following the climax of the hostility between Thomas and this world (the slap and the curse), it is this very Thomas who breaks out in song in praise of the world (as shekinah). Does this imply a radical transformation of Thomas's attitude?

5.2 Thomas's Transformation as Initiation

We must observe first, of course, that there is no necessary implication of a transformation of Thomas in the fact that it is he who sings the song. One could suppose that the redactors merely put their own sentiments in the mouth of Thomas. It is partly a problem of how to construe the text. Should we take the apparent logic of all the narrative progressions seriously? We met a similar problem when the selling of Thomas in a vision apparently, but puzzlingly, led to his willing assent to go to India.

There are three passages in the text which indicate that we actually should pay serious attention to the apparent change in Thomas's attitude to the world. First, there is the statement following the hymn that Thomas drew attention to himself by his "changed appearance" ($\epsilon\hat{\iota}\delta\sigma$ $\dot{\epsilon}\nu\alpha\lambda\lambda\alpha\gamma\dot{\epsilon}\nu$, 111.3). As Klijn has noted, this represents some kind of divinizing transformation of Thomas.[3]

One could look upon the transformation as being due to the act of (ecstatic) hymn singing. But there is also, secondly, the sacramental anointing that precedes the hymn which is conventionally associated with spiritual transformation.

However, the main evidence that there is a transformation of Thomas prior to the hymn lies in the scene of the servant's slap. Argumentation on this third point will be somewhat extended, due to the nature of the evidence. It will consist of some observations about the scene in its context here and also some comparisons with other material both within the *Acts Thom.* and outside it.

Internally, what is noticeable is that each of the banquet episodes prior to this one has portrayed the Andrapolitan characters in relation to Thomas in a double role. They are ungodly figures persecuting the apostle and coercing (seducing) him into compromising involvement with the world that is foreign to God. And they also represent the offering of divine gifts to Thomas. The attentive reader will approach this episode expecting that the servant's slap will also have some such double function. This expectation is furthered by the plausible connection of the servant's hand with the hands of Thomas and the flutist, already deliberately paralleled in the preceding scenes.

What I want to propose is that the servant's slap, representing the climax of the hostility between Thomas and the world, is also part of an initiation experience for him. It is associated with the idea of painfulness of entry into the shekinah in connection with the images of the reed decorated doors of the bedroom and the "gates of the city." In this reading, a particular interpretation is being given by the redactors to the contemporary idea that initiation entails passing through an experience felt as dangerous or painful. This experience is particularly

[3] Klijn, *Acts of Thomas*, 179–80.

organic under the circumstances here in that the antagonism felt is simply the other side of the mystery of the shekinah into which one is entering.

Internal evidence points in the direction of this interpretation. What adds a good deal of support to it is comparison with another text, a Gnostic (Ophite) tradition mentioned by Origen, dealing with the theme of the hostile forces that bar the soul on its way to fulfillment. Because of its importance in several details, Origen's report needs an extended treatment here.

An Ophite Comparison

Origen's account of what he knows of the Ophites occurs in scattered fragments[4] in the course of an argument with Celsus, a person of anti-Christian sentiment who counts the Ophites among Christians. Of central interest, for our purposes, is the following:[5]

If one wishes to learn the inventions of these sorcerers (the Ophites) . . . let him hear what they are taught to say after (μετά) passing through what they call the "barrier of evil," the gates of the archons sealed forever.

7. "Solitary king, bond of blindness, unconscious oblivion, I greet you, first power, preserved by the spirit of providence and by wisdom. From there I am sent in purity, already a part of the light of the son and father. Grace be with me; yes, father, be with me. . . . "

6. Then, passing through the one they say is Ialdabaoth, they are taught to say, "You, Ialdabaoth, first and seventh, born to have power with boldness, being the ruling word of a pure mind, I, a perfect work for the father and the son, bearing a symbol of life by the image of the imprint, and having opened for the world the gate which you closed for your eternity—I pass by your power, free again. Grace be with me, father, be with me."

5. They think that the one passing through Ialdabaoth and reaching Iao must say, "You, ruler of the hidden mysteries of the son and the father, one who shines at night, second and first, lord of death, part of the innocent one, I am bearing already, as a symbol, your own . . . beard,[6] and being ready I pass by your power, having overcome

---

[4] Orig. *Cels.* 6.25–36.

[5] For convenience in reference, I shall number the formulas for the different "gates" through which the person passes in reverse order as they occur in Origen's account.

[6] The text has ὑπηνουν (sic) here, a word unattested elsewhere. The translation

the one born of you with a living word. Let grace be, father, let it be."

4. And then next Sabaoth, to whom they think one should say, "Ruler of the fifth authority, powerful Sabaoth, defender of the law of your creation destroyed by grace, by a more powerful pentad, let me pass, seeing a blameless symbol of your art protected by an image of an imprint, a body released by a pentad. Grace be with me father, be with me."

3. And after him Astaphaios, to whom they believe one should say these things, "Ruler of the third gate, Astaphaios, overseer of the first beginning of water, let me pass, seeing the initiate, one cleansed by the spirit of the maiden, seeing the essence of the cosmos. Grace be with me, father, be with me."

2. And after him Ailoaios, to whom they think one should say, "Ruler of the second gate, Ailoaios, let me pass, bearing for you a symbol of your mother, a grace hidden from the powers of the authorities. Grace be with me, father, be with me."

1. Last they mention Horaios, and they think one should say to him, "You passed fearlessly over the barrier of fire, Horaios, designated power over the first gate, let me pass, seeing a symbol of your power released by the imprint of the tree of life, having been taken over by an image in the likeness of the innocent one. Grace be with me, father, be with me."[7]

There are a number of peculiarities in this passage which have given difficulty to previous commentators.[8] First, there is the introduction to it given by Origen concerning "what they are taught to say after passing through what they call the 'barrier of evil,' the gates of the archons sealed forever."

People are taught these formulas "after" ($\mu\epsilon\tau\acute{\alpha}$) they have passed through the gates of the archons. Yet the wording of the formulas themselves makes it clear that they are to be recited *as* one is passing through seven "gates of the archons." This is especially evident in

---

"beard" accepts the emendation ὑπήνην. Others have suggested ὑπήκοον νοῦν (obedient mind). See the textual notes in Marcel Borret, s.j., ed. *Origène Contre Celse* Tome III (SC 147) 256.

[7] Orig. *Cels.* 6.31.

[8] See R. A. Lipsius, "Ueber die ophitischen Systeme," *ZWTh* 7 (1864) 37–57; and the notes in Henry Chadwick, trans., *Origen: Contra Celsum* (Cambridge: Cambridge University Press, 1953) 346–48.

the formulas for the second and third gates. It seems clear that two separate passages through the gates are envisioned.[9] Looking to the formulas themselves, several of them indicate that the one passing through is already an initiate: "Let me pass, seeing an initiate, one cleansed by the spirit of the maiden . . ." (third gate). "Being ready, I pass by your power, having overcome the one born of you by a living word" (fifth gate). "Let me pass, seeing . . . a body released by a pentad" (fourth gate). One begins to suspect that there has been a previous passage through these gates that served as an initiation preparatory to the one envisioned here. The hypothesis that the previous initiation involved a similar passage through seven gates is supported by the fact that the one passing through frequently appeals for protection by virtue of something related to the ruler through whose gate passage is being made. Passing through the fourth gate, the initiate is referred to as a "body released by a pentad." At the fifth gate the initiate claims to have "overcome the one born of you (the ruler)."

In several other formulas the initiate appeals to a "symbol" related to the ruler: "a symbol of your art" (fourth gate); "a symbol of your mother" (second gate); "a symbol of your power" (first gate); and "a symbol of your own beard" (fifth gate).

We can note that in a previous account of Ophite teaching (*Cels.* 6.27) Origen mentions a "sealing" ceremony in which among other things instructions are given as to what happens to the soul at death. This suggests a plausible sense of the double passage through the seven gates. That is, there is one initiatory passage during life that is believed to prepare the initiate for successfully negotiating a similar passage at death. It is the latter passage for which these formulas are given.[10]

We can get a more specific picture of the character of the preparatory initiation by looking at the use in the formulas of the words σύμβολος and τύπος. The key passage here is the formula for the fourth gate: "Let me pass, seeing a blameless symbol of your art (σύμβολον ὁρῶν σῆς τέχνης), protected by an image of an imprint (εἰκόνι τύπου), a body released by a pentad (πεντάδι λυθὲν σῶμα)." Chadwick sees in this "symbol" a reference to a magical amulet, stamped with a secret

---

[9] Chadwick (*Origen*, 346) wants to translate, ". . . taught to say *at* the . . . gates of the archons after passing through the barrier of evil." Lipsius ("Ueber die ophitischen Systeme," 41) wants to make "gates of the archons" an addition by Origen. These are clearly attempts to avoid the natural sense of the passage because of the substantive difficulty.

[10] Theodor Hopfner ("Das Diagramm der Ophiten" in *Charisteria Alois Rzach* [Reichenberg: Stiepel, 1930] 87) also gives this interpretation.

image which the initiate bears as protection while passing through the gates.[11]

But there are several complications to this interpretation. First of all, note that "symbol" here is in apposition to a "body released by a pentad." Is the amulet a "body released by a pentad?" "Body" seems a more likely reference to the person's body, and the apposition is some indication that "symbol" is, too.

This is admittedly an odd usage for "symbol," but it has a parallel in the first-gate formula where we have a "symbol . . . released by an imprint of the tree of life" (σύμβολον καταλυθὲν τύπῳ ζωῆς ξύλου). Not only is this a verbal parallel to a "body released by a pentad" (σῶμα λυθὲν πεντάδι), it also enables us to make sense of the otherwise puzzling notion of a symbol's being "released." More conclusive support for reading "symbol" as a reference to the person of the initiate comes in the following phrase concerning a "symbol taken over by an image in the likeness of the innocent one" (σύμβολον . . . εἰκόνι καθ᾽ ὁμοίωσιν ληφθὲν ἀθῴου). The notion of a symbol "taken over"[12] by an image is even more unusual than that of a symbol "released" by an image, and several scholars have for this reason suggested that the case and gender of ληφθέν be emended in order that it might modify something else. Chadwick suggests ληφθέντα which would modify "me" (the initiate).[13] Understanding "symbol" as already being a reference to the initiate solves the difficulty and gives Chadwick's interpretation without a necessity of emendation.

But we should not abandon altogether Chadwick's idea of the stamping of a symbol with an image. The same basic motif, metaphorically understood, lies behind the idea of giving the "seal" (σφραγίς) as a rite in a passage about the Ophites in Orig. *Cels.* 6.27. And the notion of the stamping of an image on a person's soul was common among early Christian writers on the sacraments.[14] And the language of some

[11] Chadwick, *Origen*, 347 n. 1.

[12] "Received" would be a more usual translation of ληφθέν. I choose the more active "taken over" as making more sense here. I take it to suggest a transformation of the person, a parallel to what is implied in the third-gate formula where the initiate claims to be the "essence of the cosmos" after having been purified by the maiden. Taking the "maiden" as a figure representing the "essence of the cosmos," the initiate is claiming to have been "taken over" by the maiden, to have taken on something of her own character.

[13] Chadwick, *Origen*, above n. 11.

[14] See G. W. H. Lampe, *The Seal of the Spirit: A Study in the Doctrine of Baptism and Confirmation in the New Testament and the Fathers* (2d ed.; London: Longmans, Green and Co., 1967) 153, 250; the image is also used by Philo in a different context (p. 17).

of the Ophite formulas themselves seems to point unmistakably to the ideas of stamping with an image. For example, the fourth-gate formula has σύμβολον ... εἰκόνι τύπου τετηρημένον. Τύπος here must have its original sense of "imprint," otherwise we would have the meaningless "image of an image."[15] See also the sixth-gate formula, "bearing a symbol of life by the image of the imprint" (χαρακτῆρι τύπου ζωῆς σύμβολον ἐπιφέρων).[16] The word χαρακτήρ is connected with the stamping of images (it shows up later in Christian sacramental "character"), and again the particular combination with τύπος suggests the sense of "imprint" rather than "image" for the latter.

The indication is that the stamping of an image on an amulet or a coin is being taken as a metaphor describing the effects of the previous initiation on the person. In the course of the previous passing through the gates, the initiates claims to have been "stamped" with various "images" by which they were "released," and also "taken over," in a purification and transformation, and now they claim protection by these images.

We saw earlier that the initiate claims to be a symbol closely related to the rulers through whose gates he or she is passing. Does this mean that these rulers who bar the way are also the ones who impart a protective seal? There are several indications that this is actually what is meant.

To begin with, one can notice that in the formulas the rulers of the gates are described in both positive and negative terms. Most obviously negative is the characterization of the "gates of the archons" as the "barrier of evil" (φραγμὸν κακίας) in the introduction to the formulas. In the formulas themselves, both positive and negative descriptions of the rulers are given, sometimes within the same formula. The ruler of the seventh gate is called "bond of blindness" and "unconscious oblivion," as well as "first power, preserved by the spirit of providence and by Sophia." The next, Ialdabaoth, seems surely negative since the initiate claims to have "opened . . . the gate which you closed for your eternity,"[17] yet he is also "born to have power with

---

[15] Wilson ("Acts of Thomas," 97) translates the phrase, "by the imprint (εἰκόνι) of the blow (τύπου)," taking τύπος in a sense even closer to its origin in τύπτειν.

[16] One could take the dative χαρακτῆρι to mean "with" the image. The parallel with the other formulas suggests that the symbol is stamped rather than that one bears both a symbol and an image. I take "bearing a symbol" to mean "marked by a symbol," similar in sense to being a symbol.

[17] Theodor Hopfner ("Das Diagramm der Ophiten" in *Charisteria Alois Rzach* [Reichenberg: Stiepel, 1930] 98) points out that "Ialdabaoth" means "son of chaos," thus suggesting a negative valuation even in the name.

boldness," which may be a positive description. "Being the ruling (ἄρχων) word of a pure mind" may also refer to this ruler.

Sabaoth of the fourth gate is a demonic "defender of the law of your creation destroyed by grace." Astaphaios of the third gate is "overseer of the first beginning of water," which is ambiguous but sounds more positive than negative. As to Ailoaios, his mother is at least a positive protectress of the initiate. And finally, Horaios of the first gate seems positively a hero who has "passed fearlessly over the barrier of fire."

What strengthens this interpretation of the rulers as having a double character is, secondly, a comparison with another bit of Ophite lore connected with these seven gates by Origen (*Cels.* 6.25). He speaks of an Ophite diagram. It consists of "seven circles of the rulers (ἀρχοντικῶν)" that are surrounded by one larger circle "which they say is the soul of the universe (τῶν ὅλων ψύχη) and Leviathan." Earlier he has spoken of a similar diagram of ten circles, and in these circles "Leviathan, the soul of the universe" is marked twice, once at the circumference and once in the middle.

In the formulas for the third gate, on the other hand, we read, "Let me pass, seeing an initiate, one cleansed by the spirit of the maiden (παρθένου), seeing the essence of the cosmos (οὐσίαν τοῦ κόσμου)." As Origen himself remarks, the implication of the diagram markings is that the soul that permates the universe is evil, since it is named Leviathan the chaos monster and enemy of God in the Old Testament and Semitic lore generally. In the formula just quoted, the initiate claims to be the "essence of the cosmos," and this is connected with the fact that he or she has been "cleansed by the spirit of the maiden." The maiden here is almost certainly the "maiden Prunikos," a figure mentioned in Ophite teachings given by Origen shortly after the report about the seven gates. She is a familiar figure elsewhere in Gnosticism (as "Sophia Prunikos") and represents, according to Jonas, the world (the cosmos) as fallen ("Prunikos" means the "whore"). However, her connection also with the divine Sophia is one of the more difficult problems one has to deal with in interpreting Gnosticism.[18] In the Ophite formula in question she appears closely related to the "essence of the cosmos," hence also to "Leviathan the soul of the universe," and yet she is the one who has "purified" the initiate in a previous initiation.[19]

---

[18] Jonas, *Gnostic Religion*, 176–77.

[19] This involves a general problem related to accounts of Ophite teachings in which the serpent Leviathan is assigned both positive and negative roles.

What would make sense of this double character of the rulers is that passing through this "barrier of evil" is a test of strength. One who successfully passes the test has overcome the rulers in their negative aspect.[20] A metaphorical way of expressing what has happened is to say that winning out in this test has stamped the initiate with an image related to the respective ruler which now serves as protection. That is, it has made the ruler a positive force for the initiate.[21] The fourth-gate formula, "seeing a symbol of your art," suggests rather directly that the ruler has imparted the image. (In fact another passage in Origen's account of the Ophites speaks of the "seven angels who give the seal," although in a different context.) This is probably also the meaning of "symbol of your power" (first gate), "symbol of your beard" (fifth gate), and perhaps "symbol of your mother" (second gate). Assuming that "essence of the cosmos" has both a positive and negative side, the third-gate formula also suggests that it becomes positive and protective after one has passed through it (being "purified by the maiden").

Bornkamm, in some passing comments on these formulas, understands them in a similar way. He gives them a slightly different interpretation than that proposed here, but he too sees that passing through the gates has a "double meaning . . . the overcoming of the powers and . . . the process of fulfillment."[22] This tradition can be compared with a line from the Syriac text of the *Acts Thom.*: "The heavenly marriage founded on the bridge of fire, on which is sprinkled grace. . . ."[23] Bornkamm states, "The place of the wedding lies on a bridge of fire, that last barrier, which by the sprinkling of grace is rendered free from danger for the soul."[24]

Several points of comparison between the Ophite ritual, thus interpreted, and the banquet passage in the *Acts Thom.* are clear. In the *Acts Thom.* we also have indications that Thomas is encountering a force that has both a positive and a negative side; part of what is portrayed is his initiation (into the shekinah, similar to the "essence of the cosmos"), and the character of what confronts him changes after a

---

[20] See esp. the sixth-gate formula where the person claims to have "opened for the world the gate which you closed for your eternity (or: with your Eon)." Similarly, in the fifth-gate formula the person claims to have "overcome the one born of you with a living word," which also suggests some contest of strength.

[21] The metaphor of "stamping" may be suggested by the combative and hence violent character of the initation.

[22] Bornkamm, *Mythos*, 78.

[23] W. Wright, *Apocryphal Acts of the Apostles* (2 vols.; London: Williams and Norgate, 1871) 2. 261.

[24] Bornkamm, *Mythos*, above n. 22.

hostile encounter (the servant's slap and Thomas's curse).

What supports the parallelism of the *Acts Thom.* with the Ophite material is the use of τύπτειν (cognate of τύπος) to describe the servant's "striking" Thomas. This slap has a double quality, both a hostile attack and a divine gift. The fact that a document like that of the Ophites both shows close parallels to the *Acts Thom.* and uses the "stamping" metaphor with τύπος to refer to initiation suggests that this theme and this use of τύπος/τύπτειν were familiar in circles common to both texts. Hence there is an intended play on words where the *Acts Thom.* speaks of the servant's "striking" Thomas. There is support also for this thesis also in that τύπος occurs in the wedding hymn (109.10–11) in the odd phrase, "her neck lies in the form of steps (εἰς τύπον βαθμῶν)." Together with the other evidence, the facts that the use of τύπος here is awkward and that it is associated with βαθμοί (initiation grades) is an indication that the redactors want to associate τύπτειν/τύπος with the idea of initiation.

The observation that internal evidence in both the Ophite material and the *Acts Thom.* indicates similar ideas and word usage is of course also supportive evidence that the interpretation of each proposed here is correct. Further support for using the Ophite material to illuminate the *Acts Thom.* comes from the facts that the Ophites are the Gnostic group which shows the closest motif parallels to the wedding hymn[25] and that the *Acts Thom.* in another passage presents the theme of the dangerous passage through hostile powers at death.[26]

Finally, in support of the initiatory character of the servant's slap, two other passages in chapters 1–10 of the *Acts Thom.* show parallel progressions of events. The selling scene and the Christ prayer with its introduction also represent events in which, through forced contact with the world, Thomas's attitude is changed and he comes to see the divine presence in the world.

These observations all point to the fact that the wedding hymn is very deliberately placed where it is. The narrative, according to one strand, represents Thomas's coming into the world to be initiated. The

[25] Preuschen (*Hymnen*, 35–44) points out the Ophites as the most apt group for comparison with the material in the wedding hymn.

[26] Thomas, in his farewell speech before his death says, "Let not the powers and dominions perceive me ... When I am borne upward let them not venture to stand before me, by thy power, Lord Jesus, which enwreathes me ... Grant me now ... that in quietness I may pass by, and in joy and peace cross over and stand before the judge" (chap. 148). The Ophite material regarding the dangerous passage is also closely related to the "descent to the Merkabah" of early Jewish mysticism (See Scholem, *Major Trends*, 50), another point of contact between the *Acts Thom.* and the Ophites.

wedding hymn, as presented by the redactors, centers on the idea of initiation. In the mouth of Thomas it also represents his own initiatory change of attitude toward, and perspective on, the world.

5.3 The Imaginative Logic of The Text

Taking for granted for now the above interpretations of the relation of the wedding hymn to its narrative setting, we can turn to some reflections on the implications this has for our understanding of the logic and imaginative style behind the use of motifs and images in this work.

First of all, it is clear on several accounts that Thomas and the situations and events in the narrative are representative and meant to have significance for a broader range of issues than those involving a particular ascetic apostle at a banquet. The myth of the descent of a heavenly figure to the earthly realm which is evoked, for example, traditionally has to do with the nature of the human condition and human destiny.[27] Further, the fact that the Andrapolitan banquet represents the earthly realm tends to generalize the significance of Thomas's attitudes. They represent aloofness from the world in general rather than specific acts of abstention.

Secondly, we can now make sense of the double presentation of the world in the narrative. It now appears that both the positive and negative aspects of the world are parts of allegorical schemes, the descent from heaven to an ungodly world on the one hand, and initiation into the shekinah on the other. The two schemes overlap in a peculiar way, and this is what has important implications for our understanding of what the text is ultimately about and of the related issue of the kind of logic underlying the use of imagery in this work.

As to content, the purpose of the overlap seems fairly clear. It represents an attempt to take up two apparently opposing contemporary conceptions of the world—as an ungodly realm,[28] and as a revelation of God[29] —and place them in a coherent relation to each other. That is, it explains the concept of the ungodly world as a function of a limited (uninitiated) mind. This image of the world can be gotten through (literally) and gotten over in an initiatory experience, after which the

---

[27] This is particularly true, of course, when the myth has to do with the descent of the soul, but the myth of the heavenly redeemer also is mainly, if less directly, concerned with human destiny. Both these myths are involved in these chapters.

[28] See Hermann Sasse, "κόσμος," *TDNT* 3 (1965) 892–95.

[29] See Rom 1:19–20 and Wis 13:1–9.

world appears in its opposite aspect. The cryptic references in the narrative to the world as a divine offering are adumbrations of the positive possibilities of the encounter with the world, possibilities that come to full expression in the images of the wedding hymn.

It must be said here that the image of the world as revelatory does not simply replace that of the ungodly world. As will appear, the concept of the world as ungodly is given emphatic expression in the latter part of the Christ prayer where we find the Andrapolitan world described as "Hades . . . the prison of darkness" (115.1–7).

As to the logic involved in this use of imagery, here we can make modified use of a distinction referred to by Hans Jonas. He distinguishes two ways of understanding myths. On the one hand, a myth can be understood as the expression of a "thought system . . . theory or a system of beliefs about the nature of things,"[30] or "a projection of an existential reality which seeks its own truth in a total view of things" and attempts to "satisfy its aspirations in such objective-symbolic representations."[31]

On the other hand, a myth (or rather some myths) can be understood as maps of "immanent programs of psychic discipline," of "stages of being" that are possibilities for "subjective realization." The prime example Jonas gives this latter understanding is the use, in certain mystery cults, of the myth of the soul's ascent to heaven in seven stages. Here the myth becomes not simply "a belief . . . expressive of the conception of man's relation to the world," but is translated, via ritual, into a "psychological technique of inner transformations." The elements of the myth then represent "subjective phases of self-performable experience . . . stages of an intra-psychic progress," in which the "*eschaton* is taken into the range of the subject's own faculties and becomes a supreme possibility of existence itself."[32] Since Jonas thinks that the former "theoretical" understanding of myth generally represents a chronologically prior stage, he speaks of this latter approach as the " 'psychologization' of the [myth of the] ascent."[33]

In the light of our previous discussion, it is clear that the redactors' use of myth approximates this latter, subjective-psychological process-oriented use of myth rather than the former theoretical one. That is, the myth of the descent from heaven to an ungodly earth does not

---

[30] Hans Jonas, "Myth and Mysticism: A Study of Objectification and Interiorization in Religious Thought," *JR* 49 (1969) 326.
[31] Ibid., 315.
[32] Ibid., 315–18.
[33] Ibid., 318.

represent a fixed evaluation, a belief about what is objectively the case regarding the world we live in. It represents rather a particular way of experiencing the world, explicitly recognized as relative to a certain state of consciousness, a certain perspective which can change. The mythical shekinah, likewise, represents not a belief about the world but, in Jonas's words above, "the *eschaton* . . . taken into the range of the subject's own faculties," an eschatological possibility which can, however, be experienced in this life by one who has taken on an "initiated" perspective. What the text represents then, is an idealized progression of intrapsychic events and experiences. And this is accompanied by symbolic and mythological images that are the correlates of the various stages in the progression rather than fixed beliefs about the way things are.

An objective look at several other aspects of the text confirms this view and suggests some elaborations on it. First of all, the narrative genre itself is one that tends to draw the reader into an identification with the progression of events and experiences the hero undergoes. The redactors have left this aspect of their material largely intact, preferring to inject allegorical meanings by subtle suggestion rather than by obvious intrusion.

An analogous observation can be made about the hymn, that stylistically the emphasis is on the lyric praise of the bride, the bedroom, and the banquet. Sensual beauty, erotic attraction, glorious radiance, joy and pleasure, great privileges and satisfactions—the images are weighted toward these emotionally loaded impressions, while the symbolic representation of *ideas* stylistically takes second place. This shows in the diversity of interpretations the hymn has undergone in relation to this latter aspect. It is relatively obscure, while no one can mistake the emotional tone.

Here it can be mentioned in addition that the hymn does not function only as a more explicit mythical interpretation of narrative themes. It is also an emotional climax. This is most true of the erotic imagery of the hymn in relation to the image of the seductive flutist in the narrative.

Additionally, the particular way in which the initiation scheme disrupts the framework of the myth of the descent and destroys its objective quality has several analogies in other passages in the *Acts Thom.* which shed further light on the particular use of myth and allegory in this work. Because of the importance of this point to the establishment of a perspective of reading competence, it will be worth treating it at some length.

First, it can be pointed out how the double, contradictory presentation of world in the banquet episodes tends to work against any tendency of the reader to take this narrative as an allegorical reference to a set of mythical "facts" about the descent of a heavenly figure to an earthly, ungodly realm. The presentation of the world as a divine offering disrupts the consistency of the framework upon which the myth, as a set of facts, depends. A descent from heaven to the shekinah makes no sense as a myth because heaven is already the traditional place where God's presence is obvious. The overlap of the two themes, contradictory on a factual level, leaves as a consistent object of the reader's attention only what the images convey about the quality, structure, and progression of Thomas's subjective experience. "Heaven" can no longer be conceived of as the familiar realm with its conventional positive and divine associations. It is neutralized and psychologized into a representation of that in which Thomas feels at home, the locus of his personal (limited) religious allegiances. One can speak of a certain deliteralization of images such as this, a de-emphasis on possible objective referents they might have and an emphasis instead on what they convey about subjective experience.

Here is where comparison with several other passages of the *Acts Thom.* can help us, serving both as supportive evidence that this way of reading follows a paradigm found elsewhere in the work, and as a clarification of the character of the particular aspect of reading competence proposed here.

The first passage is from a conversion speech (chapter 34):

1 I became free from worry and guilt.
2 There was a sunrise for me from the night's worry.
3 I rested from the day's busyness. (151.10–12)

Lines 2 and 3 here are clearly parallel. The parallelism of the first two lines indicates that "sunrise" comes as a relief, making it parallel to "rest" in line 3. And "night's worry" is parallel to "day's busyness" as representing a harried period.

One tends at first to take the second line allegorically. Light represents the divine and night represents the dominion of the devil. But the allegorical code breaks down in the third line where day is the negative period and evening is associated with divine "rest," a name for God and eschatological completion in the *Acts Thom.*[34]

---

[34] See Bornkamm, *Mythos,* 34.

The breakdown of the allegory takes place on a different level here than in the case of the banquet scenes, but the result is the same. What is left as coherent for the reader to focus on is the kind of experience represented by both lines 2 and 3, relief from a troubled situation. Light and darkness cannot be regarded as mythical "facts" but only carriers of the experiential quality of the event.

A different kind of breakdown in coherence on the level of mythical facts is visible in the bride's speech of chapter 14. Here (119.13 – 120.2) the bride first portrays herself in the position of an unmarried woman who has Jesus for a lover, whom she now wants to marry: "I will ask my Lord that the love I have experienced tonight may remain, and I will ask for the man I have experienced today." At the end of the same speech, however, she presents herself as being already married to Jesus: "I am joined in another marriage . . . united with the True Husband." Again, both statements are clearly carriers of the feeling the woman has about her conversion experience. And their inconsistency as descriptions of the mythical facts of the case prevents the reader from focusing attention on the supposed mythical facts and forces attention to language as carrier of experience, emotion, and attitude rather than of information.

Finally, one can point also to the lines of the address to the demon in chapter 44. Thomas first speaks of the "Enemy" as the force behind the demonic apparitions plaguing the woman. But then this "Enemy" as a literal figure disappears in an implied group of sinister "Aliens" (161.17 – 18): "O one from the devil who fights for the Aliens. . . ." One is left feeling an evil presence without being able to focus on a real figure.

In all these cases, as with the banquet scenes, it is clear that the mythic dimension is an important aspect of the text. The emotional impact would be lessened without it since the sense of the cosmic level on which the events take place would be lost. But this mythic dimension is in the service of the emotional impact of the text rather than vice versa. The mythic figures and events simply take place in a different than normal dimension and are deprived of any possible status as objective realities.

Here it will be useful to further clarify the position proposed here by contrasting it with another way of understanding myth proposed by Jonas. As one possibility of the "subjective" approach to myth he mentions W. Völker's thesis that in some cases the myth itself is the expression of a feeling which stems directly from mystical experience, and it is therefore to be read as a "coded confession rather than [as a] manifest thought system."[35]

The allusion to initiation which is undoubtedly present in the *Acts Thom.* passage in question raises the possibility that this passage is just such a "coded confession" (a very cryptically coded one) giving expressive representation to some spontaneous or deliberately induced mystical experience. Can we say that the text is indeed allegorical, the ultimate referent being some such concrete mystical experience?

Put in this way, the thesis seems unlikely. What tells against it most of all is the lack of any attempt to evoke the concrete circumstances or the actual content of a visionary experience.[36] The allusion to initiation is managed entirely by the particular combination of images and themes employed; there is no direct mention of the idea itself. The place of what would be an account of the contents of the mystical vision is taken by excerpts from traditional material.

What we seem to have is something of a middle ground between Jonas's objective-theoretical account and the fully subjective-experiential type described above. That is, the text does mean to represent a series of experiences in which subjective and emotional elements play an important part. But on the other hand, it has no specific reference to any particular concrete events, mythical or mystical. Rather, it represents an idealized progression of subjective experiences meant to be of general applicability to a broad range of specific concrete instances.[37] One could imagine contracting a sickness which appears to keep one from fulfilling what is thought of as religious duties (e.g., Paul's "thorn in the flesh," 2 Cor 12:7). This passage in the *Acts Thom.* would encourage a person to look for ways in which the experience of sickness itself could be a revelation of God. But the passage could also be used as a kind of guide as to what one can expect as the sequence of events, and especially as the outcome, in certain kinds of visionary experiences.[38]

---

[35] Hans Jonas, "Myth and Mysticism: A Study of Objectification and Interiorization in Religious Thought," *JR* 49 (1969) 327.

[36] Such an attempt is visible, for example, in the Ophite material cited above or in the Hermetic tractate from Nag Hammadi, *Discourse on the Eighth and Ninth* (NHC 6,6).

[37] Semantically, this is a similar conception to the "concrete universal" of W. K. Wimsatt, Jr. This is a kind of meaning he ascribes to certain kinds of poetry where the "real subject of the poem [is] . . . an abstraction . . . for which there is no name and no other description than the [several] members of [a] metaphor pointing, as to the center of their pattern" (*The Verbal Icon: Studies in the Meaning of Poetry* [Lexington: University of Kentucky Press, 1954] 80).

[38] The Ophites may have tried to induce such experience, as did the Merkabah mystics according to Scholem, *Major Trends*, 49.

In this case, the text does to some extent represent a "theoretical" view, and it reflects theorizing on the part of the redactors. (This seems to be indicated by their apparent attempts to reflect on and reconcile diverse traditions with which they were familiar.) But the "theory" is not about the nature of the world but about the psychology of religious experience. And it is couched in terms that reflect as much as possible the reality of these experiences in their many dimensions, representing the concepts, the traditional themes and ideal figures, the concurrent emotional states, and the sense of participating in a cosmic drama associated with the kinds of experiences to which the passage is applicable. These elements are, again, not so much objective information as ways of drawing the reader into a certain kind of experience.[39]

In the interpretation proposed here the text is a kind of mimesis of actual experience (though expressed in terms "abstracted" from any specific experience). Thus the logic behind its particular image combinations is a substantive logic derived from the character of the real experiences to which it is applicable. Ultimately, the double presentation of the world in the banquet scenes reflects the mixed character of the world as we perceive it. It can be both an ungodly hindrance and a divine revelation. "World" as an implied category in this passage has a meaning somewhat peculiar to this work. From now on in this study this concept will be represented by a capitalized World.

A good comparison to what is said here though somewhat different in specifics is the example of the obviously "psychological" understanding of myth in the conversion speech of chapter 34. There we read: "I have lost that one (the Enemy) who darkens (σκοτίζοντα) and blinds his subjects so they don't know what they are doing, and being ashamed (αἰσχυνθέντες) of their works, they depart from them" (151.17–19). The context makes it clear that what is spoken of is the common progression of experiences in which a person does something that, under the influence of passion, appears good. However, afterwards it appears shameful, and the persons dissociate themselves ("depart") from it. A few lines later we are given an obviously mythicized version of the same sequence: "I have changed over from him whose lie is eternal, before whom darkness (σκότος) goes as a veil and shame (αἰσχύνη) creeps after" (151.22–152.3).

---

[39] It is, in the categories of Greek rhetoric, ψυχαγωγία (soul leading) and is related also to Reitzenstein's proposed "literary mystery," a kind of vicarious mystery-initiation in which the "reader is to experience [the mystery] . . . in . . . imagination" (*Mystery-Religions*, 51–52).

5.4 The Gnostic Problematic

In concluding this Chapter, it will be helpful to relate what has been said here to several other characterizations of Gnosticism in general that have been made by Hans Jonas.

First of all, it is clear that the experience of alienation from the world that Jonas sees as the cultural basis for Gnosticism[40] is reflected in the *Acts Thom.* as well. This is an experience in which one identifies subjectivity with the divine. Hence the world that is given apart from subjectivity and limiting it appears not only as hostile to the self but theologically as opposed to the true God. This way of experiencing the world is, however, in the *Acts Thom.* not proclaimed as the message of the redactors. It is, rather, their starting point. They assume, in their religious psychology, that their readers experience the world in this way, but their message consists (in chapters 1–10 at least) in outlining ways this polarization between self and world can be overcome.

This is different from what Jonas proposes as the general case with Gnosticism. He sees the typical Gnostic solution as escaping from the world into some acosmic reality.[41] Nevertheless the experience of the self-world polarization is important in our account of reading competence in the sense that the reader must whether actually, or imaginatively and vicariously, be able to enter into this experience in order to understand the problematic with which the redactors are trying to deal. This is all the more necessary given the important part played by the emotional aspects of experience portrayed in the text.

Secondly, in Jonas's view, Gnosticism as a religion is based on a mistaken "objectified" interpretation of categories which have their real reference in subjective experience.[42] In actuality the character of subjective consciousness and that of the objective world experienced by consciousness are mutually determining realities in a given cultural milieu. The Gnostic who imagines she or he can escape this world has mistakenly applied the logic of objective entities to these two categories and so imagined that they are potentially separable and hence that one can escape from one into the other. In addition, of course, those Gnostics

---

[40] Jonas, *Gnostic Religion*, 326–31.

[41] Ibid., 327, 332–33. I suspect that further studies of other Gnostic texts concentrating, like the present one, on imaginative logic might well modify this common "world-hating" interpretation of Gnosticism. The analysis of the Ophite account given above suggests this. One could also think of an assessment of the double (fallen and divine) character of Sophia along lines presented here.

[42] Hans Jonas, *Gnosis und spätantiker Geist*, vol. 2. 1: *Von der Mythologie zur mystischen Philosophie* (Göttingen: Vandenhoeck & Ruprecht, 1954) 1–23.

who imagined acosmic existence as a concrete possibility of human experience have involved themselves in the contradiction of a completely unworldly state that is yet concrete and so worldly.

In regard to this assessment of Gnosticism in general one can say first of all that the *Acts Thom.* passage analyzed here does not present one making an escape into an acosmic reality, but undergoing some kind of transformation in which the character of the world changes. This in turn implies, secondly, that the logic followed in this text is in fact the one Jonas assumes to be in accord with the real referents of the categories used.[43] Far from treating the categories of subjective consciousness and the objective world as completely objective and hence separable entities, the text emphatically cuts across a logic of discrete objects (it is "inconsistent" from this point of view) and adheres to a logic derived from subjective experience. From the latter point of view the character of the objective world and the character of subjective consciousness are mutually determinative. Taking this latter point of view the redactors clearly assume the inseparability and mutually determinative character of the two categories and portray a change in consciousness as involving a change in the world this consciousness perceives.

We may pursue these ideas further in that Jonas holds that the Gnostic attempt to bring eschatological reality within the realm of concrete experience not only involves an internal contradiction, but robs this reality of its transcendent character by making it subject to conscious control. That is, he sees an opposition between what is transcendent and what is capable of being experienced concretely.

Several things can be said here in relation to the *Acts Thom.* First, if the interpretation above is correct, it is not certain that the redactors believe that eschatological reality in its fullness is capable of being concretely experienced. Thomas's apparently direct experience of the shekinah may be only a kind of limit case, an ideal concretely realizable only in more-or-less limited ways. Concrete, limited experiences would then be regarded as participating in the events Thomas undergoes as an ideal, "mythical" figure in a cosmic dimension.

Secondly, the redactors work with a notion of transcendence and its relation to concrete experience different from that of Jonas, and their view deserves some consideration. Their view shows partly in their use of the "Mother of Wisdom," a figure clearly related to the world and yet also a transcendent being equal to the "Father of Truth." (The world as bride is among those who sing their praises.) It also shows in

---

[43] Ibid.

their view that the divine power which consciousness has is at the same time inherent in it and a divine gift. There is some respect in which the influx of transcendence into the world is a product of consciousness, hence partly at its disposal.

Finally, it seems likely that the redactors' use of language reflects their particular attitude to objectivity, subjective consciousness, and transcendence. They use concrete (worldly) images but in combinations that break down their character as bearers of objective information and emphasize what they convey about subjective experience.[44] And the way in which these subjective experiences participate in transcendence is also conveyed by locating them in a cosmic dimension. That is, they probably evoke in the reader some experience of what the redactors regard as transcendent.

---

[44] One might profitably consider here the analysis of language usage in certain kinds of modern poetry made by Philip Ellis Wheelwright (*Metaphor and Reality* [Bloomington: Indiana University Press, 1962] 78–86) who states that they emphasize what he calls the "diaphoric," nonreferential aspect of metaphor.

6

THE CHRIST PRAYER
AND THE EVENTS PRECEDING IT

This Chapter completes the exegetical work undertaken in this study with an interpretation of the Christ prayer and the narrative events preceding it. Just as the wedding hymn was shown to be a climax to the narrative thread giving a positive evaluation to the World, the Christ prayer is shown to be a climax of the narrative thread evaluating the World negatively as a demonic realm to which Thomas comes as a divine savior and liberator. In the course of this discussion all the major techniques and ideas of the editors pertinent to this section of the text come to light, and the major problems and puzzles left unsolved in earlier discussions are taken up again and given solutions.

6.1 The Events Following the Hymn

The narrative recounting the events that follow the wedding hymn incorporates material from the story of the flutist and the story of the wine pourer. Since the redactors have woven this material into a complex series of interrelated events, it will be best to treat the material up to and including the final conversion of some of the guests as a single unit. (Redactional additions and alterations are given in italics.)

> *And when he had sung and completed this song, all who were present were looking at him. And he was silent.* They were looking at his changed appearance, but what was said by him they did not understand, since he was Hebrew and what was said by him was in Hebrew.
>
> *The flutist alone heard it all because she was a Hebrew by race.* And moving away from him she fluted for the others, but she often looked away and looked at him. Because she loved him very much, *as a man of her own race. And* he was in his appearance more beautiful than all who were there.
>
> And when the flutist had completed everything and fluted, *she sat opposite him, looking and gazing at him.*
>
> *But he was looking at no one, nor did he pay attention to anyone, but having his eyes on the earth he paid attention, waiting for when he would depart from there.*
>
> And *that* wine pourer *who had slapped him* went down to the spring to draw water. *There happened to be there a lion, and he killed him and left him lying in the area, having torn apart his members* (τὰ μέλη). *And dogs right away took his members, among whom one black* (μέλας) dog took hold of his right hand in his mouth and brought it into the banqueting area.
>
> And seeing this, all were upset, asking who it was among them who had left. And when it became clear that the hand was that of the wine pourer who had struck the apostle, the flutist broke her flutes and threw them down, and went and sat at the apostle's feet saying, *"This man is either a god or an apostle of God. Because I heard him saying to the wine pourer in Hebrew, 'I will soon see the hand that struck me being dragged by dogs.' This is what you have seen. Just as he said, so it happened."*
>
> And *some* believed *her,* others did not. (111.1–113.7)

Aside from a few particulars, the separating of traditional from redactional elements in this section either has been treated earlier or obviously belongs to a stage at which the different originally independent units are being woven together.

The events recounted in this section represent something of a change from the state of affairs at the banquet prior to the hymn. Thomas is now shown exerting his influence. The guests are impressed by his hymn, the flutist even more so. His curse is carried out, and the visible evidence of this leads the flutist and some of the guests to conversion and recognition of Thomas's divine status.

In relation to the two opposing strands of redactional interpretation, it is clear that as a story of divine wonders and conversion this section has to do with that strand evaluating the apostle positively, and giving a negative value to the World. The World's negative value is especially evident as an implication in the story of how the servant is punished and killed by the lion.

The general story line in this passage is complicated by a number of factors. Most obvious, as a general feature of the narrative here, is the gradualness with which Thomas's divine status comes to be felt and recognized. The guests are at first struck by the hymn (111.1–2) and Thomas's changed appearance (111.2–3), but they do not understand the content of the hymn. They are initially "shaken" by the sight of the hand-carrying dog who signals the carrying out of the curse, but they do not realize the significance of this until the flutist translates Thomas's curse for them—then some of them are finally won over.

The flutist understands the hymn right away (she already had some recognition of Thomas in 108.1–5), but the redactors also represent her conversion as gradual. This is done partly by the device of picturing her moving progressively closer to Thomas: "After she had . . . fluted, she sat down opposite (ἄντικρυς) him" (111.9–10). Then seeing the fulfillment of the curse "she broke her flutes . . . and came and sat at his feet" (113.1–2). In the redactors' story we see her then initially attracted to Thomas, drawn even more by his song, and finally won over to complete recognition by seeing the evidence of the curse's fulfillment.

It is the redactors who represent both the hymn and the curse as having been spoken in Hebrew. They also make the flutist into a mediating figure, translating and bringing the guests to a recognition of Thomas. This is most likely the significance of the paralleling of the flutist's fluting with Thomas's singing:

When he had sung and completed this song. . . . (111.1)

When she had completed everything and had fluted. . . . (111.9–10)[1]

---

[1] This mediating function of the flutist is perhaps also suggested in that "she fluted for the others, but she often looked away at him" (111.6–7).

The flutist's relation to Thomas is also, however, emphatically paralleled to that of the guests via the "looking" motif prominent throughout this section. This is related to the earlier presentation of the flutist as both Thomas's kin and part of the worldly banquet. Many of these features will be taken up and reinterpreted by the Christ prayer. Several other features of this section will also be given special attention in that prayer, one of which it will be useful to mention now: the opening lines of this section seem to combine a number of allusions to traditional motifs. Thomas's "transformed appearance" (111.3) is part of an initiation schema. But it now appears also to be part of the process by which Thomas's divine status is revealed to the guests. It serves as something of an epiphany.[2] The following statements that the guests did not understand the hymn but the flutist did resemble, in fact, a theme found elsewhere in the *Acts Thom.* as well as in the New Testament: an epiphany which is fully perceived only by one person, and partially perceived by many others (*Acts Thom.* 142.9–11; Acts 9:7; 22:9). Finally, the "looking" motif following the ῦmn resembles a typical ending of an ἀρετή episode,[3] a miracle or wonder achieved by a figure of divine or semi-divine stature. That is, we have here in condensed form a compositional technique observed elsewhere: the act of wording a passage so that it recalls one or several traditional themes. Here the effect would be to overlay two motifs, the hymn as an ἀρετή and the transformation of Thomas's appearance as an epiphany.[4]

These preliminary observations will be supported by later analysis of this passage based on the Christ prayer's interpretation of it.

The one puzzling element in this narrative section that seems unrelated to any of the above ideas is the statement that Thomas "looked at no one, nor paid attention to anyone, but having his eyes on the earth, paid attention waiting for when he would depart from there" (111.11–112.1).

In the light of what we now know about the allegorical meaning of the Andrapolitan World, it seems clear that there is a play on words here. "To return" (ἀναλύειν) is a common metaphor referring to death as "departing" this world. The metaphor is based on a ship's

---

[2] A parallel here would be the passage in Apuleius, *The Golden Ass* (11.24) where Lucius, after being initiated, is shown to the crowds in glorious apparel.

[3] See Rudolf Bultmann, *History of the Synoptic Tradition* (New York: Harper & Row, 1963) 225–26.

[4] This overlaying is probably visible structurally in the duplication involved in the first two lines following the hymn: "When he had . . . completed this song, they were looking at him . . . and they were looking at his changed appearance" (111.1–3).

departure. It means literally "release," and this is a meaning that will come into play later. Thomas "has his eyes on the earth (γῆν: this world)" waiting till he will be able "to depart from there" (i.e., from the earth, the Andrapolitan World he so reluctantly entered).

This line seems a throwback to the earlier theme of the world-estranged ascetic who would like to have nothing to do with the world and wants out. This is a bit of a puzzle given the interpretation above that Thomas has undergone a transforming initiation that has brought him to see the divine presence in the World.

6.2 The King's Request

And when the king heard these things he came forward and said to the apostle, "Get up and come with me and pray over *my daughter. I have her as an only daughter and today I am giving her away.*"
    But the apostle did not want to set off with (συναπελθεῖν) him, because the Lord had not yet been revealed to him there. But the king led him unwilling into the bridal chamber, so that he might pray over them. (113.7–114.3)

This passage is really the beginning of a new series of episodes having to do with the conversion of the newlywed couple. After Thomas's prayer in the bedroom Jesus appears there in his likeness and converts the couple, who then give the conversion speeches analyzed in Chapter 1.

The request that Thomas come into the bedroom serves as an opening for this new conversion story.[5] But the present form of the opening does not appear to be the original one in all respects. The present form speaks only of the king's asking Thomas to come into the bedroom and of his leading him there forcibly. The narrative following Thomas's prayer, however, speaks as though Thomas came in with a whole group of attendants. Immediately after the prayer the "king asked the attendants to come out of the bedroom" and later the bridegroom, upon seeing Jesus who he thinks is Thomas, says, "Didn't you leave before all the others?" As we shall see shortly, there are good reasons to

---

[5] It may actually be the continuation of the story begun at the invitation scene, though without the intervening scenes from the anointing scene through the guests' conversion. The abrupt introduction of the king here is evidence of new reworking. It is probably significant that the king's statement "I have her as an only daughter and today I am giving her away" is verbally almost identical to a line in the invitation scene (105.2–3). This may be a redactional technique to indicate the taking up of a story previously left off. See 103.8–104.2; 108.4–5; 111.5–6; and 125.1–8.

suppose that the explanation given for Thomas's reluctance to go and also for the king's forcibly leading him into the bedroom are redactional touches in the story. We may suppose that there was a different original which had the king's prayer request but spoke simply of Thomas's entering the bedroom with the attendants (probably with no reluctance). The present text has left out the reference to the attendants in order to put the entire emphasis of the passage on the elements they have added: Thomas's reluctance and the reason for it, and the king's leading him forcibly into the bedroom.

These elements are certainly, on the face of it, peculiar. The reason given for Thomas's reluctance is especially strange. They will come up once more in connection with certain ideas from the Christ prayer. Here we can simply list the essentials of what has been, or will be, spelled out in detail elsewhere:

1) Thomas's reluctance to enter the bedroom is an allegorical representation of his (ascetic) unwillingness to be involved in the World (already represented by the image of a bride's bedroom in the wedding hymn, 109.14–110.3). It is thus parallel to his refusal to participate in the banquet and to his initial refusal to go to India.[6]

2) His reason for not wanting to go, that the "Lord had not yet been revealed to him there," corresponds to the implied problem he originally had at the wedding banquet: he could not yet (before his initiation) see the divine presence in the World.[7]

3) The king's forcing him to go is parallel to his being sold by Jesus (forcing him into India) and the servant's slap (forcing him into contact with the World). Like the line about waiting to depart from the earth, these lines call up once more Thomas's negative attitude to the World, and here also we seem to be back at a stage before his initiation. The redactors want to keep this train of thought before the reader's mind even while the predominant trend in the narrative preceding this is to present the very different theme of Thomas's making his influence felt.

The final piece in our study, the prayer to Christ, follows a conventional scheme:[8] the recitation of the divine reputation (qualities, deeds)

---

[6] Catchwords help draw attention to the latter parallel: οὐκ ἐβούλετο ἀπελθεῖν in 100.5 corresponds to οὐκ ἐβούλετο συναπελθεῖν αὐτῷ here.

[7] This is also the reference of μὴ δύνασθαι μήτε χωρεῖν of 100.5–6.

[8] The same scheme is found in some of the prayers from the magical papyri found in Karl Preisendanz and Albert Henrichs, eds., *Papyri Graecae Magicae: Die Griechischen Zauberpapyri* (2 vols.; Stuttgart: Teubner, 1973–74) 1. 77–78, 161–65; 2. 11–12, 16–17, 31–32, and 148–49.

followed by a request for help cast here in very general terms (115.9–10): βοηθοῦντα, συμβαλλόμενα, and συμφέροντα.

This piece has not drawn much critical comment, and presumably this is due to its appearance as a string of fairly conventional phrases thrown together somewhat loosely. The last section is an exception to this. It gets special attention in Bornkamm's study because it is a very clear, short summary of the so-called Gnostic redeemer myth.[9]

Here we shall treat only the recitation section of the hymn, and it will be shown that a cycle of the redactors' presentation comes to a close with it. For purposes of analysis, it is divided into 3 sections: 114.5–10; 114.10–17; and 114.17–115.8. Reasons for this division will be given as we proceed.

6.3 The Metaphors of *Acts Thom.* 114.5–10

> *My Lord and my God,*
> *The fellow traveler of his servants,*
> *The leader on the way and guide of those who believe in him,*
> *The refuge and rest of the oppressed,*
> *The hope of the poor and redeemer of the captives,*
> *The healer of souls lying in sickness,*
> *And savior of all creation,*
> *The one who gives life to the cosmos,*
> *And empowers the souls. . . .*   (114.5–10)

Leaving out the first line, the organization of the section is of a kind we have observed in other speeches. Several units are visible: the first lines center around the travel metaphor, the last four are arranged according to a chiastic parallelism[10] that makes them appear to be a

---

[9] Bornkamm, *Mythos*, 8–16. This myth recounts the descent of a heavenly savior and his reascent with those he has liberated. Neither the debate about the origins of this myth nor how widespread it was need enter our discussion here. It will suffice to notice that this mythic scheme is used as an outline for epithets praising Christ and his deeds in the hymns in *Acts Thom.* 195.19–196.12 and 265.3–7. The Hymn of the Pearl, chaps. 108–13, follows a like schema, and thus it can be presumed to have been familiar to the redactors of the *Acts Thom.* as a common theme. On the other hand, Bornkamm's attempt (*Mythos*, 8–12) to portray this scheme as the context in which the majority of metaphors and mythologoumena in the *Acts Thom.* are to be understood almost certainly claims too much for it. This should be evident from the interpretation of chaps. 1–10 given here in which several other themes play equal or more important roles.

[10] The seventh and eighth lines here are parallel, while the fifth and ninth deal with helping souls. The parallelism between "healing" and "empowering" will appear more clearly below at the end of this section (6.3).

unit, and there is a middle section concerned with help for those in trouble. But there is also a blurring of the boundaries. "Refuge" (καταφυγή) could be considered a continuation of the theme of help for travelers, but "refuge of the oppressed" also belongs with the next lines about help in trouble. The same can be said about the "healer of souls lying in sickness." Coming immediately after "redeemer of the captives," it seems to continue the theme of help in troubled situations, but it is also clearly related to the following section (from which the explicit mention of trouble has disappeared) by the chiastic construction. These preliminary, formal observations will be supported by the substantive analysis in what follows.

Earthly Life as a Dangerous Journey

To begin with the first lines, comparison to several other passages in the *Acts Thom.* suggests that there is a conventional association in this work between the theme of the journey and that of difficulty and danger.

Three passages can be cited here, in each of which we have the same juxtaposition of the guide-for-travelers motif with that of rescue from danger:

> Believe in . . . Jesus . . . so that your hope may be in him . . . so that he will be a fellow traveler for you in this land of error and will be a harbor for you on this troubled sea. (155.11–15)

> Jesus . . . will turn aside the anger of Charisius . . . and will become for you a fellow traveler on this frightful highway and will himself guide you to his kingdom. (216.4–8)

> Do not be afraid . . . Jesus will not leave you. . . . Look at the light because the Lord will not leave those who love him to walk in darkness. (229.9–10)

> Look upon the fellow traveler of his own servants, because he is for them a fellow fighter in dangerous situations. (229.15–18)

This association of the guide-for-travelers motif with danger can be supported and made more specific by bringing into our analysis a general stylistic feature of the long monologues in the *Acts Thom.*: the convention whereby the speech or prayer is unified by using the same motifs at the beginning and at the end of the piece.

At the end of this hymn we have the Gnostic redeemer myth presented partly under the metaphor of Jesus' leading out prisoners he has freed and showing them the way leading to the heights. Given the fact that the competent reader approaches the text looking for motifs connecting the beginning and end of prayers, the similarity between the idea of freeing prisoners implied in the last section and the phrase "redeemer of the captives" (λυτρωτὴς τῶν αἰχμαλώτων) in the first is clearly significant. The attentive reader looking for such connections would probably also notice the double repetition of cognates at the beginning (114.6) and end (115.7–8): ὁδηγός and ἄνοδος ἀνάγουσα ("leader on the way" and "way leading up").

The suggestion of these comparisons is that the opening metaphors of Jesus as guide for the traveler have to do with Thomas's journey in the World of Andrapolis, which has been presented as hostile and foreign to him. That is, we have in the last section of this prayer the climax of the negative interpretation of the World of the wedding banquet: here it is "Hades . . . the stronghold of darkness."

This suggestion is confirmed by part of Thomas's farewell speech later in the *Acts Thom.* (264.18–266.6) which shows striking similarities to the Christ prayer both in general thought and specific motifs:

Farewell Speech	*Christ Prayer*
Companion and ally	Fellow traveler
Hope of the weak	Hope of the poor
Refuge and lodging	Refuge and rest
for the weary . . .	of the oppressed
for those traveling through	Voice heard by
the lands of the archons	the archons, shaking
	all their powers
The unpaid healer	Healer of souls
The one who went down to Hades	Reaching to Hades
with great power	Unfallen power destroying
	the Enemy
The sight of whom the rulers	Shaking the rulers' powers
of death could not bear	
And you ascended with	You showed the way up
great glory	The one leading to the heights
And gathering all who	
took refuge in you,	
you prepared a way.	
And all those whom you redeemed	
traveled in your footsteps.	
(264.18–265.7)	

The farewell speech ends with a prayer:

Be for them a guide in the land of error.	Leader on the way
Be a healer for them in the land of sickness.	Healer of souls lying in sickness
Be for them a rest in the land of the weary. (266.1 – 3)	Rest for the oppressed

Reading this piece in the light of the general use of catchwords and recurrent motifs, it seems clear that the people traveling in this "land of error-sickness-burdens" are likened to those who are "traveling through the lands of the archons," who are the same "archons of death" in "Hades" to which Christ descends to "prepare a road" for those to whom he is a "companion and cofighter, a comforter dwelling in the midst."

What all this indicates is a treatment, somewhat familiar in the milieu of the *Acts Thom.*, of life in the world as a dangerous journey in the realm of hostile forces. This of course is very similar to the initiation journey through the threatening gates of the archons.

Other Metaphors for Earthly Life

Note that "poor" (πενήτων—occuring here in "hope of the poor") is also a conventional characterization of earthly life in the *Acts Thom.* It is often used in relation to Jesus' earthly state in the incarnation.[11] Thomas also says of his earthly sojourn, "I became poor and needy and a foreigner and a slave and despised and a prisoner" (151.9 – 10). Most explicitly he says of Jesus, "You are the one who brought me into the poverty of the world (πενίαν τοῦ κόσμου, 251.16)."

Similar observations can be made about "healer of souls lying in sickness." It is more obvious here than in the other cases that the metaphor is concerned with the soul's plight as such rather than, say, with a particular social situation. Sickness as a specific reference to earthly life is an idea implied in the last three parallel lines of the farewell speech just quoted (266.1 – 4): "Guide in the land of error (χώρᾳ πλάνης) . . . healer in the land of sickness (νοσήματος) . . . rest

---

[11] Note the statements, "He fooled us (demons) by his . . . poverty and need . . ." (162.18 – 19) and "Jesus, the one who is needy, and saving as one without need . . ." (164.6 – 7).

in the land of the weary (καμνόντων)." The fact that this is Thomas's farewell prayer for those he is leaving behind in this world makes it clear that error, sickness, and weariness are being spoken of as characteristics of earthly life.[12]

The main support for this interpretation, however, comes from the connection of this phrase and its chiastic parallel, "empowering souls," with the intial sending scene.

To speak first of all of the indications of this connection, they consist in a combination of identical motifs. Thomas's refusal (101.5–6) in the sending scene reads: λέγων μὴ δύνασθαι μήτε χωρεῖν διὰ τὴν ἀσθένειαν τῆς σαρκός. We saw earlier how this sentence contains several double meanings. One could read, "He could not travel because of a weakness of the flesh (sickness)," or it could be read, "He did not have the (mental) power, could not comprehend because of the weakness of the flesh (human limitation)."

In the Christ prayer passage we have a like combination: an explicit reference to sickness and a reference to his "empowering" (ἐνδυναμῶν—a remedy for the previously expressed μὴ δύνασθαι). The latter word also implies, of course, a previous "weakness" on the part of souls. Finally, as we have seen, there is a likelihood that the entire passage in the Christ prayer has to do with a freeing from the limitations of earthly life, matching precisely the implication of "weakness of the flesh." The implication is that "healing" and "empowering" souls speaks of the same matter as the previous metaphor, "hope of the poor." That is, all three images have to do with the act of freeing from the limitations imposed on the soul by earthly existence.

The remaining two lines of this section, "Savior of all creation" and "enlivening the cosmos," are concerned with a different theme: the saving of the World rather than salvation from the World. These lines weave into the first section of the prayer a theme closely related to later sections.

Finally, it should be clear from this analysis how this section is composed. The individual motifs are all conventional, and even their formulation shows very little originality. There is little apparent substantive unity to the section apart from its relation to trains of thought and motifs presented in the narrative context, which shows that as a unit it is entirely a redactional composition.

In these respects it is much more characteristic of the long monologues recorded in the *Acts Thom.* in general than is the wedding hymn which incorporates much larger blocks of traditional material.

---

[12] Elsewhere healing from sickness is a metaphor for conversion; see 208.19.

6.4 The Initiation Schema

With the link between the Christ prayer and the sending scene, we have come to the final element in what can now be shown to be a very important group of three parallel progressions in the text: elements in the sending scenes, in the banquet scene and wedding hymn, and in the Christ prayer with the immmediately preceding scene. All repeat a common schema dealing with the idea of initiation. This theme has already been treated extensively in relation to the banquet scenes. Because this whole group of parallels provides an important formal paradigm for the interpretation of the rest of the Christ prayer, it will be useful to treat this matter at some length here.

Since most of the individual elements of these parallels have already been treated and since evidence for the connections involved lies mainly in the coincidence of a number of features, it will be best to simply outline the schema (in five steps) and the elements related to each step of the schema in each of the three progressions. The scenes will be numbered: 1) the sending scene; 2) the banquet scenes; and 3) the Christ prayer and the immediately preceding narrative.

A) Thomas is reluctant to involve himself in the world:

1) He did not want to set off (ἀπελθεῖν) to India. (100.5)
2) As they were eating . . . the apostle tasted nothing. (106.5 – 6) The flutist fluted . . . the apostle was looking away at the ground. (108.3 – 6)
3) He did not want to set off with (συναπελθεῖν) the king into the bridal chamber. (113.10 – 114.1)

B) The reason for the reluctance is Thomas's limited state:

1) He was not able nor did he comprehend (μὴ δύνασθαι μήτε χωρεῖν) because of the weakness of the flesh. (100.5 – 6)
2) This step in the schema is unstated but implied in the train of thought critical of Thomas's ascetic attitude representing him as being in need of initiation.
3) Healer of souls lying in sickness . . . empowering (ἐνδυναμῶν) souls. (114.8 – 10)

C) Thomas's problem is being unable to see the divine presence in the World:

1) He was not able nor did he understand because of the weakness of the flesh. (100.5 – 6) [13]

---

[13] In the first scene, this element is not directly evident. But the language implies that

2) This step is implied in the content of the hymn, a praise of the shek-inah, and the contrast this represents to Thomas's previous attitude.
3) He did not want to set off (into the bedroom) because the Lord had not yet been revealed to him there. (114.1–2)

D) Thomas is forced into contact with the World:

1) Jesus sells him into slavery (101.3–102.9).
2) Thomas goes to the banquet under coercion from the invitation-threat (105.7–8), and the servant's slap forcibly initiates him (108.6–7).
3) The king led him away unwilling into the bedroom. (114.2–3)

E) The result of the forcing is a change in Thomas's point of view:

1) After the dream-vision of the selling, Thomas goes to India willingly: "Thy will be done." (102.10–103.1)
2) The content of the wedding hymn shows a radical change in his atti-tude to the World. Afterward he also has a changed appearance (111.2–3).
3) Before the Christ prayer the "Lord was not yet revealed to him there" (114.1–2), but in the course of it, he comes to confess, "You are Lord, in all things, showing in the energies of all." (114.15–17)

The elements in each case cited above are the result of redactional work, and in two cases especially, Thomas's initial refusal of his mis-sion (110.5–8) and his refusal of the king's request (114.10), they draw attention to themselves as being peculiar in their wording and in their lack of appropriateness to their context. That is, we can now see that, besides altering traditional material to draw parallels between adja-cent episodes, the redactors also work to present a parallel line of thought in three groups of elements that are larger and farther apart. This aspect of their compositional principles probably explains the pecu-liarity that the motif of Thomas's inability to see the divine presence in the World occurs also after he has apparently been initiated. Here the presentation of parallel themes actually produces inconsistency in the sequential logic of the narrative.

In the light of the parallels mentioned, it is even more clear now that the journey implied in the first lines of the Christ prayer is an ini-tiatory journey. The danger of the journey implied here relates to the foreignness of India in the sending scene and the hostility Thomas

---

there is some difficult mystery Thomas cannot comprehend, a suggestion that needs some clarification as to the subject of the mystery. The other parallels between the scenes suggest that it be clarified in precisely this way.

encounters at the banquet. The sending scene also implies a correlation between traveling and understanding: one negotiates the dangerous journey in the World by penetrating through its alienness and seeing the divine presence there.[14]

On the other hand, the statement in the sending scene that Thomas "cannot understand because of the weakness of the flesh" implies that his inability to see the divine presence in the World is partly a result of limitation by that same World (flesh).[15]

The corresponding metaphors of sickness and weakness in the latter part of the first section of the Christ prayer also imply intrinsic limitations rather than external difficulties. In this context we should probably also understand "captives," "poor," and "oppressed" in a similar sense as limitations on understanding due to being in the World.

Initiation means not only passing through difficult barriers to get into the World (as shekinah), but also being able to break out of the World (as limitation). Here there is probably a relation between the earlier image of Thomas's waiting "to depart" (ἀναλύειν) from the earth and the metaphor in the Christ prayer, "redeemer (or: releaser) of the captives" (λυτρωτὴς τῶν αἰχμαλώτων).[16]

We can now see that the gradual sliding from one theme to another is a prominent stylistic feature of this section of the prayer that also applies to the substance. The initial travel metaphor which has to do with the soul's difficult journey through the World undergoes a gradual transition to the later metaphors (particularly "sickness") referring to the soul's difficulties involved in being in a body. (It is becoming more obvious that Thomas represents not simply a person, but specifically a "soul," over against a "body.")

This literary merging of themes, in turn, implies that the redactors' imaginative vision lumps together the soul-world and soul-body polarity in a single problematic. The soul's weakness, the limitation of its ability to understand because it is in a body, is seen as in some way the same problem as that of the external world's impenetrability to understanding, the difficulty it presents to the mind looking for the divine in it.

---

[14] The double meaning of χωρεῖν therefore actually implies an overlaying of the two meanings involved, "to travel" and "to understand."

[15] See Wis 9:14: "The reasonings of mortals are unsure . . . a perishable body presses down the soul, this tent of clay weighs down the teeming mind."

[16] The Ophite initiatory "journey" also implies a double process. One both becomes free of ("released from") the power of the rulers, and also becomes allied with them.

This continues the pattern of presenting different images representing many different facets of "world" as traditionally conceived. It is also evident that this particular linking of the soul-body problem with the soul-world problem can only be made coherent on the assumption that these clashes on a literal level are to be resolved by attending to the experiential commonality that links the categories from a certain perspective. On a conceptual level the body impeding the functioning of the mind can seem to be a different problem than that of the external world's meaninglessness. But from the point of view of the kind of consciousness to which this text is addressed, the two are experientially similar.

6.5 The Prayer and the Narrative

For reasons that will become clear as we proceed, it will be best to treat the two remaining sections of the Christ prayer together (114.10–17 and 114.17–115.8) making at first some preliminary remarks about each of the two separately.

The first of these sections reads:

> *You know what is to come,*
> *And through us you bring it to completion,*
> You, Lord, the one revealing hidden mysteries
> And making manifest secret sayings.
> You are, Lord, the planter of the good tree,
> And through your hands all good works are brought to birth.
> You are, Lord, the one in all things,
> And coming to completion through all,
> And lying on all your works,
> And made manifest in the energies of all. (114.10–17)

This section is set off stylistically from what precedes and what follows by the introductory formula of each of its lines ("You . . ."), and this is accompanied also by a change in the themes around which it and the other sections are focused. "You know the future" is a clear break from "empowering souls." Likewise, "Son of compassion" on the surface is a clear break from the idea of Christ as manifest in the elements of the World, "showing in the energies of all."

Several of the formulas in this section closely resemble formulas used of Wisdom in the Wisdom of Solomon:

Acts Thom.	*Wisdom of Solomon*
You know what is to come.	You know what is ancient and show what is to come.
. . . making manifest secret sayings. (114.10–13)	You understand verses and sayings and solve riddles. (8:8)
. . . revealing hidden mysteries. (12)	You teach me wisdom regarding those things that are hidden. (7:21)
	She [Wisdom] is an initiate in the knowledge of God. (8:4)
The one in all things and coming to completion through all. (15)	She lives and goes about through everything. (7:24)
. . . lying on all your works. (16)	Wisdom . . . who made all things. (7:21)

In view of the close resemblances and the connection already established between the wedding hymn and the traditions of the Wisdom of Solomon, it seems likely that the redactors are consciously drawing here on the wisdom tradition. (This point is not essential to the following argument, though my ultimate interpretation of this passage tends to support this connection with Wisdom on other grounds.)

The line about the "planter (or: grower) of the good tree" is somewhat enigmatic. But some clarifying suggestions can be gleaned from the context. The lines preceding ("Revealing hidden mysteries, making manifest secret sayings . . .") and following ("Lord . . . made manifest in the energies of all") this line speak of something hidden becoming manifest. The line itself reads, "Planter of the good tree, by your hands all good works are brought to birth." The context suggests that we take the metaphors in this line in a sense similar to those in Matt 7:16–20: "A good tree cannot bear bad fruit . . . By their fruits (actions) you will know them." The good tree is something relatively unmanifest which manifests itself in good works which are its produce.

This would make the entire section unified around a single theme, which is to be expected on stylistic grounds. The first line of the section, "You know what is to come, and through us you bring it to completion," taken by itself is not so clearly connected with this theme. But it, too, actually does deal with the manifestation (through concrete fulfillment) of what is initially unknown to any except Christ. Stylistic considerations indicate that the parallelism should be taken as significant.

This latter line also happens to be the one in this section with the most obvious narrative correlate: Thomas's curse is in fact a prediction of the future which is later "brought to completion" by creatures acting as divine agents.

This coincidence seems to be related to a third feature of the text. According to the redactors' narrative presentation, the curse and its fulfillment are the major factors in making manifest Thomas's previously unrecognized divine power and status.

Finally, the last line of this section begins, "You are, Lord, the one who is in all things" (114.15). We saw earlier that the line preceding the prayer ("He did not want to set off with him because the Lord had not yet been revealed to him there," 113.10–114.2) is an allusion to the doubting-Thomas story of John 20:24–29. And we know that the statement that the "Lord had not yet been revealed to him there" refers to Thomas's inability to see the divine presence in the World. Given this, it is clear that the last line of the section, quoted above, represents Thomas's difficulty (doubting) as having been solved. He now has come to see the divine presence in the World. It has already been noted how this reading of the passage fits the initiation schema. And there is some support for this interpretation in the opening formulas of the lines in this section as well. There is a progression from σύ . . . (114.10), to σὺ εἶ . . . (114.11), to σὺ εἶ κύριε . . . (114.15). The last formula sounds like a confessional formula, and the progression leading up to it makes it sound like a climax.

The final section of the prayer which concerns us reads:[17]

> *Jesus Christ, Son of the Compassion and Perfect Savior,*
> *Christ, Son of the living God,*
> *Unfallen Power, the one destroying the Enemy,*
> *And Voice heard by the rulers, shaking all their powers,*
> *Messenger sent from the heights and reaching to Hades,*
> *Who, opening the doors, led up from there those shut up for long ages*
>   *in the prison of darkness,*
> *And showed them the way up leading to the heights.* (114.17–115.8)

---

[17] The final lines (115.8–10) are a plea for help, cast in very general terms, and they do not seem to carry forward any of the specific themes of the earlier sections.

This section is made up, again, of short phrases and statements of traditional motifs. It is clear, even without much analysis, that the summary of the Gnostic redeemer myth (115.4–8) is the principal organizing factor of the piece. That is, the description of Christ's divine origin (115.1) is meant to be read as parallel to "Messenger sent from the heights" (115.4), and the statement about destroying the Enemy (115.1–2) is meant as parallel to "reaching to Hades . . . opening the doors."

The general relation of this mythic theme to the narrative is fairly obvious. The redactors mean to present the World in both a positive and a negative light. We know, too, that the journey of Thomas in the narrative is a journey into the World. It seems clear that just as the shekinah and related images in the wedding hymn form the climax of the positive presentation of World, so Hades and the prison of darkness form the climax of its negative presentation. In this light the "foreigner" motif takes on its conventional meaning of otherworldly, that is, heavenly. Hence the Hebrew Thomas coming from Jerusalem can be said to be a "messenger sent from the heights." Likewise the saving mission of this redeemer is easily seen as a mythicized version of the narrative as a conversion story, a compositional device to be seen elsewhere in the *Acts Thom.* (The fact that a reascent of the heavenly redeemer is not explicitly mentioned here may be a deliberate mirroring of the fact that there is no reascent of Thomas represented in the narrative.)

At this point two more specific relationships between lines in this section and the narrative can be noted. The first involves "Unfallen Power, the one destroying the Enemy." A connection of this line with the event of the lion's killing the servant is suggested by the combination of two motif associations: (1) the conventional association of the lion with strength ($\delta\acute{\upsilon}\nu\alpha\mu\iota\varsigma$) and (2) the fact that the servant represents the climax of the World's hostility to Thomas. Given that we are dealing here with a negative, demonic interpretation of the World, this makes him a fit representative of the mythic "Enemy." Secondly, the parallel of "Power . . . destroying" and "Voice . . . shaking (the) powers" suggests an exercise of power through the Voice. And this in turn recalls the fact that it was Thomas's exercise of divine power through his curse ("voice") that eventually converted ("liberated") the flutist and the guests. So we seem to have a reference in this section, too, to Thomas's curse and its fulfillment.

These two examples are mutually supportive, and this also makes up for the fact that there are no catchword connections to draw attention to the motif recurrences. Finally, two peculiar word uses can be mentioned here. "Unfallen Power" is a bit peculiar in that one says "unfallen" only where fallen-unfallen is an issue. It is not at all clear as yet why one would bring up this issue in this context. On the other hand, the following line speaks of "shaking the powers" (ἐξουσίαι) of the "rulers" (ἄρχοντες). The "rulers" in the context are clearly evil beings. In the light of the fact that both ἄρχοντες and ἐξουσίαι are elsewhere names for angelic or demonic classes of beings,[18] it seems likely that there is an intended contrast here between an "unfallen power" and the fallen ἄρχοντες and ἐξουσίαι.

Given these general relationships between prayer and narrative, we can begin to build toward a more substantive interpretation.

6.6 Making the Divine Present in the World

First, let us look at two lines with a similar thought pattern:

You know what is to come and you bring it to completion through us. (114.10–11)

You are, Lord, the planter of the good tree, and by your hands all good works are brought to birth. (114.13–14)

The first line, as mentioned earlier, is a fairly clear reference to the curse and its fulfillment, here interpreted as an example of the fact that Christ-Wisdom (repesented by Thomas) knows the future and also brings it about through created agents (the lion and the dog of the story).

The second line quoted presents a similar train of thought. Christ is responsible for the beginning (planting) of a process as well as for the final completion, and he uses intermediary agents for the completion ("By your hands all good works are brought to birth"). The parallelism in thought is an initial indication that this line also refers to the curse.

With some analysis we can see a similar implication in two parallel lines of the last section of the prayer:

Unfallen Power, the one destroying the Enemy . . .
Voice heard by the rulers, shaking all their powers. (115.1 and 4)

---

[18] See Gerhard Delling, "ἄρχων," *TDNT* 1 (1964) 488–89 and Werner Foerster, "ἐξουσία," *TDNT* 2 (1964) 571.

The first line is a reference to the lion who killed the servant. The second line has its narrative correlate in the powerful curse (Voice).

These two parallel lines see Christ's presence both in the curse (Voice) and in the lion (Power), the agent who carries out the curse. That is, it implies a thought similar to the first two lines examined: "Christ" is a presence to be seen both in Thomas's cursing of the servant and in the actions of the figures who actually carry out the curse. This, of course, is a thought already present in the narrative itself as it would have been interpreted in comtemporary culture: the curse would be understood as having a divine power in it, and the lion and the dog would have been seen as moved by God to fulfill the curse. What is important is that the redactors choose to focus on this particular aspect of the narrative rather than others.

The Curse as Revelation, a Parallel to the Hymn

What can be pointed to next is several indications that the curse-and-fulfillment sequence is interpreted by the redactors specifically as a revelation event.

We already saw some evidence of this in the fact that the reference to the curse ("You know what is to come and through us you bring it about") occurs in a section the rest of whose lines focus on the theme of making manifest what is hidden.

We can now point out also that the reference to the curse in the last section ("Voice . . . shaking all their powers," 115.2–4) stands there as a parallel to "Messenger sent from the heights and reaching to Hades" (115.4–5). That is, the "Voice" is represented as coming from an otherworldly realm, a "hidden" one so far as the World is concerned, and entering the (demonic) World, becoming manifest. This would imply that the narrative theme of Thomas's journey from Jerusalem to Andrapolis ("from the heights . . . to Hades") is being made parallel to the gradual manifestation of his initially unrecognized divine power and status to the Andrapolitans. These kinds of parallels drawn between narrative sequences by the redactors are something we have seen before.

Secondly, there are a number of indications that the redactors want to draw a parallel between the wedding hymn and the curse and to represent them both as revelations of hidden mysteries.

There is a certain parallelism between the curse and the hymn already in the narrative. Both are (according to the redactors) spoken in Hebrew, and both serve to make Thomas's divine status known to the flutist and the guests. Their staring at him after the wedding hymn is parallel to the later confession of the flutist and conversion of the guests following the curse's fulfillment. This parallelism is also indicated by the juxtaposition of two lines in the Christ prayer:

> *You know what is to come* (τὰ μέλλοντα) *and you bring it to completion through us,*
> *You are the one revealing hidden mysteries.* (114.10–12)

The first line's narrative correlate is the curse and fulfillment whereas the second more aptly refers to the wedding hymn in which Thomas speaks of the mystery of the shekinah, the hidden divine presence in the World. Does this mean that the redactors want the line to refer to both the hymn and the curse, implicitly paralleling them?

There are in fact some very cryptic suggestions in the episode of the servant's death that hint at such an idea. The suggestion is that the grabbing of the servant's hand by the black dog is meant to represent a particular "eschatological mystery" found elsewhere in the *Acts Thom.*, the final self-destruction of evil.

The passage reads:

> *A lion . . . killed him and left (him) lying in the area having torn apart his members* (τὰ μέλη). *And right away dogs took his members, among which one black* (μέλας) *dog, grabbing* (κρατῶν) *his right hand in his mouth, brought it into the banquet area.* (112.2–6)

First of all, speaking specifically of a "black" dog gives the dog a likely relation to the demon, elsewhere manifested in the *Acts Thom.* in the guise of "black" men (171.15; 180.15–16).

Secondly, we have already seen evidence that assonance is used by the redactors as an indication of significant connections.[19] Here we have a similarity between τὰ μέλη (members—repeated twice) and μέλας (black). The servant himself represents the Enemy according to the Christ prayer, supporting the suggestion by assonance that both the dog and the "member" that slapped Thomas represent the force of evil.

---

[19] The examples treated so far are περιηχοῦσαι—περιήρχετο (104.6–7 and 108.2), κόρη—κορυφή (109.1 and 5), and σμύρνη—μυρσίναι (110.1 and 2). In each of these cases there are some other grounds for seeing a connection, though none is conclusive. The present case is the one where outside grounds for seeing a connection are strongest. See also the similar wordplay involved in θέαμα—θεά (110.9 and 16) and γένειον—γέννειον (107.4).

The passages in which the self-destruction of evil is explicity mentioned as an aspect of the endtime occur in the Third and in the Fifth Acts. In the Third Act, Thomas demands that a serpent representing a demon suck out the poison with which he has killed a young man (150.3–6). The serpent replies, "If my father draw forth and suck out what he cast into creation, then is his end" (150.9–10). In the Fifth Act, after an exorcism, a demon disappears amid fire and smoke, and the apostle comments (163.17–19), "That demon showed nothing strange or alien, but his own nature (τὴν φύσιν αὐτοῦ) in which he will be burned up (ἐν ᾗ καὶ κατακαυθήσεται)." The latter passage is especially clear in its statement that the devil will be destroyed by his own nature.

What all this points to is that Thomas's curse, stating that the hand that struck him would be "dragged by dogs" is interpreted by the redactors as the enunciation of one of the mysteries of the eschaton that is actually fulfilled ("revealed" in the apocalyptic sense of ἀποκαλύπτειν) when the black dog grabs the servant's hand.[20] It is in this sense that the whole sequence of curse and fulfillment forms a parallel to the revelation of mysteries that takes place in the singing of the hymn.

This understanding of the curse's fulfillment as the making manifest of a divine mystery enables us to make sense of several more features of the middle section of the Christ prayer:

> *You know what is to come,*
> *And through us you bring it to completion.*
> *You, Lord, are the one revealing hidden mysteries*
> *And making manifest secret sayings* (λόγους ἀπορρήτους).
> *You are, Lord, the planter of the good tree,*
> *And through your hands all good works*
> (ἀγαθὰ ἔργα) *are brought*
>   *to birth.*
> *You are, Lord, the one in all things,*
> *And coming to completion* (διερχόμενος) *through all things,*
> *And lying upon all your works* (ἔργοις),
> *And manifest in the energies* (ἐνεργείαις) *of all things.* (114.10–17)

The first and third lines of this section express a formally similar thought, and we can now see how the third line as well as the first is a reference to the curse and fulfillment. The Andrapolitan figures who

---

[20] "Grabbing" (κρατῶν) in the account may have some significance in this respect. It has connotations of overpowering, seizing by force.

fulfill the curse are Christ's "hands" bringing to completion and manifesting (bringing to birth) the "good works," the actions that make manifest the eschatological mystery. "Hands" here has a special reference to the servant's hand which played a prominent role in the slap and continues to play a prominent role in making this mystery manifest. Thomas, in speaking the curse, is represented as planting a good tree which ultimately bears fruit in these good works.

We can also see now how to interpret another peculiarity: these lines represent Christ as both revealer ("revealing hidden mysteries") and revealed ("manifest in the energies of all"). Several features suggest that this is an extension of the thought that Christ initiates the revelatory process. It is he who acts through created agents to carry it out, and it is he who is actually in the end made manifest.

What suggests this thought is the fact that Christ is the one who comes to completion through all things—giving here a full sense to διερχόμενος. The repetition of ἔργα (works) and its cognate ἐνεργείαι (energies) suggests that Christ is made manifest in the energies of the Andrapolitan figures whose good works fulfill the mystery expressed in the curse and who manifest him also because they are his works (i.e., his creation) in whom he is present (ἔγκειται).

The suggestion is then that Christ himself is also the mystery who is made manifest, according to an expression we also find in the New Testament (Eph 3:4, 9).[21]

What this would imply about the formal composition of the speech is that there is a gradual shift of emphasis in this section. The thought of Christ as initiator of the revelation and the one who activates created agents to carry it out moves toward the thought that he is the one who is being made manifest in the process.

Finally, "making manifest secret sayings" (ἐκφαίνων λόγους ἀπορρήτους, 114.12–13) has its natural place in the context of the mysteries where it would refer to the part of the initiation where the candidates are told the secret sayings that are partial keys to the mystery into which they are being initiated. Given the correlation of being hidden

---

[21] It is probably significant in this respect that in the passage quoted above where the demon disappears amid fire and smoke as an illustration of the mystery of the self-destruction of evil (163.14–16), a speech follows that begins, "Jesus, the mystery that has been revealed to us . . ." (163.21–164.1). If the parallel holds, this too is a reference to the fact that this mystery of the self-destruction of evil is a manifestaion of Christ the mystery. See also the probable connection between "I shall see (θεάσομαι) the hand of the one who struck me dragged by dogs" (108.11–12), and the woman of the hymn as manifestation (θέαμα) of the divine (109.3; 110.9)—another suggestion that the content of Thomas's curse is something that will make God manifest.

and being Hebrew, the natural narrative reference of this line is the flutist's making known (translating) to the guests Thomas's secret (Hebrew) sayings which actually contain a mystery.

The paralleling of this phrase with "revealing hidden mysteries" (referring to the wedding hymn) is then another indication that the redactors want to parallel the wedding hymn as revelation with the process by which Thomas's curse comes to reveal his (Christ's) initially hidden divine status.

Three Presentations of the Revelation Schema

We saw above that the redactors interpret their material partly as a threefold presentation of an initiation schema that is the major organizing framework for the strand of their work picturing Thomas as in need of enlightenment rather than as a savior figure. What the above observations are building toward is that the redactors use a similar device to organize the opposite strand of their interpretation representing Thomas as Christ the heavenly redeemer. That is, there is also a revelation schema (represented so far in our analysis by two narrative sequences), the curse and fulfillment and the wedding hymn with the events that surround it.

Before presenting the case for this thesis more fully, I want to go to yet a third narrative sequence which, with the help of some of the ideas above, can be shown to be a third presentation of essentially the same schema. The evidence from this passage is especially valuable since it rests on what are quite obviously peculiarities introduced into the narrative by the redactors to make their point.

The passage in question is the one in which Thomas joins Abban and leaves India:

> And *he set off* to Abban the merchant, carrying with him nothing at all *except only his price* (τίμημα). *For the Lord had given (it) to him saying, "May your authority* (τιμή) *be with you, with my grace, wherever you may set off for."* And the apostle caught up with Abban, like-wise *carrying his baggage* (or: *equipment*—σκεύη) *onto the boat. And he began also himself to carry (it) on up with him.*
>
> *And when they had embarked on the boat and had sat down,* Abban asked the apostle, "What work do you know?" And he said, "In wood: plows and yokes and balances *and boats, and oars for boats and masts and pulleys.* And in stone: pillars and temples and royal palaces." And Abban the merchant said to him, "Yes, we have need of that kind of a craftsman." (103.1–104.2)

We have already noted in Chapter 2 the very peculiar set of correspondences suggested in this passage: price (τίμημα) = status (τιμή) = grace (χάρις) = equipment (σκεύη) = ship's tackle (the oars and masts and pulleys that Thomas makes as a craftsman). Likewise, we noted the fact that Thomas speaks of boat building while he is sitting in a boat bound for India.[22]

We can speak first of the last point: Thomas the boat builder boards a boat for India. Understanding now the journey to India as a representation of an entry into the World, this idea implies a train of thought similar to that described above: Thomas is the one who travels to India, and he is also the one who builds the kind of vehicle which gets him there. The parallel lies in the fact that Thomas-Jesus is the one making the hidden manifest (manifest = incarnate, worldly), the one activating the agents (vehicles) of the manifestation, and the one who himself becomes manifest (enters the World).

This line of thinking can also be seen to make sense of another peculiar equation in the passage: τιμή = χάρις = σκεύη. Thomas's original objection to going to India (100.6–8) was the fact that he would be a foreigner there: "How can I, a Hebrew man, go to the Indians to preach the truth?" The use of the motif "foreigner" in the Andrapolitan scene connects it with being vulnerable, at a social disadvantage.[23]

Hence Jesus' bestowal of τιμή on Thomas at his departure is quite plausibly connected with this general situation. That is, Jesus is giving Thomas the status, the authority which will later enable him to actually exert power in Andrapolis rather than remain a vulnerable foreigner.

This reading is supported by the connection of τιμή and χάρις (grace). Immediately after Thomas's protest against being a foreigner in India, Jesus appears and says, "Do not be afraid, Thomas. Go to India and preach the Word there because my grace is with you" (100.9–11). Thus, in the departure scene Jesus is conferring on Thomas the grace which actually remedies the cause of his fear—a grace which is authority. Although χάρις occurs here in a very conventional phrase, we have other instances in the *Acts Thom.* of conventional phrases which are given very particular interpretation in reference to the immediate context.

---

[22] Note the repetition of πλοῖον. They embark on a πλοῖον and Thomas makes πλοῖα καὶ κώπας πλοίων.

[23] See especially Abban's comment on the king's invitation-threat: "Let us set off then, too, so that we give no offense to the king, especially since we are foreigners" (105.9–11).

Assuming then that τιμή refers to Thomas's being a person of status in the World, his ability to make his presence felt in the World, the equation τιμή = σκεύη = ship's gear (oars, masts, and pulleys) has a natural place in the train of thought being spoken of: the ship's gear is part of the equipment Thomas constructs in order to enter the World, which is the same as exerting his τιμή there, making his presence felt.

There is in this interpretation some confusion as to whether Thomas is given this τιμή/σκεύη by the Lord, or whether he himself makes it. But this confusion has its analogue in the confusion elsewhere between Jesus and Thomas. Specifically, in the selling scene prior to this one we find the connection of both Jesus and Thomas with the "craftsman" motif.

The connection between the ship by which Thomas journeys to Andrapolis and the authority that makes his presence felt there matches perfectly an observation made earlier about the last section of the Christ prayer: Thomas's journey is interpreted as that of a "messenger sent from the heights reaching to Hades," and this is parallel to the idea that the powerful voice-curse (δύναμις/φωνή as τιμή) makes itself felt by destroying the enemy.

Given this interpretation, we now have three groups of textual elements using different imagery that are parallel presentations of a single schema, a specific view of the process by which the divine becomes manifest in the World. Like the parallel presentations of an intiation schema, these three presentations are mutually clarifying.

The three presentations of this common schema can be represented in the same fashion as before. Letters again indicate the main elements of the schema, and numbers represent the three different groups of elements presenting it: 1) the departure on the journey; 2) the wedding hymn and connected events; and 3) the curse and fulfillment.

A) There is a figure who is divine and otherworldly whose presence is intially not perceived in the worldly realm:

1) Thomas is initially in Jerusalem (spoken of as ὕψος in the Christ prayer, 115.4) representing himself as vulnerable, a foreigner without status (100.6 – 8).
2) His true status is only gradually recognized at the banquet; his hymn is in Hebrew, unintelligible to the guests (111.3 – 5) and contains "hidden mysteries."
3) His curse likewise gives expression to a "hidden mystery," is spoken in Hebrew, and only gradually comes to be understood when its effect is seen and it is translated.

B) This figure produces a vehicle by which his presence comes to be felt:

1) Thomas makes the boats and boat equipment which get him to Andrapolis and are also equivalent to the authority (τιμή) he exercises there.
2) Thomas sings the words of the wedding hymn, which "reveals hidden mysteries," and is a wonder (ἀρετή) in the eyes of the guests, contributing to the flutist's recognition of Thomas (111.5 – 6).
3) Thomas speaks the words of the curse whose power (δύναμις/φωνή, 115.1 – 2) activates other figures to vindicate his previously unrecognized divine status and thus to make it felt among the Andrapolitans. The curse and the fulfillment also motivate the flutist to explain the words and the wonder to the guests.

C) The end result of this process is to render the divine figure present in and to the World:

1) The ship carries Thomas to Andrapolis.
2) The hymn as a wonder is parallel to the image of Thomas's divinely transformed appearance, an epiphany for the guests and the flutist.
3) The fulfillment of the curse (114.15 – 17) is a rendering present of Christ the mystery (i.e., Christ's "coming to completion through all . . . manifest in the energies of all things") in the Andrapolitan World. The final result of the curse (and hymn) is to make Thomas's divine status known to the guests.

This outline of the revelation schema and its three presentations will serve as a summary of our interpretative work so far on the middle and last sections of the Christ prayer. What has not yet been included is: (a) the relation of the ideas of the destruction of evil and salvation as liberation (present in the last section of the prayer) to this revelation schema, and (b) some further aspects of the idea of the divine presence in the World.

6.7 Salvation as Destruction of Evil and Liberation

The narrative as such ends with some conversions, implying at least a beginning of salvation for those involved. This applies especially to the flutist in that the original story of the flutist was about the salvation of a degraded soul by a heavenly redeemer.

That the redactors want to emphasize this idea is clear most of all from the last part of the Christ prayer:

> *O messenger sent from the heights and reaching to Hades,*
> *Who also, opening the doors, led up from there those shut up for*
>   *many years in the prison of darkness,*
> *And showed them the way up, the way leading up to the heights.*

Given that the descent "from the heights . . . to Hades" (115.4–5) refers to the different ways in which Thomas enters the World, the redactors clearly intend the liberation imagery of the last part of this passage as a reference to the conversions that his entry into the World brings about.

This draws our attention back to the first part of the Christ prayer. There the theme of liberation is also a focal point. Even though we earlier interpreted the liberation imagery there as references to Thomas's liberation from Worldly limitation in the process of his initiatory journey, there is clearly an attempt by the redactors to draw parallels between Thomas's liberation and that of the flutist and the guests. This is most evident in the interweaving of themes in the first section:

> *The healer of souls [Thomas] lying in sickness*
> *And savior of creation (the World).*
> *The one giving life to the cosmos*
> *And empowering the souls.* (114.8–10)

It is also evident in the parallel motif (114.8) occurring in the first and last section. "Redeemer of the captives" (114.8) is a fairly exact correlate to the motif in the last section (115.5–8) concerning freeing the prisoners from the prison of darkness.

Finally, we may note that the idea of liberation is closely related, in the last part of the prayer, to the idea of the destruction of evil. That is, "destroying the enemy" (115.2) and "shaking the powers of the Rulers" (115.3–4) are clearly related in the context to the statement, "Reaching to Hades, you opened the doors and led up from there those shut up . . ." (115.4–6). It is implied that the Enemy and the archons are holding people as prisoners.

Though it is clear that liberation from evil is an idea the redactors use to interpret the narrative, it is as yet not at all clear how this idea relates to the other themes of the Christ prayer. We have observed earlier many cases where the redactors take seemingly diverse themes and connect them in unusual ways to integrate them into their presentation. So here also we should ask whether this theme is not to be integrated with the others in some way.

This problem, however, can best be solved by first dealing with another one: the relation of the theme of Thomas the revealer to that of Thomas the recipient of revelation. This amounts to the same thing as the relation of the revelation schema to the initiation schema.

The Relation of the Revelation Schema to the Initiation Schema

We can begin by saying more precisely now how it is that Thomas comes to see the divine presence in the World. The section of the Christ prayer in which he makes confession of his belief in this divine presence is the one in which he is speaking of the Andrapolitan figures (the lion and the hand) as representatives of Christ. That is, the implication is that Thomas comes to see Christ's presence in the World by seeing the activities of these figures. They are for him, as well as for the guests, a revelation.[24]

This presents a rather enigmatic picture. Thomas, representing Christ the revealer, is the activating force in several Worldly figures and through the medium of these figures reveals Christ the mystery to Thomas as initiate, the one receiving this revelation of Christ in the World.

This is a very odd train of thought, but there are actually two passages in the wedding hymn which have very similar implications. The redactional practice observed earlier of presenting parallel and mutually clarifying images at several points in the text justifies comparisons of such passages to get at the specific interpretative ideas of the redactors.

The first of these hymn passages is in the second section which opens by speaking of the woman with her mouth open, out of which comes the songs of the thirty-two eons (109.7–9). The third line reads, "Whose tongue is like the curtain of the door which is shaken by those going in" (109.9–10).

The most natural explanation of the imagery is to suppose that those going in are shaking the woman's tongue in song, that is, they are partly the cause of the song's coming out of her mouth.

---

[24] This is similar to the parallel between Thomas's and the guests' liberation just noted. We can also mention here what is probably a literary trick of the redactors: drawing a parallel between the revelation to Thomas and that to the guests. The flutist reports the words of Thomas's curse to the guests (113.4–6): "*I* will see ($\theta\epsilon\acute{\alpha}\sigma o\mu\alpha\iota$) the hand." She then immediately says, "*You* have now seen ($\dot{\epsilon}\theta\epsilon\acute{\alpha}\sigma\alpha\sigma\theta\epsilon$) it."

The passage goes on, however, to suggest that "those going in" are doing so in order to be initiated through the βαθμοί (the thirty-two eons) represented by her neck. Initiation, as we saw, is the idea the redactors use to join the various sections of the hymn together. The implication is that those going in both activate the woman (the World) to manifest the divine by the songs of the thirty-two that proceed from her, and they are also the ones who are the recipients of the divine revelation made manifest by these thirty-two eons who are in her.

The second passage is:

> *Her bridegrooms surround her* . . . having their gaze *and vision* toward the bridegroom that through *the vision of* him they might be enlightened. (110.3−9)

We saw earlier how θεάματος αὐτοῦ refers to the bride (the World) as manifestation (θέαμα) of the bridegroom. This is a redactional modification of material that originally spoke of the bride (Earth) with her attendants (planets and stars) being enlightened all together by the bridegroom (the rising sun).

The redactors specifically want to present the attendants as being enlightened through the bride-World, a manifestation of the bridegroom who is still understood as enlightening her. But they also add a very odd line about another group of "bridegrooms" who also await enlightenment by the coming "bridegroom."

The motivation for both these redactional alterations is not hard to see if we have in mind the other two cases where a single figure or group (Thomas and those entering in) both serve to activate the World to a revelation of the divine, and are the recipients of such a revelation through the medium of the World. This case is slightly different in that there is only one bridegroom who reveals himself to seven bridegrooms through the medium of the World. But the appearance of two sets of bridegrooms in a wedding scene is striking enough in itself to call attention to the fact that a single name is being given both to the enlightener and those who are being enlightened.

These two passages in the wedding hymn make it clear that it is not arbitrary on our part to focus on the relation of Thomas the revealer and Thomas the initiate as a problem. The fact that the peculiarities in both hymn passages can be explained precisely as an attempt to bring these two trains of thought into relation to each other shows that the redactors themselves have this issue in mind.

The implication in both hymn passages as well as in the Christ prayer is that initiation does not take place merely through forced contact with the foreign World. Contact with the World is only genuinely initiatory when the World is made into a vehicle of revelation under the influence of a revealer. Those who enter shake the curtain, the bridegroom enlightens the World, and Thomas's revelatory curse activates Worldly figures to act out the revelation. It is necessary that the revelatory act overcome the World's foreignness by transforming it and making it into a manifestation of the divine. It is then that contact with it can become an initiatory experience.[25]

The notion that there is something about the World that needs changing in order that it can be a vehicle of revelation directs our attention to the theme of the World's foreignness. In the wedding hymn the hostility of the World to Thomas was interpreted in a rather positive light: it is connected with the painfulness and humiliating quality of the experience of initiation. One could note the role of the servant's slap, connected with the play on τύπτειν, and also the reed decorated "barred doors" (κλειστάδες) of the bride's bedroom.

But the Christ prayer makes it obvious that the World's hostility is also to be interpreted as genuine ungodliness. This is especially evident in the interpretation of the servant as the Enemy (115.2) and in the treatment of Thomas's journey to Andrapolis as a descent into Hades (115.4–5). The worldliness of the Andrapolitan banquet that stands in opposition to the apostle is given a mythical interpretation as the realm of the Evil One.

Going further, we can note that this characterization of the World as a demonic realm occurs in a passage (115.1–8) whose focal point is the destruction of the Evil One, the shaking of the power of the demonic archons, and the freeing of those formerly held captive. And it is precisely Thomas's journey into the World that effects this destruction of evil and liberation, a journey which is equivalent to the entrance of divine revelation into the World. It is even explicitly said in this passage that it is Thomas's (revelatory) "voice" that "shakes the powers" of the archons.

What all this points to is this: the World as initially encountered is experienced as ungodly and hostile to the religious person. The revelatory activity of a heavenly figure, however, destroys this ungodly character of the World (destroys the Enemy's hold on it) and transforms it into a vehicle of revelation. That is, the liberation of the World from

---

[25] Something similar is probably meant by the line in the first-gate formula of the Ophite ritual quoted earlier (5.2): "I have overcome the one born of you by a living word." The "living word" here is a parallel to Thomas's powerful "voice . . . shaking the powers of the archons" (115.2–3).

the power of the Enemy is an intrinsic part of the process by which it becomes a vehicle of divine revelation. This notion solves the earlier problem of how the idea of salvation and liberation is related to the theme of revelation.

Several other groups of elements in the text also converge toward this way of relating the themes to each other. We have first of all the particular interweaving of themes in the early parts of the Christ prayer:

> *Redeemer of the captives,*
> *The healer of the souls lying in sickness, and the savior of all creation.*
> *The one enlivening the cosmos, and empowering the souls.*
> *You know what is to come, and through us you bring it to completion. . . .*
> *Through your hands all good works are brought to birth.*
> (114.8 – 14)

Given the fact that the last section of the prayer speaks of salvation as liberation of prisoners, it is clear that the "redeemer of the captives" and the "savior of all creation" are linked substantively.[26] The next line concerns the "one enlivening the cosmos," which one naturally reads as equivalent to the "savior of creation," but then this implies that the way the World is saved is by Christ's enlivening it. Following this we have the section of the prayer which speaks about Thomas's activating created agents as vehicles of revelation. The particular juxtaposition of lines here, plus the earlier evidence that the interweaving of themes in prayers is an intentional device, suggests that there is a deliberate connection between the activation of created agents, the enlivening of the cosmos, the salvation of the creation, and the liberation of the captives. That is, there is an intrinsic connection between freeing the World, saving it, enlivening it, and making it a vehicle of revelation.

The elements of the second group that show the redactors' explicit intention to connect these themes in this way are certain catchword connections between the wedding hymn and the last section of the Christ prayer: "doors" (θύραι) in 109.10 and 115.5; and "barred

---

[26] They are connected also with the freeing of Thomas from Worldly "sickness" and limitation. There is also probably a link between "redeemer of the captives" and the earlier image of Thomas with "his eyes fixed on the earth, waiting for when he would return (ἀναλύσῃ) from there."

doors" (κλειστάδες) connected with "shut up" (ἐγκεκλεισμένους) in 110.3 and 115.6.

Our analysis in Chapter 1 suggested that competent reading of this work includes looking for motif and catchword recurrences between speeches or prayers that occur in sequence. This general principle is supported in this case in that one of the words involved, κλειστάδες, is unattested elsewhere and probably coined. It is quite likely that it is a word made up by the redactors to indicate a connection to ἐγκεκλεισ-μένους in the Christ prayer (115.5–7). The intention would be precisely to indicate a connection between the reed decorated doors (κλειστάδες) of the bedroom that bar the initiate's entry and the evil forces that keep elements of the World "closed up" (ἐγκεκλεισμένους) in the prison of the Evil One. This connection in turn is supported by another catchword recurrence involving "doors."

In a redactional line (109.9–10), the "curtain of the door" (παρα-πέτασμα τῆς θύρας) is shaken by those entering the singing woman, while the heavenly redeemer in the Christ prayer opens the doors of the prison of darkness.[27] The implication is that shaking the tongue of the woman-World (the "curtain of the door"), causing her to manifest the divine presence, is the same as opening the doors by which the Evil One shuts up the elements of the World in the prison of darkness.[28] Activating the World as a vehicle of revelation is the same as freeing it from the power of the Evil One.

Finally, this train of thought is implied generally in the way several elements in the story, particularly the black dog and the servant's hand, serve as representations of evil and yet also act out concretely the mystery expressed in the curse, as vehicles by which the divine manifests itself in the World. Their character as evil (i.e., the hold the Evil One has on them) is destroyed precisely when they are activated by the revelatory curse. In the light of the above interpretation of what it means to break the Enemy's power in the World, the last lines of the Christ prayer should be seen as being related to this kind of freeing of those in the prison of darkness as well as the freeing involved in the conversions of the flutist and the guests.

---

[27] These motifs are all probably connected with the motif of the "gates (πύλαι) of the archons" in the Ophite ritual. We noted that "gates (πύλαι) of the city" (109.14) is a motif parallel to "barred doors" in the wedding hymn.

[28] There is probably a similar thought expressed in the Ophite sixth-gate formula: "I, having opened for the world the gate which you closed for your eternity. . . ." The initiate claims that his passing through the gate has had a more universal salutary effect.

6.8   The Divine Presence in the World

The final major aspect of the redactional presentation with which we have to deal concerns certain ideas related to the theme of God's presence in the World. The treatment of these ideas will also lead us to an analysis of the redactional interpretation of the lion, the flutist, Abban the merchant, and the king.

We treated the idea of the divine presence in the World earlier in relation to the themes of revelation and liberation-salvation of the World in the Christ prayer: the divine presence is something brought about in the World through a freeing of the elements of the World from the hold the Evil One has on it, and they are used as vehicles for divine revelation. This idea is also present in the wedding hymn where those entering in and the bridegroom activate and enlighten the World (Bride) so that she becomes a means of contact with the divine.

But there is also in the wedding hymn the notion of the World as something divine in its own right. This is evident most of all, so far as the redactional presentation is concerned, in the treatment of the Mother of Wisdom as a Goddess-consort who is the manifestation (θέα) of the Father of Truth, but is also placed on equal footing with him.   That is, she seems to be an etherealized essence of the World who is actually the manifest aspect of the divinity.

There are indications that the Christ prayer also reflects this notion in some of its lines.   The phrases concerning the "one who is in all things" and "lying upon all your works" (114.15 and 16) would both, as isolated phrases, be taken simply to mean that Christ is everywhere and always present in creation.   The allusion to the figure of Wisdom in this passage would also strengthen this notion.

Going a step further, Bornkamm concludes that in the *Acts Thom.* "compassion" (εὐσπλαγχνία), a divine title in 114.17, is a reference to the divine (World related) "Mother" also met in this work.[29] His case rests chiefly on two instances (166.7 and 142.14) where this title (or σπλάγχνα) occurs in epikleses clearly addressed to this Mother.[30]

Bornkamm's view gains added support when we look at the context of this phrase in the Christ prayer: "Jesus Christ, the Son of Compassion (εὐσπλαγχνίας) and Perfect Savior (τέλειος σωτήρ), Christ, Son of the living God (τοῦ θεοῦ τοῦ ζῶντος) . . ." (114.17–115.1).   There

---

[29] Bornkamm, *Mythos*, 79.

[30] He (*Mythos*, above n. 29) cites also 156.24; 164.11; 232.4; 239.26; and 265.8. But it is not really clear in these cases that the "Mother" is being addressed. Wilson ("Acts of Thomas," 342) accepts Bornkamm's opinion.

is already some unlikelihood, in a work as tightly organized as the *Acts Thom.* appears to be, that this line merely repeats the same thoughts. We have already seen how "giving life" (ζωοποιῶν) in a previous line (114.10) of this prayer expresses a thought similar to that the enlightening activity of the bridegroom-Father in the wedding hymn. Given the use of catchwords as organizing devices, it is not unlikely that the "living" of living God (θεὸς ζῶν) here is meant to suggest that this Father-God is being alluded to, and that here also the redactors mean to present a divine pair, the Compassion-Mother and the "living" Father, both as parents of Christ.

Additional support will be given for this interpretation of "living" in the ensuing treatment of the living Spirit (110.19–20). Here we can mention another argument from the context. As Klijn remarks, we meet the phrase "Perfect Compassion" four times elsewhere in the *Acts Thom.* (142.14–15; 157.1; 164.12; and 166.7).[31] So the title, "Son of Compassion and Perfect Savior," would probably be heard by the original readers as a striking transposition of the adjective "perfect" (τέλειος). We noted, on the other hand, that an earlier use of τελεῖν in this prayer (114.11) is related to a train of thought which represents Christ both as using creatures to "bring to completion" (τελεῖν) a revelation, and also is himself the one who "comes to completion (διερχόμενος) through all things" (114.15). It is likely then, that the picture of Christ as "son of compassion" refers to the fact that it was elements of the World who "brought him forth" (ἀπογεννᾶται, 114.14) and that Christ as mystery is thus "brought to completion" as a "perfect (τέλειος) savior" of the Andrapolitans.

Formally speaking, this interpretation continues to read the speech according to an organizational pattern observed twice already in our study of this speech. There is a gradual sliding from one theme to another in the lines, and this process also operates across the lines of individual sections. Here "son of compassion and perfect savior" functions as a kind of climax to a line of thought that progressively unfolds itself in the previous section.

Substantively, this interpretation implies that the redactors consistently want to give equal time to the divine Mother-World and not to present salvation as originating completely with the heavenly Father who uses the World only as a vehicle.[32] This same trend can be

---

[31] Klijn, *Acts of Thomas*, 186.

[32] As will appear imnmediately below, "Christ" is represented in this prayer both as a heavenly and as a worldly figure. It is possible, then, that the Christ prayer itself is meant to portray stylistically a union of mind and World corresponding to the content of

observed in the redactional interpretation of the lion, the flutist, and Abban the merchant as representatives of a saving divine presence in the World itself.

The lion is interpreted as a representative of Christ in the line, "Unfallen power destroying the Enemy" (115.1–2). "Unfallen" is meant to contrast the lion as a power with evil rulers. Given this contrast, and the fact that the lion is earlier treated as a worldly figure, it seems evident that reference is being made explicitly to an aspect of the World which has never come under demonic control (never "fallen"), and this unfallen power is seen as a representative of Christ the savior.

There are some indications that Abban the merchant also is interpreted as a divine aspect of the World, though here the text is not so clear and our analysis is somewhat more conjectural.

One indication of this interpretation of Abban is the second line (114.5–6) of the Christ prayer which addresses Christ as the "fellow traveler of his slaves." In the narrative as we have it, Abban in fact acts more as Thomas's fellow traveler than as his master.[33]

Another indication comes from the consideration of the selling scene in the light of the initiation schema. We saw earlier that the other two groups of elements in this schema represent Thomas as coming to see the divine presence in the World, but in our analysis so far this element is missing in the selling scene. This is somewhat surprising since it seems most likely that Thomas's original inability "to comprehend" ($\chi\omega\rho\epsilon\hat{\iota}\nu$, 100.6) refers to his inability to see the divine presence in the World, and this dream-vision of the selling comes as part of his mental struggle with this problem.[34]

What is happening generally in this scene is a metamorphosis of a religious relationship (between God and the servant of God) into a commercial one, a process that is paralleled by the wider narrative event of the Hebrew (heavenly) Thomas's being made to enter India-Andrapolis (the World). And on the other hand the play on "Lord-master" ($\kappa\acute{\upsilon}\rho\iota\sigma\varsigma$ / $\delta\epsilon\sigma\pi\acute{\sigma}\tau\eta\varsigma$) involves precisely the confusion between a heavenly Lord and an earthly master. It may be that what is suggested here is an equivalence between the heavenly Lord (Jesus) and the earthly master (Abban),[35] and the verbal trick played on Thomas also

---

the wedding hymn (presented there in erotic imagery). Perhaps then this prayer is a "completion" of the mystery spoken of in the wedding hymn, as the dog carrying the hand is a "completion" of the mystery spoken of in the curse.

[33] See 103.5–7; 104.5–8; and 105.9–12.

[34] The scene is introduced by the line, "And saying and thinking over these things . . ." (101.3).

[35] Note also the possible connection of Abban with the divine "Father of Truth" at the

cryptically indicates here his coming to see the divine presence in the World, that is, Abban as a representative of Christ. This provides the real motivation for Thomas's change of mind and willingness to travel into the World: "I shall go wherever you want" (102.11). If this is so, the indication is of course very cryptic, but not implausible: the three presentations of the initiation schema are probably meant to be mutually clarifying. And the example of the play on τύπτειν, along with that of the black dog's grabbing the hand as a representation of an eschatological mystery, already show the use of cryptic suggestions that need to be clarified in the context of larger schemata.

There are a few more indications pointing to this interpretation of Abban. Several involve a comparison with a passage from the wedding hymn. In the fourth section of the hymn (110.3–9) we have the seven bridegrooms presented as having been chosen by the bride and as being subject to her. The seven bridegrooms represent figures in need of initiation. In other words, we seem to have here something of a contrast with the idea that Thomas is one of those under the control of the Enemy and the rulers in their prison of darkness (115.1–8). One's subjection to the World can also be a saving subjection to the divine presence in the World (shekinah).

This could make sense of two features of the selling scene. First, Thomas is called "Judas" only here, a reference to Judas Iscariot's selling Jesus.[36] He is a degraded soul being made subject to the divine presence in the World (Abban) for the sake of initiation and salvation. One could note that Jesus is called the "Savior" as he leads Thomas to Abban. Secondly, Abban's mission is to bring back (to India) a carpenter (101.6) and it is (redactionally) described in a way that parallels it to Thomas's mission. This is possibly related to the idea that the bride "chose" the seven bridegrooms. That is, both these passages are related to the Gnostic theme of the desire of the World for what is otherworldly (or, as we shall see later, for mind).[37] This desire relates to salvation and is attributed by the redactors to a divine presence in the World (Abban and the bride).[38]

---

end of the wedding hymn by the use of the catchword δεσπότης (110.16).

[36] It will be shown below that the redactors play on the double name "Judas Thomas," a common name for this apostle elsewhere in Syrian tradition.

[37] See Jonas, *Gnostic Religion*, 182–86.

[38] "Desire" (ἐπιθυμία) occurs in a peculiar phrase at the end of the wedding hymn (110.18–19), "wine which gave them no thirst and desire," and there are some suggestions that the word here does relate to the Gnostic theme just mentioned. We have noted already that the pair bride-bridegroom are matched by the pair Mother-Father. We have also noted that "living," which occurs here in the next line as "living Spirit" (an

To return to Abban, note that he (101.3–4) and the lion (112.2) are both introduced in the work by the same phrase, "there happened to be there." The first occurrence of the phrase is redactional and may well be an attempt to link the two figures as being divine presences immanent in the World.

Finally, the redactors have Abban saying that he is also a foreigner in Andrapolis: "Let us set off to the wedding . . . especially since we are foreigners" (105.10–11). We have observed a redactional tendency to present the flutist and the guests grouped both *with* Thomas and with the World over against Thomas, so it is likely that this, too, is deliberate. Probably what is meant is that, as a divine presence, Abban is like Thomas in that he is foreign to the ungodly World. The basis for comparing and grouping is obviously then a shifting one.

The case of the flutist is somewhat more complex. In the original story she represented a heavenly soul or divine spark sunk into the ungodly world below and saved from it by a heaven-sent apostle. The redactors have emphasized both her heavenly aspect, as Hebrew, and her Worldly aspect, as part of the Andrapolitan banquet.

Beyond this, they introduce the idea that she is a mediator between Thomas and the guests. She understands his hymn when they do not, she is the first to understand the curse and hence the significance of the hand-carrying dog, and upon her conversion, she translates and explains for the guests thus converting them. Her role in doing this is ascribed to Christ in the prayer: "You, Lord, are the one . . . making manifest secret words" (114.11–13). The prayer also draws an implicit parallel between this revelatory act and Thomas's hymn singing as well as the making manifest of the curse-mystery by the lion, the dog, and the hand. The former parallel is also suggested by the parallel pleonastic phrases in the narrative: "when he had sung and completed this song" (111.1) and "when she had completed everything and had fluted" (111.9–10).[39]

---

unusual title), is most likely related in this work to the masculine image of God. So the suggestion is natural that this passage represents the redactional alteration of two traditional themes ("wine giving no thirst or desire" and "Holy Spirit") to suggest a further pairing of two salutary motivating forces related to the masculine ("living") and feminine ("desire") images of God. In this interpretation both desire and the living Spirit motivate the songs to the Mother and Father.

[39] It is probable that reference is also made to her role as Christ the mediator in the third line of the Christ prayer (114.6): "You (Christ) are the one leading and setting straight those who believe in you ($\tau o \grave{v} \varsigma$ $\epsilon \grave{\iota} \varsigma$ $\alpha \mathring{v} \tau \grave{o} \nu$ $\pi \iota \sigma \tau \epsilon \acute{v} o \nu \tau \alpha \varsigma$). Immediately above in the narrative (113.7), the guests' conversion is indicated by "they believed in her" ($\epsilon \pi \acute{\iota} \sigma \tau \epsilon \upsilon o \nu$ $\alpha \mathring{v} \tau \mathring{\eta}$).

But it appears that she is not only a mediator of Thomas's influence to the World. In an earlier scene the redactors have introduced the peculiar image that she is fluting at Thomas's head (108.4). This image is related to two others in nearby passages: Thomas's anointing the top of his head (107.5–6) and the king-truth seated on top of the head of the woman in the wedding hymn (109.5).

The anointing scene pertains to an idea involved in the initiation theme: the worldy oil is a medium of divine grace. The fluting is, for Thomas, an element of the World that is seductive and inviting but also painful. The present parallel suggests that, like the oil, it is also a medium for contact with the divine.

The parallel with the image of the truth-king seated on the woman's head in the hymn is harder to explain. We seem in fact to have a reversal of the elements. It is the top of the World's head that is being spoken of rather than worldly elements in relation to the top of Thomas's head. The solution to this problem will have to wait until later in our investigation when more will also be said about the flutist and what she represents.

The figure of the king of Andrapolis also receives some redactional elaboration. In the earlier passages (104.4; 105.4–10) he represents the Gnostic evil God of this World,[40] who also has for the redactors a positive aspect. In the scene just prior to the Christ prayer he fulfills a role parallel to that of Christ in the selling scene and the servant in the banquet scene, forcing Thomas into contact with the World by leading him unwilling into the bedroom. In this case, as in the selling scene, the role seems to be an entirely postive one of leading Thomas to see the divine presence in the World. The pleonasm in the prayer, "Lord . . . leader on the way (ὁδηγός) and guide," probably contains a reference to the king's leading (ἀνάγειν) Thomas into the bedroom, hence making even more explicit the parallel between the king here and Christ-Abban as he appears in the selling scene.[41] The king seems to represent the coercive power the World has over the person, a power that has both a divine and a demonic aspect.

---

[40] The Gnostic mentality would probably perceive the threat accompanying the wedding invitation as a representation of God the (evil) lawgiver; see Jonas, *Gnostic Religion*, 142.

[41] Another parallel would be that between "Judas" (as a mind in need of salvation-enlightenment) in the selling scene and the "doubting Thomas" probably alluded to in the Christ prayer scene. The fact that the latter theme fits very well in this scene which represents Thomas in need of initiation coming to see and acknowledge the divine presence in the World gives added support to the literary evidence presented above for seeing an allusion to it here.

Finally, for the sake of completeness, something should be said of the motif of "rest of the oppressed" that occurs in the first part of the Christ prayer (114.7). The evidence here is skimpy, but a comparison to the story of the colt (chapters 39–41) can help us here with some likely conjectures. Evidence points to the fact that the World itself (the colt) is being treated as giving rest to the soul. In the light of the positive evaluation of World by the redactors, this seems not unlikely. And at the end of the invitation scene (105.11–12), we read of Thomas's "resting a little in the inn (ξενοδοχεῖον)." The word ξενοδοχεῖον means literally "receiver of foreigners." Seeing that "foreigner" is a theme in the nearby context (105.11; 106.3) and that "inn" is elsewhere a Gnostic term for the world,[42] it seems likely that there is some hint here of the World's giving rest to Thomas. The Christ prayer, then, probably sees Christ as present in the inn.

I suspect that this rest motif in the prayer also has to do with the repeated statement (102.9 and 111.2), "And he (Thomas) was silent (ἡσυχάζεν)." The verb ἡσυχάζειν is used of praying elsewhere, specifically prayer connected with the Sabbath rest.[43] Both these occurrences come after prayers. The meaning I suggest is that the soul finds a kind of rest in the concrete (worldly) images of the prayers that help to solve its problems. This is of course conjectural, awaiting further research on the use of these themes in the *Acts Thom.*

6.9 The Ultimate Significance of The Christ Prayer

We have now covered the main features of the Christ prayer together with those features of the previous narrative of which it offers an interpretation. Throughout this Chapter, I have tried to stay as close as possible to the images of the text and the traditional themes (e.g., revelation and liberation) which they more-or-less directly evoke. We saw earlier (Chapter 5) that these kinds of traditional themes are ultimately in the service of a yet further level of meaning, and it remains now to do for the material of this Chapter the same kind of translation that was carried out in Chapter 5 for the analyses preceding it.

In the preceding Chapter, I described the ultimate subject of the work as the psychology of certain kinds of religious experience, a psychology fundamentally determined by the culturally conditioned

---

[42] See Jonas, *Gnostic Religion*, 55.
[43] See BAG, *s.v.* ἡσυχάζω.

alienation from the world that characterizes Gnosticism generally. The basic polarization involved in this alienation has to do with subjectivity as such—not simply self as distinct from external world, but subjective consciousness as opposed to what it feels as given to it, including the conditions under which it exists. This latter point has been confirmed in the present Chapter in that World includes the body itself in which consciousness (the soul) inheres.

What we now have to consider is how this subjectivity represented by Thomas can also have the functions and interrelationships with the World that are represented by the images analyzed in this Chapter. They have to do primarily with Thomas as mediator of the divine to the World, presented via the themes of revelation, transformation, the destruction of evil, and liberation.

Features Pointing to a Noetic Interpretation

That subjective consciousness is allied with the divine is implicit in the self-World polarity as described in Chapter 5. The self belongs with God over against the ungodly World. This thought receives explicit expression in the Greek philosophical notion that the mind (νοῦς, λό-γος) is a semidivine entity, a tradition taken over and given emphasis in Gnosticism where Νοῦς becomes a divine title.[44]

The text implies that consciousness is not only allied with the divine but mediates God's presence to the World and transforms it making the World itself a manifestation of the divine. This thought, too, has a partial parallel in Gnostic thought, as interpreted by Jonas.[45] The mind's act of gaining "Knowledge" in Valentinian speculation, he says, is not only a way to salvation for the individual soul, it also has cosmic effects, moving the "objective ground of being." In Valentinus's thought, "Ignorance . . . is the begetting principle as well as the abiding substance of the lower world." Hence:

> Knowledge . . . assumes an ontological status far exceeding any merely moral and psychological importance granted to it . . . (It is) the sole and sufficient vehicle of salvation, and this salvation itself in each soul is a cosmic event. For if not only the spiritual condition of the human person but also the very existence of the universe is constituted by ignorance, then every individual illumination by "knowledge" helps to cancel out again the total system

---

[44] See, e.g., *Corp. Herm.* 1.6 and 9.
[45] *Gnostic Religion*, 175.

> sustained by that principle . . . Knowledge affects . . . the known
> itself . . . by every "private" act of knowledge the objective ground
> of being is moved.

The adoption of this line of interpretation in the *Acts Thom.* would entail a much more specific notion of what Thomas stands for in this work. He would represent not simply "self" or "subjective consciousness," but specifically mind, consciousness as a knowing faculty. And the interactions between Thomas and the World would be played out in a specifically noetic realm. There are actually several indications that some such interpretation is appropriate to these chapters.

First, we can mention an implication of the initiation schema. The change in the character of the World implied in Thomas's shekinah vision is not the result of external changes in the World (on a phenomenal level at least). It is primarily due to a change in Thomas's consciousness, the new mental perspective from which he views the World.

The sending scenes are shaped so as to reflect the schema of initiation also. The present discussion brings us back to an as yet unexplained aspect of the initial scene, the fact that it evokes a particular Gnostic literary opening: the scene of someone puzzling over a difficult mystery. Thomas's not being able to travel ($\chi\omega\rho\epsilon\hat{\iota}\nu$) is also an inability to understand ($\chi\omega\rho\epsilon\hat{\iota}\nu$), and what he cannot understand is the divine presence in the World. This is a more explicit reference to the noetic character of what is going on. We can now, in fact, expand on the particular theme evoked here in reference to several other passages.

Immediately following the play on $\chi\omega\rho\epsilon\hat{\iota}\nu$ which involves the conjunction of traveling and understanding, we find the twice-repeated redactional phrase, "As he was saying ($\lambda\acute{\epsilon}\gamma o\nu\tau o\varsigma$) and thinking over ($\delta\iota\alpha\lambda o\gamma\iota\zeta o\mu\acute{\epsilon}\nu o\upsilon$, 100.8 / $\acute{\epsilon}\nu\theta\upsilon\mu o\upsilon\mu\acute{\epsilon}\nu o\upsilon$, 101.3) these things." Thomas is mentally struggling with his problem of not being able to enter the World which is the same as his not being able to see the divine presence there.

These phrases are the redactional frame for Thomas's transformative vision (the epiphany and the selling scene). The redactors represent them as in some sense the product or content of Thomas's internal dialogue, his thinking about his problem. In the light of our earlier characterization of the relation between the revelation schema and the initiation schema, we have here a representation of Thomas the thinker revealing the divine presence in the World (through the equation Lord = master) to Thomas the initiate.

A related passage presents a similar train of thought. We have already noted numerous parallels between the sending scenes and the Christ prayer with the scene immediately preceding it, and we can now note one more. Immediately following the dream-vision of the selling we read: "And the next morning, having prayed (εὐξάμενος) and entreated the Lord . . ." (102.10). The line contains a familiar pleonastic construction, but unlike most of the other examples of this construction which we have observed neither member occurs in the nearby context.

However, "to pray" (εὔχεσθαι) does occur immediately preceding the Christ prayer, and attention is called to it by its being repeated three times (113.9; 114.3, 4). In the last of the occurrences the Christ prayer is characterized as "praying," and the occurrence also involves a pleonasm: "He began to pray and to speak like this. . . ."

Thomas in the course of this prayer comes to see and confess the divine presence in the World, apparently as a result of seeing Christ's presence in the worldly Andrapolitan figures who bring about the fulfillment of the curse. We can note that, given the earlier equivalence of King's daughter-bride = World, the king's request, "Pray over my daughter" (113.9), plausibly represents a request that Thomas pray over the World. It is Thomas's reflecting on the events in the World that bring him to see the divine presence there, and this reflection is characterized as a prayer over the World.[46]

This reasoning gives a plausible explanation for the redactors' calling attention to εὔχεσθαι. It is another parallel that relates the sending scenes to the scene of the king's request and the Christ prayer. The phrase, "having prayed and entreated the Lord," following the dream-vision is meant to refer not only to Thomas's morning prayers but also to the epiphany and the selling scene as the concern of a prayer: religious reflection on the problem of the apparent foreignness of the World, the absence of God in it. In this line of thought, it is the thinking process which transforms the character of the World for Thomas, somewhat parallel to Jonas's account of the transformative effect of knowledge in Valentinus.[47]

---

[46] The connection between reflecting and praying is familiar in Judaism, as the form of many psalms shows: they are often theological reflections on national or personal events with which it has been found difficult to deal. For contemporary examples, see *Ps. Sol.* 1, 2, and 9.

[47] There are, of course, important differences between what is said here and Jonas's interpretation of Valentinus. In the latter, divine self-ignorance causes the world of matter, and salvation through gnosis means that the individual repairs this lack. Gnosis "transposes the individual self to the divine realm . . . reintegrating the impaired god-

This of course assumes that the change in the World is primarily a change in the way the world is experienced. The question as to whether this is to be regarded as a real change or as a merely noetic change will be treated below. First we must treat more elements of the text related to the noetic hypothesis proposed here.

What we can mention first in this respect is the rather odd notion that Thomas is both revealer and the recipient of revelation. Now that we have established some case for seeing Thomas specifically as a representative of mind, it can be pointed out that a very similar notion concerning the mind exists in Plotinus and earlier in the Aristotelian commentator Alexander Aphrodisias.[48] Two quotations from Philip Merlan will bring out the parallels. He summarizes the ideas of Plotinus in *Enn.* 5.1:

> The soul has intelligence—double intelligence, to be precise—one which thinks (λογίζεσθαι) and another which supplies with thinking (λογίζεσθαι παρέχων)—incorporeal, operating without a bodily organ, and transcendent (χωριστόν) . . . The ability of the soul to investigate the justice or beauty of a particular phenomenon reveals that there is something which is permanently just, permanently beautiful. They are what stimulates the soul to think about them.[49]
>
> When he speaks of a double intelligence . . . we immediately recognize Aristotle's doctrine of double intelligence—in his own words ὁ μὲν νοῦς τῷ πάντα γίνεσθαι, ὁ δὲ τῷ πάντα ποιεῖν.[50] (*Anima* 3.5, 430a 13–15)

Merlan describes the thought of Alexander Aphrodisias in similar terms:

> We are born with potential intelligence (δυνάμει νοῦς) . . . this intelligence can be called material intelligence (ὑλικὸς νοῦς) because receptiveness is a mark of matter. Material intelligence can be compared with the 'unwrittenness' of a blackboard . . .

---

head itself" (*Gnostic Religion*, 175). The implication is that gnosis does not transform the world into a divine manifestation (as in the *Acts Thom.*). It makes it (as something alien to God) vanish. The analogy extends only to the ability of the act of knowing to cause a radical change in the character of the World, not to the specific change brought about.

[48] Connections between Gnosticism and Middle and Neoplatonism have often been suggested before. See Kurt Rudolph, "Gnosis und Gnostizismus, ein Forschungsbericht," *ThR* 38 (1973) 12–25.

[49] Philip Merlan, *Monopsychism Mysticism Metaconsciousness: Problems of the Soul in the Neoaristotelian and Neoplatonic Tradition* (The Hague: Nijhoff, 1963) 6.

[50] Ibid., 10.

After this material intelligence has been instructed, it is the form and perfection (εἶδος καὶ ἐντελέχεια) of the uninstructed intelligence. In this context it can also be called acquired (ἐπίκτητος) intelligence . . . Whereas the material intelligence can perceive intelligibles (νοητά) only in the presence of sensibles in which they are embodied, the acquired intelligence can perceive intelligibles even in the absence of corresponding sensibles . . . In addition to this material intelligence . . . there must exist another, the productive intelligence (νοῦς ποιητικός). It is this intelligence which is the cause of the material intelligence turning into able (acquired) intelligence. This productive intelligence is immaterial. It is . . . transcendent (χωριστόν), pure (ἀμιγές), changeless (ἀπαθές) . . . eternal . . . Man becomes like god . . . whenever his material intelligence becomes transformed into the productive intelligence.[51]

There are striking correspondences between the "double intelligence" spoken of here and the peculiar double role of Thomas in chapters 1–10 of the *Acts Thom.* In both cases we have an active mind that is also transcendent and a receptive mind connected more with the material world. The latter receives impressions only from the material world (though this is only true of its initial state, according to Alexander). In both cases it is the active mind which causes the divinizing transformation of the receptive mind.[52]

The correspondences are rather exact despite some differences, and in both cases the notions presented are not very common. (There is in Gnosticism the concept of the redeemed redeemer, but it is not elaborated in the specific way we find here.) This suggests that there is some kind of connection between the *Acts Thom.* and a particular strand of Greek philosophical thought. And this in turn offers considerable support for the thesis that these chapters of the *Acts Thom.* do ultimately have to do specifically with noetic processes.

Several other elements of the text make good sense when considered in this light. For example, we have seen how the departure scene

---

[51] Ibid., 14–16.

[52] Assuming that the original readers of the *Acts Thom.* were familiar with this idea of the two-sided character of the mind, it is very likely that they would have read the introduction of Thomas ("Judas Thomas, the Twin," 100.4–5) as an intimation of this theme. This is the more probable since later a play is made also on the "Judas" component of the name in reference to Judas Iscariot. In the context of the two-sided mind, this "Judas" would represent the receptive, material mind. "Judas Thomas" is a common appellation of this apostle elsewhere (see Klijn, *Acts of Thomas*, 158–59). There is some possibility that here we actually have the origin of this rather puzzling name, though it could also be a novel interpretation of a traditional name.

represents Thomas, originally otherworldly and hidden, as building the kind of vehicle by which he enters the World. The images correspond well to the character of the mind, an intangible reality that can, however, make its creative power tangible. It does so partially in images and ideas (the hymn, impressive but still Hebrew, i.e., mental and incomprehensible to the worldly guests). And secondly it becomes more completely tangible by effecting a transformation in the World outside itself.

The notion that there is a mind-made reality (images, ideas) that mediates between mind and World draws attention to the other mediating figure in the text, the flutist. Her fluting is in fact paralleled to Thomas's hymn singing. On the other hand, despite the fact that she is kin to Thomas, she is primarily a worldly figure. The Greek philosophical tradition has a category that corresponds well to the role of the flutist as the redactors represent her here: the Aristotelian forms inherent in matter. According to this notion, physical reality has two basic components, matter ($\H{v}\lambda\eta$) and form ($\mu o \rho \phi \acute{\eta}$). The former is unintelligible as such; the latter is what makes things the kind of things they are, and they are like ideas embedded in things.[53] In terms of the imagery of the *Acts Thom.* this is an aspect of the World in which it has "kinship" with mind. As "matter" ($\H{v}\lambda\eta$), it is completely "foreign."

A line found elsewhere in the *Acts Thom.* seems to refer explicitly to a "mental" part of the World. It calls Jesus the "mental aspect of the Perfect Compassion" (156.24 – 157.1). "Compassion" is again taken as a title for the World as divine.

And this notion seems to solve the earlier puzzle about the image of the "top of the head" of the woman-shekinah. The suggestion would be that the World has a "head," an aspect akin to mind, and it is primarily this part of the World which is able to mediate the divine presence to mind. It is "on top of [the World's] head" that the "king is established, feeding ... those who are established upon him" (109.5 – 6). The flutist's "fluting at Thomas's head" is a parallel image to this one, and this fact confirms the suspicion that she represents an aspect of the World according to which it is akin to mind.[54]

---

[53] They are the "$\nu o \eta \tau \acute{\alpha}$ embodied in sensibles" mentioned by Merlan above.

[54] The thirty-two eons-steps who are in the shekinah (109.8 – 13) probably also represent intelligible aspects of the World. This would suggest that the seven dancing planets who surround her do as well (110.5 – 6). And this would explain the literary merging of these figures with the "seven bridegrooms." The latter represent the (receptive) mind, and the merging of mind with forms received from the World is a familiar idea in Greek philosophy, as is evidenced by Aristotle's $\nu o \H{v} \varsigma \ \tau \H{\omega} \ \pi \acute{\alpha} \nu \tau \alpha \ \gamma \acute{\iota} \nu \epsilon \sigma \theta \alpha \iota$ (*Anima* 3.5, 430a 13 – 15).

The Question of Allegory

But this connection with Greek philosophy raises some questions about our previous interpretation. The correspondence of the images in the *Acts Thom.* with certain philosophical categories (the double mind, ideas, forms) might lead us to think that we are dealing here with allegory after all. The ultimate referents of the text are perhaps the elements not of a myth but of a conceptual scheme involved with the psychology of perception.

What still tells against this view, however, is the content and character of the images in the text themselves. These are personalistic to an extent that goes beyond simple dramatization of an abstract scheme. The text emphasizes images having to do with welcoming, seduction, social pressure and resistance, insult and vindication, power relationships, deliverance from danger, erotic attraction, enjoyment, humiliation, and fear. The lyric and erotic representation of the World's beauty in the wedding hymn can be mentioned as especially overdone unless one is really trying to evoke not simply concepts but also the experiences involved in divinizing contact with the World. The same can be said for the life-and-death context in which destruction of evil and liberation from the World are portrayed in the final section of the Christ prayer.

Additionally, if the basic categories governing the composition are actual concepts originating in philosophical speculation, one would expect that the interrelation of images would be governed by some logic related to the definitions of these categories to which there would be a consistent adherence. One would not expect, for example, logical inconsistencies such as the mind's having "equipment" which is both something given to it and something it produces. At least one would not expect these images to be placed simply side by side with no attempt to relate them by establishing distinct aspects.

In the present context it seems plausible to suggest that this logical confusion mirrors the fact that, for actual introspective experience, the aspects of the exercise of active intelligence under which it is felt as a divine gift most often blends indistinguishably with the aspect under which it is felt to be due to our own activity.

These features of the text support our thesis that the images and the logic which joins them reflect an attempt to mirror the quality of actual experiences rather than a simple allegorical clothing for an abstract conceptual scheme. Further observations will be made below on the ways in which the logic of the images in the text mimes concrete experience rather than abstract schemes. The conclusion, as far as the present

problem is concerned, is that the correspondences between textual elements and Greek philosophical categories (hymn-curse=ideas;
flutist=forms) represent a phenomenon stylistically similar to the use
of religious themes and images from the Judeo-Christian tradition. In
both cases the categories or themes evoked are not themselves the ultimate referents of the language but carriers and guides leading the
prepared reader to a further level of meaning dealing with psychological
processes as concretely experienced.

Finally, we may note that the connection with Neoplatonism can be
regarded, in one sense, as a support for this reading. Neoplatonist phi-
losophers, guided by previous philosophical thought, worked out their
own concepts in direct relation to introspective perceptions about the
psychology of their own religious and mystical experiences. This often
led them to express themselves in imagery and mythologoumena causing difficulty for those who want to interpret their thought along the
lines of abstract and consistent systems of doctrine.

In this light, the foreignness of the World undoubtedly relates to its
unintelligibility, but this needs to be understood specifically as existential unintelligibility, its meaninglessness for the person encountering it.
"Understanding the world" in the sense of modern science, or even in
the Aristotelian sense, would not necessarily help Thomas in his predicament.

The Question of Noetic versus Real

We need now to raise the question as to whether our noetic interpretation of the text is really to be extended to all the events in the narrative. And this relates also to the question concerning whether or not
the change that occurs in the World, represented by the curse and
fulfillment sequence, is regarded by the redactors as a real one.

There seems, on the one hand, no reason to exempt the curse-and-
fulfillment sequence from the kind of interpretation that extends to so
much of the rest of the text, including the figure of the flutist who
figures in this sequence. Further, the formal implication of this
interpretation is that the curse-and-fulfillment sequence is parallel to
Thomas's praying over the World. This matches a familiar organizational paradigm of the redactors in which parallels are drawn between
elements that in the text appear sequential.

On the other hand, it seems unquestionable that the redactors regard
the transformation of the World represented in the curse-and-
fulfillment sequence as a salvation of the World on a cosmic level. It is
not only a change related to Thomas's initiation, taking place only in

his own mind. This is brought out by the images in the Christ prayer (114.9–10; 115.1–8) and also by the fact that this representation of the cosmic transformation of the World follows rather than precedes the central account of Thomas's initiation.

Several interrelated observations can be made in the face of this dilemma. The first is that the redactors are working from a basic model of what they regard as a radical change in consciousness. The kind of change in Thomas's perspective on the World they envisage does not primarily involve a minor shift in mood, attitude, or habits of thought that might be even consciously brought about by willing it, without any fundamental change in the person. Rather, they think of a very basic change in the person such as (supposedly) happens in initiation. We might pursue this initiation-experience model further. For one who has undergone such an experience, the World with which they actually interact afterwards is likely to be felt as having changed its basic character, and one might naturally interpret this phenomenon as a very real, cosmic change in the constitution of things. Implicit in this view would be a philosophical view according to which subjectivity and the objective World are on a basic level mutually constitutive realities, and consequently a fundamental change in one necessarily involves a fundamental change in the other.[55] Secondly, it must be remembered that the events represented in the narrative, although they are not in every respect an allegorical representation of myth, do have this character to a certain extent. This means they are to be understood as occurring in a cosmic dimension. (My use of the word "cosmic" here has nothing to do with the category World.) Thomas is then in some sense a mythical-cosmic figure, and the changes portrayed in the relation between him and the Andrapolitan World also take place on a cosmic, ultimate level. This makes it easier to explain why the change in the World is regarded as a real one—easier than if Thomas were merely a representative of an individual initiate. In this light individual initiation experiences would be looked upon as participation in the cosmic and very real process by which humankind is being enlightened and the World is being transformed into a more perfect manifestation of God.

Finally, what was said in Chapter 5 about the general applicability of images and sequences in the text can be recalled here. Although the redactors' presentation is modelled on extraordinary religious experiences such as radical changes brought on by initiation, they most likely are meant to apply to more normal, everyday activities as well. In the

---

[55] This is suggested by Jonas (*Gnostic Religion*, 175), and it has already been partly outlined in our discussion in Chap. 5.

case of the present themes, the idea of the World's transformation by the mind might apply to ordinary activities that change the world in tangible ways. These would include one's own conduct, the social relationships one helps to form, the artistic products one creates (such as the *Acts Thom.* itself), or even the kind of houses (or boats) one builds. What is required in order that these activities fit the model is simply that the reordering of the world which they bring about does in some sense, in some small way, represent an actual change in the (existential) constitution of things. It is not merely a reshuffling of the deck, so to speak, leaving the basic character of things unchanged.

7

GNOSTIC HERMENEUTICS
IN THE
ACTS OF THOMAS

This concluding Chapter returns to the subject of hermeneutics. This study has tried to work out an improved and more exact method for exegetical hermeneutics. But as it turns out, the stretch of text chosen from the *Acts Thom.* for analysis also has some important things to say about hermeneutics—about the way religious language, and human experience, ought to be interpreted. I attempt here to describe that in which this "Gnostic hermeneutics" consists and to suggest some religious trends in the Hellenistic world out of which it grows. Finally, I would like to place this study in the context of a larger project, that of constructing a genuinely "pluralist" hermeneutics able to lead us to an appreciative understanding of texts and religions whose presuppositions we ourselves do not share.

7.1 A More Exact Method of Exegetical Hermeneutics

A major ambition of this study has been to advance the science of hermeneutics, chiefly on its exegetical side. My aim has been to demon-
strate, first, how the fact that a given text is meant to suggest meanings
below the surface can be established by controlled argumentation.
Secondly, I have shown how the presuppositions required for the adequate understanding of such a suggestive text can also be established
with some certainty by careful study of indirect indications given in the
text itself. The *Acts Thom.* has proved to be a very good test case for
such a project for the following reasons.

1) The presuppositions which prove necessary in this case are highly
   unusual when compared to ordinary literary conventions, even for
   ancient literature. Therefore, the simple application of refined
   literary sensibility is clearly inadequate in this case. If the interpretation of the *Acts Thom.* arrived at here is substantially correct, a way
   of discovering some very unusual presuppositions is absolutely
   essential to an adequate understanding of this work.
2) With a proper grasp of the kind of investigation and argumentation
   required, these presuppositions can in fact be derived in a very controlled way from indirect evidence clearly present in this text. This
   gives us a way of making sure that we are getting at the text's
   intended meaning and a way of avoiding arbitrariness in our interpretation.
3) The application of the exegetical methods worked out here leads to
   results that are rather spectacular in the case of this text. The initial
   impression of a poorly constructed text which is disconnected and
   incoherent gradually yields to the realization that it is a very intri-
   cately designed literary work, reflecting an extraordinarily sophisticated development within the tradition of Gnostic thought.

7.2 Gnostic Philosophical Hermeneutics

The *Acts Thom.* does show rather sophisticated thinking, and this brings
up an additional way in which the study has implications for hermeneutics: it shows us a text whose authors have clearly reflected at some
depth on questions of hermeneutics. I am speaking here not of the
exegetical side of hermeneutics but of its more philosophical aspects
which have come increasingly to the fore in recent discussions.
Specifically, the thought expressed in the *Acts Thom.* is interesting as a
"hermeneutics of experience." It advocates a certain way of

interpreting and making sense of human experience generally. Secondly, it also suggests a hermeneutics of religious tradition, implicitly advocating a certain way of getting at the substance of traditional religious images and employing them in the interpretation of our experience.

In order to highlight the specific character of the Gnostic hermeneutics suggested in the *Acts Thom.*, it will be helpful to contrast it with the prevalent assumptions of prevailing, non-Gnostic Christianity about how human experience and religious images ought to be interpreted. According to the prevailing view in Christianity, religious tradition is regarded as teaching "doctrines" about certain realities beyond the empirical world—realities such as God or a coming reign of God where the righteous will be rewarded. These realities form the context in which the attitudes, decisions, and actions constituting the drama of human life receive their true meaning. It is in this sense that the otherworldly context represented by religious doctrine indirectly "interprets" for us the meaning of our experience. Given that this is the function to be served by this otherworldly context, it is crucial that the context be both self-consistent and unchanging. This context lies beyond immediate experience which often deceives one about the true meaning of events in one's life. One comes to know about this otherworldly context in a way which is set very much apart from ordinary experience. It is something one knows of and believes in "by faith."

The Gnostic thought represented in the *Acts Thom.* differs in some fundamental ways from the prevailing hermeneutics just described, both in the way it uses religious images to interpret experience, and in its interpretation of the realities represented by religious images.

Gnostic Interpretation of Experience

So far as the interpretation of experience goes, the basic categories of the "Gnostic hermeneutics" implied in the *Acts Thom.* are certain constituent elements of experience, elements which are not so much objective realities but rather certain constant elements making up the "perceived character" of our experience. So, for example, the category "World" in this thought does not refer to the physical world in its objective reality. It refers to what resists the understanding and control of consciousness in its felt character as something resistant or beyond control. Whatever is felt as resisting or being alien belongs in this category. And this can include not only the physical world but also such realities as religious demands which "call on us" to do things and the fixed structures and dynamics inherent in the psychological makeup of human beings. Both of these can belong to the category "World" insofar as they can have a reality and power over us independent of our own completely conscious understanding and deliberate acceptance. Such categories as these are the basic elements this type hermeneutics offers us for interpreting our experience.

Though different in context, these categories are similar to Martin Heidegger's "existentials,"[1] in that they are the most general and fundamental determinants of the character of human existence, and they determine the way in which a person experiences more concrete and specific individual elements of their own being and of their surroundings. The difference in their content from Heidegger's "existentials" reflects some important differences between the Gnostic thought of the *Acts Thom.* and Heideggerian existentialism, again despite some striking similarities of the kind to which Hans Jonas has drawn attention with respect to Gnosticism in general.[2]

As to their content, the categories in question are variations on, or nuances of, three fundamental categories: (a) Mind; (b) World; and (c) an intermediate realm of Forms-Ideas mediating between Mind and World.

At the most fundamental level, these basic categories are neutral. They are not given a fixed evaluation as positive or negative. Rather, each category is capable of having either a positive or negative value. "World" as that which resists understanding and control can be something negative, something in our experience which cannot be infused with meaning. And it can also be something positive, something in our experience which is beyond our complete grasp because its great meaningfulness transcends the comprehension and control of the limited ego.

Religious tradition supplies various ideas and images (e.g., "God," "prophet," and "worldliness") each of which usually has some specific, very positive or very negative value attached to it. In this hermeneutics, each of these ideas or images is to be attached to one of the basic categories mentioned above. The same element of experience can have both a positive and a negative image attached to it, as for example World is represented in the text here both by the positive image of the shekinah and by the negative image of a prison ruled by demonic archons.

---

[1] Martin Heidegger, *Being and Time* (New York: Harper and Row, 1962) 70.
[2] Jonas, *Gnostic Religion*, 326–31.

Religious images seen in this light function in a way similar to Platonic Ideas. They picture archetypal Ideas[3] in which our ordinary experience "participates" to greater and lesser degrees. A relatively ordinary sunset, so far as it brings more meaning to someone's life, participates in the archetypal shekinah, while depression and anxiety, so far as they are barriers to a meaningful life, participate in the archetypal prison of the archons. The emotive connotations of these religious images capture the perceived character of these elements of our experience, and their religious and otherworldly associations give us a sense that our everyday experiences participate in some larger, archetypal reality.

In the prevailing interpretation of experience the otherworldly context which determines the significance of human conduct is unchanging, and it gives an unambiguous, unchanging interpretation to specific human attitudes and experiences. There are "laws of God" which are unchangingly good, and feelings of resistance to those laws are unequivocally negative. By contrast, in the Gnostic interpretation of experience presented here, almost any element of our experience is capable of having a positive or a negative meaning.

The basis on which some element of experience is evaluated positively or negatively is dynamic rather than static, and this is so in two ways. First of all, the evaluation which any element of experience is given depends on the positive or negative role it plays in a dynamic progression of (primarily psychological) events. Resistance to religious commandments (represented in our story by Thomas's unwillingness to take part in the wedding banquet) can be negative in that it can block an enrichment of consciousness which could have taken place through the influence of those commandments. It can be positive by virtue of its leading to a transcending of the literal content of those commandments and an appreciative understanding of the ideal meanings potentially reflected in them (represented by the destruction of evil and the "enlivening" of the World celebrated in the Christ prayer).

Secondly, as a result of these same dynamic progressions, the character of certain elements of our experience can change radically. The two main categories used in this interpretation of experience, Mind and

---

[3] This reference to the "archetypes" is not meant to identify the thought of the *Acts Thom.* with Jungian psychology on this point, nor is the reference to Platonism meant to characterize the thought here as Platonic in the ordinary sense. An image qualifies as "archetypal" in the sense I mean it here if it captures some aspect of experience in some particularly concentrated and intensely meaningful way. A wide variety of images can serve as "archetypes" in this sense, so there is no theory implied here about some particular predetermined set of images which are "universal archetypes."

World, do not stand in an unchanging relation to each other. Mind in particular can change in very significant ways, and the meaning that World has for it will change accordingly. For a "weak," uncreative Mind the otherness of World has a negative meaning as that which constricts it in its search for meaning in life. A creative Mind has the capability of enlivening this same resistant World so that its concreteness, originally experienced as resistant, meaningless otherness, becomes a support and an important source of meaning and delight.

The Gnostic thought reflected here aims not only at enhancing the meaningfulness of individual experiences but more importantly at a fundamental and more-or-less permanent personal ("initiatory") transformation of a person's consciousness. This transformation is partially brought about by the way in which the concrete World overcomes the tendency of the Mind to shun concreteness in favor of its own abstractions with which it initially feels more at home. The ultimate aim is to lead one to a permanent higher state of consciousness and so to a pervasive heightening of meaning in life in general which results from this transformation. This again is in contrast with a standard Christian viewpoint in which the interpretation of human conduct in the light of otherworldly norms has the ultimate aim of bringing about a constant moral alertness in which at every moment one decides anew to bring one's life into accord with those norms.

The Gnostic hermeutics just described is implied in the way the text is constructed. That is, the implication is that one ought to use the images which the text offers to interpret one's own concrete experience in the way just outlined. Conversely, when the reader relates the text in this way to actual experience, this imbues the (mental) images of the text with (worldly) concreteness, an essential element in the meaningfulness they have to offer.

But a hermeneutics of experience of this kind is also a large part of the content, the direct message of the opening two scenes of the *Acts Thom.* interpreted in this study. The allegory presented to us in these opening scenes outlines precisely the way in which the creative Mind can utilize Ideas to "make sense of" a World initially experienced as devoid of meaning—a "making sense" which is also an infusing of this World with meaning. It also shows the way in which a World thus made meaningful in turn transforms and enlightens a Mind whose initial tendency to avoid the concrete World left it impoverished in the midst of its own abstractions.

A Gnostic "Demythologizing" of Religious Ideas

In addition to a theory about how religious images can function to interpret our experience, the *Acts Thom.* also suggests a particular kind of interpretation of religious ideas themselves. Its "hermeneutics" in this sense is close in some respects to the "demythologizing" hermeneutics associated in our time with Rudolf Bultmann. That is, it suggests that religious ideas—particularly the idea "God"—do not refer to factual objects, positivistically conceived, in the same way that the idea "tree" refers to factual trees. Religious ideas represent realities of an existential rather than of a purely factual kind.

The idea "God" serves as a good example here. If I may, for the sake of clarity, rephrase and expand on the thought of the *Acts Thom.* on this subject, it goes something like this. In the Gnostic hermeneutics with which we are dealing, this idea represents what it is that makes life and experience meaningful. God is the reality on which human life depends. But the reference here is not to physical life as such but to the meaningfulness of human life. The foundation of meaningfulness in life is what is referred to by the name "God." In the *Acts Thom.* meaningfulness has two components—both Mind and World contribute to it—and these two components are represented as two aspects of "God."

In the first place, life is more meaningful when it is experienced with a greater depth of Mind. One way of defining this depth is that it is that aspect of Mind which is not preoccupied with egotistic interests but is in touch with the ideal possibilities of things and devoted to realizing these possibilities in actual concrete reality. We can conceive then of different layers or levels of Mind, from the most egotistic to the most idealistic, that most concerned with ideals. And in this context, "God" is a kind of limit-concept representing the ultimate foundation of the Mind's idealism and of the creative power of this idealism to transform reality as experienced and infuse it with meaning. While God remains transcendent in relation to more ordinary, egotistically tinged levels of Mind, there is no strict break between God and human consciousness. We should envisage, rather, a continuum. At the lowest level of this continuum lies that aspect of Mind which is most egocentric. One moves up the continuum to more and more idealistic levels of Mind, and at the highest level one comes to "God."

In the second place, as existentialism in our own time has pointed out, real meaningfulness demands not only depth of mind but also concrete engagement with concrete reality. There is a dimension to the meaning of human dignity, for example, which one cannot encounter in contemplating the abstract concept of it, no matter how ideal this may be. One can only experience the full meaningfulness of human dignity by actual personal contact with a concrete human being. In this sense concreteness, the "World" spoken of above, has an importance in respect to the experience of meaning in life equal to the importance of the Mind and the ideal reality with which it is at home. This World, too, has its levels which extend from its superficial surfaces—its bare givenness imposing itself on consciousness but devoid of any meaning for it—to its depths in which consciousness encounters ideal reality in concrete form. And here again "God" is a limit-concept representing the utmost depths of meaning which one meets in actual engagement with concrete reality.

For the sake of brevity and expository clarity I have tried here to describe in an analytical way the implicit views of the *Acts Thom.* on the subject of how to understand human experience and religious images. But it must be kept in mind that the difference in genre between my own expository essay and the involvement provoking narrative of the *Acts Thom.* is important and reflects a certain attitude toward interpretation as doctrine. And the sketch I have just given can easily be interpreted as an account of some Gnostic doctrines or beliefs about reality which the authors of the *Acts Thom.* for some reason chose to present in an annoyingly indirect fashion. This misses the point that the preference for an involving narrative over direct and analytical exposition reflects the central place given to experience in the thought of the authors. For them the idea and images are not expressions of doctrines which are to be imposed on experience. They are only properly understood when they can be seen to grow out of experience. So, for example, "seeing the world as divine" for these authors does not mean having a thought or belief in one's mind that exists alongside one's experience of the world, a belief which one attempts to impose on that experience. Rather, in the state of mind taken as a goal in the *Acts Thom.*, one experiences the concrete reality as intensely meaningful, and one way of expressing that character of the experience is to speak of it as an encounter with the shekinah, God in the world.

An interesting issue, which can only be raised as a question here, concerns the relation of this Gnostic hermeneutics implicit in the *Acts Thom.* to Gnostic thought generally. If we were to read other Gnostic works with this kind of hermeneutics in mind, it would undoubtedly bring about a radical revision in our understanding of what Gnostics in general were trying to say. A prime case here is the supposed Gnostic dualism which exalts a spiritual subjectivity allied with the divine and despises the material World as a demonic realm. In the dynamic hermeneutics of the *Acts Thom.*, such a dualism represents a starting point. It reflects the way in which, in one necessary stage of spiritual development of a good Gnostic, a person must experience the World as alien. This is a necessary first step in awakening from the relatively impoverished way of being which ordinary life is in the Gnostic view. But this experience of alienation is also regarded as an unfortunate state of affairs. The whole point of the text is to sketch out ways in which this dualism can be overcome. And the overcoming has partly to do with the Mind's coming to realize that its *feeling* about its own superior reality is partially unfounded arrogance and reflects an actual weakness on its part which makes it unable as yet to enliven the World with meaning and so come to see it as a divine presence.

Does this feature of the thought of the *Acts Thom.* represent a criticism of other Gnostics who in the main were indeed the die-hard dualists they are commonly thought to be? Or, on the other hand, does our impression of Gnostic thought generally rest on a failure to take into consideration some fundamental differences between the style of Gnostic thinking and the style of prevailing Christian thought? Specifically, are we justified in interpreting the Mind-World antagonistic dualism, which we see almost everywhere in Gnostic thought, as a "doctrine" of the kind we find elsewhere in Christianity concerning the unchanging character of reality as the ultimate context in which the drama of human life is played out? Or is this focus on doctrine as context something which some Christian thinkers, ancient and modern, mistakenly import into their reading of Gnostic works without justification in the Gnostic texts? Or perhaps, to suggest another alternative, does the Gnostic style of thinking sketched here exist only in incipient or rudimentary form in Gnostic writing generally? Does the thought of the *Acts Thom.* represent Gnostic thought "at its best," a sophisticated development of some ideal possibilities inherent in the specifically Gnostic approach to reality, but found only in relatively crude forms in other surviving Gnostic works?

7.3 The Community of Origin

The thought of the *Acts Thom.*, remarkable as it is, did not arise out of nowhere. One implication of the study is that this text almost surely arose in some community which already had the very unique mind-set necessary to understand it. It is practically inconceivable that it is the work of one author who single-handedly devised a completely new genre of writing. The genre is so unusual and so impenetrable to ordinary reading habits that such an author could not possibly have hoped to be understood by anyone. We must assume there was a community of people whose involvement in the activities of that community would have prepared them to be able to understand this kind of writing. And, given such a community of people with these habits of thought and verbal expression, it seems most plausible to assume that the book itself is a community product rather than the work of an individual.

Considering further the nature of such a community and the origin of its style of thinking, one thinks immediately of the allegorical interpretation of traditional literature very widely practiced in the Hellenistic world, generally using categories taken from the Platonic tradition. We can probably assume that such interpretation was regularly practiced in the community which stands behind this work. In addition to the general practice of allegorical exegesis, however, we can assume that members of this community were already familiar with the Gnostic alienation problematic which this text sets out to solve and with the main concepts used to try to deal with it. The text is clearly not written to introduce the reader to the themes with which it deals. Rather, it assumes a familiarity with quite a number of ideas (some of which, taken in themselves, strongly conflict with each other). Its main effort goes toward integrating these themes with one another. This, plus the sophistication and intricacy of the solution presented, probably implies a considerable history of thought along these lines in the community preceding the composition of this book.

The principle materials chosen for allegorical interpretation are narratives which seem to have arisen in an earlier Christian community with strong ascetic tendencies—indeed, in which a commitment to celibacy seems to be a necessary concomitant to conversion. We can assume with some probability that the ascetic Christian community in which these stories had some authoritative status was a fairly direct ancestor of the community out of which the *Acts Thom.* arose. On the other hand, we probably also have to suppose some rather radical changes which took place in the community between the composing of the original stories and the writing of this book. The asceticism motif is now interpreted completely metaphorically, as the resistance of Mind to World, so the stories can no longer be read as dealing at all with the issue of literal asceticism or celibacy. We cannot even say whether or not the redactors' criticism of Thomas's "asceticism" represents a change in community attitudes toward actual ascetic practices.

Beyond the allegorical interpretation of traditional literature, there is one more factor, religious prayer, which probably influenced the peculiar style of thought and expression in this work. Two kinds of prayer are involved here. The first is the kind of praying we find in Hebraic psalm literature: the biblical Book of Psalms, the *Psalms of Solomon*, and the psalms found at Qumran. Secondly, there is religious ceremonial of a more-or-less initiatory kind, as represented in the mystery religions and later in some Christian liturgies.

Prayers found in the psalm literature very often represent an attempt to come to grips with some acutely problematic situation, whether it be one affecting a community or an individual. One can see the psalm writer trying to come to some satisfactory religious understanding of the meaning of the situation by interpreting it in the light of traditional religious concepts and themes. Prayer in this sense really represents someone thinking over a difficult situation. It involves a dialectical process consisting, first, of interpreting emotionally problematic aspects of the situation by seeing them in religious terms. On the other side, this process involves giving existential meaning to traditional religious themes by relating them to keenly felt concrete concerns and experiences. One can easily imagine a prayer tradition of this kind leading to the same kind of dialectical relation between ideas and experience sketched out in our discussion of Gnostic hermeneutics in the *Acts Thom.* Most likely our text more-or-less explicitly makes this connection. That is, it first portrays Thomas "thinking over" (100.8; 101.3) the predicament his mission to India represents for him. Then it retrospectively refers to the sequence in which his dilemma was solved as "praying" (102.10).

The development which the *Acts Thom.* represents beyond traditional psalm literature results partly from the influence of Greek philosophical thought. This produces a fundamental shift away from considering specific problematic situations, and focuses attention instead on the most general existential problematic posed by the human condition. In this sense the text represents a merger of the concretely oriented Hebraic psalm-prayer tradition both with the tradition of Greek philosophical thought on the most general questions of human existence and with the Gnostic tradition which focuses specifically on Mind-World alienation as *the* problem defining the human condition.

Turning to the tradition of religious ceremonial, it is very likely responsible for the dynamic aspect of the thought in this work, that is, its emphasis on experiential change and personal religious transformation as the primary goal of religious endeavor. Religious ceremonial in the mystery religions and liturgy as it developed in Christian communities were more-or-less explicitly conceived of as *psychagoge*, a leading of the soul to a higher state, by means of experiences evoked by the ritual. As Reitzenstein[4] already suggested with his idea of a "literary mystery," liturgical practice and thinking of this kind could easily be developed and serve as the basis for a literary genre which has basically this same purpose. There are ample, though somewhat fragmentary, references to and descriptions of religious ceremonial in the *Acts Thom.*, suggesting again that there were some practices of this kind in the past history of the community of origin. The patterns of composition we found to be standard in the long monologues of the *Acts Thom.* easily lend themselves to extemporaneous composition, and this, too, might form part of the background in community practice that underlies this literary production. Again this liturgical tradition has been radically reshaped by the understanding of religious images as allegorical representations of concepts from the Platonic and Gnostic traditions.

I have been assuming here a community originally involved in types of prayer common in religious groups in the Hellenistic world, which then reshaped these prayer practices under the influence of philosophical and Gnostic thinking. This is, however, not the only way of accounting for the origin of our text. What is fairly clear is that there was a merger at some point between these prayer practices on the one hand, and philosophic and Gnostic thought on the other. It is not implausible to think of persons of a primarily philosophic and Gnostic bent who were subsequently taken with the prayer practices of some "Thomas-Christians" and saw in these a way of concretely solving existential dilemmas which they had previously tried to capture conceptually and a way of concretely realizing in themselves the ideal realities about which they had previously speculated.

7.4 A Pluralist View of Hermeneutics

The above description of the character and possible origin of the Gnostic hermeneutics of the *Acts Thom.* has tried to present the thought of this work in a sympathetic light. This approach to the interpretation of human experience, and of religious imagery, does indeed have a great deal to recommend it. On the other hand, it is not at all my position that this is the correct approach which everyone should take in making sense of their experience, or which provides the key to understanding the true meaning of the imagery of all religions. I do not think that this approach is in all respects superior to the prevailing Christian approach with which I have contrasted it. Similarly, I do not want to claim that the understanding of the *Acts Thom.* which results from this

---

[4] *Mystery-Religions*, 52.

study is a good one on the grounds that it allows us to understand some universally valid truth which the authors of this work have to offer us.

The claim I would like to make for this study is rather that it helps lay some groundwork for a truly pluralist method in the study of religious texts generally. The presuppositions governing our interpretation of the texts we read tend to be the same presuppositions which govern the way we understand the meaning of our lives. The question as to which presuppositions are proper to the interpretation of a given text easily becomes a question about the correct approach one should take to understanding the meaning of life. And in this way the interpretation of texts easily becomes a battleground on which conflicts between opposing worldviews (secular and religious) are played out. In the past, Gnosticism in particular has fared ill at the hands of particular Christian interpreters for this reason: Gnostic thought directly challenges some key presuppositions of mainstream Christianity, and it cannot be appreciatively understood unless one provisionally drops those presuppositions and at least temporarily adopts others when reading Gnostic texts.

The problem is only partly a practical one, that is, the difficulty which exegetes have in even temporarily and provisionally divorcing themselves from their own firmly held perspective on life. In the situation in which interpreters and exegetes have no way of impartially determining which particular presuppositions are appropriate to the understanding of a given text, it is difficult, even from a theoretical point of view, to see conflicting interpretations as anything but a competitive struggle between the worldviews represented by different scholars. Interpretations easily come to be defended ultimately on the grounds that the presuppositions on which they are based reflect some perspective which is superior, as a perspective on life, to that which underlies rival interpretations. The model of interpretation presented here offers some theoretical tools for a way out of this impasse, the basic elements of a genuinely pluralist hermeneutics. Such a hermeneutics allows for an appreciative understanding of any text on the basis of presuppositions proper to it. And it allows for an objective and impartial discussion of what those presuppositions should be in any given case, based on evidence given in the text rather than on ideological considerations. This frees hermeneutics from its heritage as the authoritative arbiter of thought or belief, frees it to be a means of listening to and learning from a given text, rather than a way of determining authoritatively how it ought to be evaluated and/or appropriated.